Elaborate Selves: Reflections and Reveries of Christopher Bollas, Michael Eigen, Polly Young-Eisendrath, Samuel and Evelyn Laeuchli and Marie Coleman Nelson

Elaborate Selves: Reflections and Reveries of Christopher Bollas, Michael Eigen, Polly Young-Eisendrath, Samuel and Evelyn Laeuchli and Marie Coleman Nelson

Anthony Molino, NCPsyA
Editor

E. Mark Stern, PhD
Series Editor

Routledge
Taylor & Francis Group
New York London

Elaborate Selves: Reflections and Reveries of Christopher Bollas, Michael Eigen, Polly Young-Eisendrath, Samuel and Evelyn Laeuchli and Marie Coleman Nelson has also been published as *The Psychotherapy Patient*, Volume 10, Numbers 1/2 1997.

First published by
The Haworth Press, Inc., 10 Alice Street, Binghamton, NY 13904-1580 USA

This edition published 2012 by Routledge

Routledge
Taylor & Francis Group
711 Third Avenue
New York, NY 10017

Routledge
Taylor & Francis Group
2 Park Square, Milton Park
Abingdon, Oxon OX14 4RN

Library of Congress Cataloging-in-Publication Data

Elaborate selves : reflections and reveries of Christopher Bollas, Michael Eigen, Polly Young-Eisendrath, Samuel and Evelyn Laeuchli, and Marie Coleman Nelson / Anthony Molino, editor.
p. cm.
"Has also been published as The psychotherapy patient, volume 10, numbers 1/2, 1997"–T.p. verso.
Includes bibliographical references.
ISBN 0-7890-0011-3 (alk. paper)
1. Psychoanalysts–Biography. 2. Psychoanalysis–History. I. Molino, Anthony.
BF109.A1E43 1997
150'.92'2–dc20
[B] 96-38178
CIP

Elaborate Selves: Reflections and Reveries of Christopher Bollas, Michael Eigen, Polly Young-Eisendrath, Samuel and Evelyn Laeuchli and Marie Coleman Nelson

CONTENTS

ABOUT THE EDITORS

Anthony Molino, NCPsyA, is a literary translator, psychoanalyst, and anthropologist. He divides his time between Philadelphia and Italy, where he will be an Affiliate Fellow at the Academy in Rome in 1997. He holds a bachelor's degree in Italian and an MA in Anthropology, both from Temple University, where he is presently a PhD candidate in Anthropology. Bilingual, he has lived and studied for many years in Italy, where he was a Fulbright grantee in 1980. The recipient of three grants from the Pennsylvania Council on the Arts for his translation work, as well as of major fellowships from the National Theater Translation Fund and The Academy of American Poets, Mr. Molino has presented in English the work of some of Italy's foremost poets and playwrights of this century. Anthony Molino is also a member of the editorial board of *The Psychotherapy Patient*. His upcoming projects include an anthology of writings on psychoanalysis and Buddhism for Farrar, Strauss & Giroux, and a new volume of interviews with psychoanalysts, for Free Associations Books in London.

E. Mark Stern, EdD, is Professor Emeritus in the Graduate Faculty of Arts and Sciences, Iona College, New Rochelle, New York. A Diplomate in Clinical Psychology of the American Board of Professional Psychology and a Fellow of the American Psychological Association, the American Psychological Society, and the Academy of Clinical Psychology, Dr. Stern has been President of the Divisions of Humanistic Psychology and Psychology of Religion, APA. He is in private practice of psychotherapy with offices at 215 East Eleventh Street, New York, NY 10003.

Introduction

> We are all made up of fragments, so shapelessly and strangely assembled that every moment, every piece plays its own game. And there is as much difference between us and ourselves as between us and others. Deem it a great achievement to act consistently, like one and the same man.
>
> –Montaigne

From a recent *Calvin and Hobbes* comic strip:

frame 1
Calvin: I got another letter from my past self.
Hobbes: What's it say?

frame 2
Calvin: (*reading*) "Dear future Calvin, I wrote this several days before you will receive it. You've done things I haven't done. You've seen things I haven't seen. You know things I don't know. You lucky dog! Your pal, Calvin."

frame 3
Calvin: (*sniffing, wiping away a tear*) I feel so sorry for myself two days ago.
Hobbes: Poor him. He wasn't you.

[Haworth co-indexing entry note]: "Introduction." Molino, Anthony. Co-published simultaneously in *The Psychotherapy Patient* (The Haworth Press, Inc.) Vol. 10, No. 1/2, 1997, pp. 1-10; and: *Elaborate Selves: Reflections and Reveries of Christopher Bollas, Michael Eigen, Polly Young-Eisendrath, Samuel and Evelyn Laeuchli and Marie Coleman Nelson* (ed: Anthony Molino) The Haworth Press, Inc., 1997, pp. 1-10. Single or multiple copies of this article are available from The Haworth Document Delivery Service [1-800-342-9678, 9:00 a.m. - 5:00 p.m. (EST). E-mail address: getinfo@haworth.com].

It seems pretty safe to say, in this age of postmodern sensibilities, that Calvin and Hobbes help illustrate and confirm a pervasive sense that American culture has finally caught up with Rimbaud and Flaubert. From the radical pronouncements of *JE est un autre* and *Madame Bovary c'est moi*, up to and through Nietzsche's pyrotechnic prophecies and the archaeologies of the psyche, initiated by Freud and revisited most recently by Lacan and his followers, the Western bastion of self-identity has been relentlessly and systematically undermined. So-called discontinuities in self experience, reflecting the fluid or fragmented self states of the "split" or "decentred" subject, are not, however, merely grist for the latest mill of abstract philosophical inquiry or ivory-tower theorizing.

There is a debate taking place in contemporary American culture of far-reaching proportions, whose effects (or symptoms?) are already manifest in the discourses and politics not only of academic disciplines, but of the mental health fields as well. It is only recently, for example, that the DSM IV replaced the longstanding "Multiple Personality Disorder" diagnosis of its earlier editions with the newly coined "Dissociative Identity Disorder." Thus, in a social space where words do define and constitute reality, as well as the relations of power inherent in the not-so Edenic naming of the phenomenological and object worlds, there is implied in such a terminological and diagnostic shift an alteration in the way we conceive, view and experience the world. (In this instance, the epistemological move is away from the *results* of severe fragmentation–i.e., "multiple" personalities–to a clearly stated assumption of the norm of *identity*, wherein dissociation is deemed a pathological feature or tendency.) But even without attending the romantic celebrations of madness and schizophrenia to which near-contemporaries like Deleuze and Guattari would invite us, there are unequivocal signs in our midst that the times, well, they are (again) a' changing.

I should point out that the "signs" to which I refer are not only, or simply, of French derivation, though I realize this might appear to be the case. In no way do I intend to suggest that the current debate around "multiplicity" is an imported intellectual fad, though I fully recognize, in accordance with what I've just stated, that words and ideas can and do give shape to the world. One of the most exhaustive and insightful studies of the advent and impact of postmodern transformations is, in point of fact, by an American psychologist, Kenneth Gergen. In examining this century's technological achievements and the resultant barrage of social stimulation, Gergen writes in *The Saturated Self: Dilemmas of Identity in Contemporary Life*:

> I was struck by the realization that the contemporary upheaval in the academic world is paralleled by major shifts in contemporary ways of acting and relating. Increasingly, people are living through the "dissolution of self" discussed within the academy–and experiencing directly the shocks of dislocation, the dilemmas of identity, and the thrills of newly opened vistas . . . (T)his massive increment in social stimulation–moving toward a state of saturation–sets the stage both for radical changes in our daily experience of self and others and for an unbridled relativism within the academic sphere. . . . With social saturation, the coherent circles of accord are demolished, and all beliefs thrown into question by one's exposure to multiple points of view. This is no less true in academic matters of truth and objectivity than in our daily experience of self.[1]

Nor are the signs restricted to the spheres of psychology, psychotherapy, or psychoanalysis. Already a decade ago, as part of its series "Studies in Rationality and Social Change," Cambridge University Press published a volume entitled *The Multiple Self*. Edited by Jon Elster of The University of Chicago, the book collects essays by economists, philosophers, and political scientists interested in considering "whether the self is a unity or whether it should be conceived without metaphor as divided–as a 'multiple self.' "[2] In contemporary anthropology, attention to what we ethnocentrically term "the dissolution of the self" is evidenced most readily in the very titles of some of that discipline's newer ethnographies. For example, in a book entitled *Crafting Selves: Power, Gender and Discourses of Identity in a Japanese Workplace*, the anthropologist Dorinne K. Kondo explains:

> Collective identities like "the Japanese" or "Japanese concepts of self" no longer seem to me to be fixed essences, but

> rather strategic assertions which inevitably suppress differences, tensions and contradictions within . . . How did the people I knew *craft* themselves and their lives within shifting fields of power and meaning, and how did they do so in particular situations and within a particular historical and cultural context? (*my italics*)[3]

Another anthropologist, Rita Smith Kipp, at the beginning of her *Dissociated Identities: Ethnicity, Religion and Class in an Indonesian Society,* asks

> Why does the postmodern self in the late twentieth century–divided, context dependent, and relational–look strangely like the selves anthropologists have been seeking and finding in all kinds of places once thought barely modern? . . . The florescence of self-and-person studies in anthropology no doubt both indexes and influences the postmodernist climate in which the "pristine unity" of the Western self seems more and more chimerical (or ideological).[4]

Is it merely coincidence, moreover, that Kipp's book, published in 1993, bears a title strikingly similar to the DSM IV's revised diagnostic category of the Dissociative Identity Disorder? Lastly, whereas neither Kipp nor Kondo adopt psychoanalysis as an interpretive frame for their researches, a final "sign" from the fields of anthropological inquiry comes from an as yet unpublished manuscript, whose editors, Susan Lepselter and Kathleen Stewart, explore the oozings of desire in the remote "otherness" of marginalized American landscapes. In their introduction to *Subjects of Enchantment: Constituting America as an Ethnographic Object,* Lepselter and Stewart write:

> Each of (the contributors), working in widely divergent contexts . . . , has come to see "the Western self" not as an internally unified reflection of "individualist" ideology but as a densely tracked and tensely constituted "split subject," torn between nostalgia and the blindly forward thrust of wish, ruins and the glimmerings of utopia, ongoing everyday banalities and shocks of experience. . . . [5]

Similarly, when in her own book *A Space on the Side of the Road: Cultural Poetics in an "Other" America*, Stewart asks us to "picture the tattered remnants of the old coal mining camps crowded into the *hollers* of West Virginia, how the decaying orchards and graveyards of the old family places sag under the weight of memory like bodies sagging and imploding under the weight of a lifetime of work too hard to bear,"[6] she brings the problematic "home," so to speak–even though the communities she describes may seem just as strange as Kondo's Japanese workplace, or Kipp's Indonesian village. Yet Stewart also brings "home" the problematic of the self in the sense that her language is one with which readers of this volume are likely to be more familiar. It is, in many ways, the language of our work, of our patients. It is the language of memory and nostalgia, of human anguish and hope. Of spatial, geographic and emotional dislocation. Or, in Blanchot's terms, of the unconscious itself:

> The negation that is not simply a wanting, but a relation to what is wanting–desire. A desire whose essence is eternally to be desire: a desire for what is impossible to attain, and even to be desire.[7]

* * *

In recent years, a number of psychoanalytic theorists and clinicians, other than the Lacanian, have begun to struggle with and incorporate notions of multiplicity in their work. An emphasis on and theorization of *selves* is becoming increasingly apparent, from angles as diverse as the Jungian (where Polly Young-Eisendrath develops the idea from a declared feminist, postmodernist and constructivist position), to those of a varied group of object relationists (i.e., Christopher Bollas, Stephen Mitchell). In the wake of these developments, a fierce, often polarizing debate holds center stage, as theory's implications for practice are juxtaposed and positioned. Whereas Jane Flax, for example, argues in her *Disputed Subjects* on behalf of "multiplicity," and against any therapeutic task of discovering or constructing "a solid, unitary, pristine and undistorted self" (echoing sentiments expressed many years ago by

Marie Coleman Nelson[8]), James Glass, in his book *Shattered Selves*, insists:

> . . . voices of psychological fragmentation are more than ideological representations or the result of social practices; they come from human beings who have lived through traumas hidden from public view, whose core sense of self has been shattered by very specific actions. The languages, then, of these victims, these survivors, signifies more than reflection on ideology, practice, biophysical structure, or the decadence of modernity. [9]

Though I've stated the two positions somewhat schematically, it's important to recognize that they do exist, and thus work to inform prevailing notions of pathology. Along with *Calvin and Hobbes* and the changes in the DSM IV, neither Flax's "disputed subjects" nor Glass' "shattered selves" have materialized in a vacuum. Both are products of culture and history, as well as of instinct and biology. Of ideology as well as of abuse. And though the opposing designations may very well serve to identify the selfsame group of suffering patients, these and the real-life hopes offered them by the likes of Glass and Flax (both therapists as well as writers), are constant reminders of just how damningly impossible–and desperately necessary–our profession remains in this day and age.

Along these lines, in conceiving and compiling this collection of interviews, I was curious to explore the ways in which a select group of therapists, from different orientations and not all psychoanalytically inspired, were understanding *and* working with concepts of the self. Of this group, all except for Samuel and Evelyn Laeuchli had evidenced in their writings a sensibility to issues and problems of multiplicity, ranging from a clear theorization of "multiple selves" (Bollas, Young-Eisendrath) to a frequent and "multiple" use of the plural noun *selves* (Eigen, Nelson). In the case of the Laeuchlis, as I had followed the development of their *Mimesis* groups and practice for many years, I knew firsthand of how their work, drawing on myth and ritual, engages the self in its multiple and complex dimensions. As a result, their own place in the collection was firmly warranted, especially considering how the interviews were not intended solely to explore theoretical concerns but to address issues of clinical practice and relevance as well.

In closing, I'd like to say a few words about the title chosen for this collection. In a chapter entitled "The Telling of Selves," from his recent book *On Flirtation*, Adam Phillips laments the paucity of available life stories from within the ranks of psychoanalysis. "There are surprisingly few occasions–or rituals–in which people are expected or invited to tell the story of their lives from wherever they think the beginning is; or to tell the even odder story that is their dream."[10] In an interview offered here, Michael Eigen adds another slant to Phillips' words: "Nowadays, I think of psychoanalysis as an aesthetic, as a form of poetry. You have all these psychoanalytic poets and singers trying to express their aesthetic experience. . . ." It is these two perspectives, at the interstices of intellectual and personal history, of influences and imaginings, that have gone largely ignored in the study of recent psychoanalytic theory. Moving from the premise that even psychoanalysis, or psychotherapy in general, thrives and is webbed in the saturated strands of Gergen's "postmodern self," I would like to propose that the stories, lives and "selves" of the therapists here represented are both worthy of investigation, as well as telling of the predicaments of the culture at-large. Accordingly, I am suggesting in this context, along with Gergen, that postmodernism be understood as "a set of interrelated dialogues on the nature of knowledge, language and politics, most focally, but by implication also concerning the self, pluralism, education, morality and other topics resulting from the rapid and continuous transformations in cultural forms."[11] Or, as Blanchot might have it, postmodernism as *infinite conversation*.

Infinite, or *elaborate*. For the idea of multiplicity, whether it connotes the generally valued qualities of fluidity and plasticity, or the questioned attributes of fragmentation and dispersion, involves in either case elements of detail, complexity and labor. There is, in any psychotherapy, an expenditure of energy that aims to reconfigure, and thus elaborate, self experience. For each of the therapists interviewed, the self in psychotherapy is a dynamic agent that literally works, or *labors*, through the calcifications of trauma and repetitions, in an often agonizing and fearful quest to discover itself as Other: other than what it's been, other than what is known. In this light, the therapeutic visions here discussed are all calls for the elaboration of experience, and of the ossified selves encased in the prisonhouses of fruitless human affliction.

Additionally, the *elaborate selves* of the title also refers to the vibrant outcome that is the life, and lifework, of each of the therapists interviewed. For all of their theoretical differences and idiosyncratic biases, and notwithstanding the vast distances that separate their respective personal origins and histories, Christopher Bollas, Michael Eigen, Polly Young-Eisendrath, Samuel Laeuchli, Evelyn Rothchild-Laeuchli and Marie Coleman Nelson all share, if you will, a common destiny. I use the word *destiny*, here, much the way Bollas does: "A sense of destiny (involves) a feeling that the person is fulfilling some of the terms of his inner idiom through familial, social, cultural and intellectual objects." In contrast with a *fated* life, the person of destiny lives out "the natural course of the true self."[12] In different ways, the therapists contributing to this project have all, over the course of their lifetimes, elaborated not only an important theory or clinical contribution, but a capacity for professional, intellectual and moral engagement with the world that attests, I believe, to the higher reaches and aspirations of our profession. In refusing to be singularly fashioned or fashionable, they have all fashioned, and transmitted, a singularly rich and manifold experience.

Finally, as any reader is likely to understand, and as the narrator of Melville's *Billy Budd* knew well, even where the conversation is *finite* the pleasure of the Other is such that "some bypaths have an enticement not readily to be withstood." Though intended as organizing themes, the concepts of *self* and *multiplicity* readily opened, during the fruitful hours spent with my hosts, any number of tempting and exquisite bypaths which, more often than not, were not withstood. Needless to say, it was along the bypaths of reflection, that my hosts lapsed, and enticed me, into the welcome and fertile waters of *reverie*. Having since emerged, enriched, from the waters, I can only hope our readers will indulge these lapses, and take delight in them.

I want to thank all those interviewed for their collaboration and generous availability. Sincere thanks go to E. Mark Stern, who invited me to edit this volume and gave me free rein in the process.

Special thanks go to three senior members of Temple University's Anthropology Department for their ongoing support of my interdisciplinary researches: Tom Patterson, Peter Rigby, and especially Elmer Miller. I also want to thank Kathleen Stewart, for making available to me excerpts from her two manuscripts, and John and Liza Di Mino, for making available newsletters from the Laeuchlis' Mimesis Institute. The generous advice of my dear colleague and friend, Wesley Shumar, an anthropologist in the Education Program of Swarthmore College, was instrumental in helping me shape the project. Similarly, Paul Krenitsky's computer expertise and frequent assistance proved timely and invaluable. Lastly, the project owes its life to the nitty-gritty efforts of two friends who helped produce the final text. They are Susan Larkin, who somehow managed to transcribe every inch of every hour of audiotape; and Christine Ware, who throughout the past months has been more than a tireless and ever-reliable editorial assistant. Being the agile thinker and able clinician that she is, her own first book is eagerly awaited.

Anthony Molino
Philadelphia, PA

REFERENCES

1. Kenneth Gergen, *The Saturated Self: Dilemmas of Identity in Contemporary Life* (New York, Basic Books, 1991, pp. x-xi).

2. Jon Elster, ed., *The Multiple Self* (Cambridge, Cambridge University Press, 1985). The quote is taken from the back cover of the second paperback edition, 1988.

3. Dorinne K. Kondo, *Crafting Selves: Power, Gender and Discourses of Identity in a Japanese Workplace* (Chicago, University of Chicago Press, 1990, p. 10).

4. Rita Smith Kipp, *Dissociated Identities: Ethnicity, Religion and Class in an Indonesian Society* (Ann Arbor, University of Michigan Press, 1993, p. 9).

5. Kathleen Stewart and Susan Lepselter, eds., *Subjects of Enchantment: Constituting America as an Ethnographic Object*, unpublished manuscript.

6. Kathleen Stewart, *A Space on the Side of the Road: Cultural Poetics in an "Other" America* (Princeton, Princeton University Press, 1996).

7. Maurice Blanchot, "The Speech of Analysis." tr. by Susan Hanson, in *The Infinite Conversation* (Minneapolis, University of Minnesota Press, 1993, p. 232).

8. Already in a 1962 paper entitled "Effect of Paradigmatic Techniques on the Psychic Economy of Borderline Patients" Nelson writes: ". . . the ego is composed chiefly of partial introjects and multiple identifications. Hence the paradig-

matic psychotherapist views the patient as a group–*an aggregate of selves*–as well as an individual" (my italics). See the journal *Psychiatry*, 25:2, May 1962.

9. James Glass, *Shattered Selves: Multiple Personality in a Postmodern World* (Ithaca, Cornell University Press, 1993, p. 27).

10. Adam Phillips, "The Telling of Selves," in *On Flirtation* (Cambridge, Harvard University Press, 1994, p. 75).

11. "An Interview with Kenneth Gergen," in *Culture and Psychology*, p. 149, 1:1, March 1995.

12. Christopher Bollas, *Forces of Destiny: Psychoanalysis and Human Idiom* (London, Free Association Books, 1989, p. 34).

Christopher Bollas

> Yet (Freud) admirably abides by his sense that the doctor plays not an enchanted role, but one more hidden . . . that of a presence-absence over and against which some ancient drama, some profoundly forgotten event, real or imaginary, comes again to take form and expression, truth and actuality. The doctor, therefore, would be there not as himself but in the place of another. By his presence alone he plays the role of another, is other, and is the other before becoming an other.
>
> –M. Blanchot, "The Speech of Analysis"

When I interviewed Christopher Bollas in his London home in January, it was the first time I'd been to England. And, much as I'd been forewarned, the weather was typically damp and cold and grey, with a prickly form of precipitation in the air that had the irksome quality of condensing around one's head and ears. When I arrived in the vicinity of Bollas' house, legs weary and chilled to the bone, I was already battling a numbing fever. Not the best way, surely, to present myself at the doorstep of a man widely regarded as one of the foremost psychoanalytic thinkers and writers of our time. So, with flu symptoms further compounding my original, deferential hesitation, I pushed up the hill to 42 Mount View Road, fantasizing outcomes, mostly catastrophic, to the work that lie ahead.

In the eternity of the dreary, one-block walk between my bus stop and now-dreaded destination, I would have been well-served had I recalled the words of Adam Phillips, who in his book, ***On Flirta-***

[Haworth co-indexing entry note]: "Christopher Bollas." Co-published simultaneously in *The Psychotherapy Patient* (The Haworth Press, Inc.) Vol. 10, No. 1/2, 1997, pp. 11-60; and: *Elaborate Selves: Reflections and Reveries of Christopher Bollas, Michael Eigen, Polly Young-Eisendrath, Samuel and Evelyn Laeuchli and Marie Coleman Nelson* (ed: Anthony Molino) The Haworth Press, Inc., 1997, pp. 11-60. Single or multiple copies of this article are available from The Haworth Document Delivery Service [1-800-342-9678, 9:00 a.m. - 5:00 p.m. (EST). E-mail address: getinfo@haworth.com].

***tion**, writes of Bollas: "(He) gets us close to the ordinary but absolutely elusive experience of making a dream." There was, indeed, something absolutely dreamlike about that walk, as if my body had somehow become suspended in a bleak and timeless space. Of much greater consequence, however, was the dreamwork to follow, around the amazingly ordinary exchanges that took place within the modest and comforting surroundings of Bollas' home and office.*

Settled and warmed by a cup of tea, I spent the next four hours mindless of my body and its ills. The sense of suspension persisted, but in a transformed state. I began to understand why Bollas, who years earlier had inspired the idea of this collection, would only agree to an interview within the familiar confines of his own space. As he'd told me before, it had to do with a penchant of his for reverie: an atmosphere of fluid, unconscious germination, not unlike, again citing Phillips, "the sleep-walking á deux" of the psychoanalytic enterprise. Something similar, I believe, was unfolding, and enfolding me. As Bollas reclined and dipped into a treasure chest of memories and other psychic objects, the serene wealth and elegance of his answers made for an atmosphere of absorbing ease. So much so that twice in the course of our time together, we both forgot the presence of the tape recorder, and failed to heed the clicking sound signalling the end of the tape. On one such occasion, it was only after half an hour that we realized how an answer of his had radiated into an essay, and been lost. Just like that, in much the same elusive and ever so ordinary way in which a dream is made.

*The following interview, which took place in London on January 9-10, 1995, explores themes taken up by Bollas mostly in **Being a Character**. His latest book, **Cracking Up**, was published soon after our conversations.*

AM: In his book, *The Postmodern Condition*, J.-F. Lyotard, citing the work of Wittgenstein, writes: "The social subject itself seems to dissolve in this dissemination of language games. The social bond is linguistic, but is not woven with a single thread. It is a fabric formed by the intersection of at least two (and in reality an indeterminate number of) language games, obeying different rules . . . the principle of unitotality–or synthesis under the authority of a metadiscourse of knowledge–is inapplicable." In a similar vein, much of your work on the self also goes against the grain of any unitotality.

And yet in an earlier book, *Forces of Destiny, Psychoanalysis and Human Idiom*, you put forth what you call a theory for the *true self*. Is there a contradiction here? As clinician and theorist, how does Christopher Bollas understand the self?

CB: It's a topic I take up in *Cracking Up*, where there's a chapter on this thing called *self*. Winnicott's concept of the "true self" and what we mean by the self are not the same. The true self was just his way of designating the presence of spontaneity: the true self as gesture. The false self, the only other "self" he wrote about in relation to the true self, indicates its presence through compliance: it describes a reactive attitude. My belief is that we have a sense of self that exists within an illusion of integration: an illusion essential to our way of life. Even those who see themselves as radical deconstructivists cannot, and do not, live a life without that illusion.

AM: Michel Foucault has also written about postmodernism and, more or less directly, about psychoanalysis, in the contexts of his "histories" and "archaeologies." In line with his thinking, where he argues for "the insurrection of *subjugated knowledges*," of what he calls *anti-sciences*, where and how do you situate your writing? Can psychoanalysis be something other than what Foucault calls a *totalitarian theory*?

CB: Already Freud's *Interpretation of Dreams*, in his writing of his self-analysis, and the reporting of his dreams to interpretation—in what was so remarkable an event, and so very fertile an occasion—doesn't support a totalitarian structure. If, like Freud, psychoanalysts write openly, if they provide enough detail, if there's enough saturation with the unconscious, then any reader will re-read and re-write a text in such a way as to undermine any thematic totality. It is those psychoanalytical writings, written with a greater degree of unconsciousness, that are, to my way of thinking, the more interesting. I include in this area the writings of Jacques Lacan, for example, where something primitive, something mythological and elusive persists, that leads one to imagine them, and open them up in so many directions. Harold Searles' writings are unconsciously rich. Each psychoanalyst must, no matter whether he or she does it consciously, re-invent psychoanalysis for themselves. It's those analysts who show the re-invention that sustain a level of creativity that's essential to the development of thinking. One can see this in certain contemporary analysts, like André Green, Adam Phillips, Michael Eigen, Harold Boris, James Grotstein, Joyce McDougall. All these people are recasting psychoanalysis, and re-creating it.

AM: Along these lines, is there an element of a "project" in your work?

CB: I can answer that question only toward the end of my life, when I look back. I don't wish to develop a "Christopher Bollas theory"; nor do I wish to re-use or echo terms which first served simply to establish a point I was intent on making in a single, earlier essay.

AM: Speaking of archaeology, Freud had already used it as a metaphor for psychoanalysis. In your book, *Forces of Destiny: Psychoanalysis and Human Idiom*, you seem to be inviting something new when you write: "perhaps we need a new point of view in clinical psychoanalysis, close to a form of person anthropology." In a post-modern world, where the self, for one, is described as fragmented, decentred, discontinuous, multiple . . . take your pick!–what would a "person anthropology" entail?

CB: It would be an analysis of any individual as a privately evolved but structured culture. It would mean that those signifiers that were currently important to an individual could be deconstructed; or, to think, when analyzing someone for the first time, that we're to enter a foreign country. It's like going into a different culture with a different language. Psychoanalysis then becomes in part a process for the translation of a person's different and changing perspectives, a way of deciphering all the many rules of foreign lives, of private cultures. . . .

AM: In *Forces of Destiny* you take issue with D. W. Winnicott's notion of the true self, where he links it with the id (in juxtaposition to the false self and its connection to the ego). Yet you rarely speak of a false self; it seems, rather, that there exist only degrees of realized potential of true self, owing to the interplay of trauma and what you later, in *Being a Character*, call "genera." Is this so? And if it is, why resort to adjectives like "true" and "core"?

CB: I resort to them because I come from a particular intellectual and analytical tradition, and have felt it important to indicate those origins.

As for Winnicott, I think my critique of the link you mentioned was an incomplete critique. I think I understand why Winnicott linked the true self up with the id, as he was trying to get to something viscerally powerful and primitive. He did not want it linked to the ego because of that. On the other hand, I believe the organizational density of the true self, what I call *idiom*–or, to reflect back on your metaphor, a language waiting to be spoken–I believe that density is too intelligent a phenomenon to be, as it were, ascribed to the id. As a seething cauldron of primitive urges, the id did not, at least in the Freudian structural theory, have the kind of dense intelligence to it that I think exists for the true self, or indeed for idiom. Conversely, when Freud theorized the unconscious ego, he got to something which had that kind of thick intelligence to it: something that really has to do with the aesthetic organization of the self, or with the self as an aesthetic organization. Ultimately I think it is understandable why Winnicott linked his idea of the self with the id; but too much of his concept of the true self would still have to find a place in Freud's theory of the primary repressed unconscious, or later, of the unconscious ego. So, it was a failed effort, I think, to link it up to the structural theory.

AM: Your reflections on the self, on idiom, have taken you to explore the realm of "character," a word which appears prominently in the title of your last book. It's not a concept usually invoked by psychoanalysts. . . .

CB: I think that "character" is an aesthetic. If our way of being refers to our very precise means of forming our world, both internal and intersubjective, then each of us is a kind of artist with his or her own creative sensibility. We know that the distinctiveness of that creation is the particular form we have brought to it. We will share many contents with other beings; we share many phenomena in common, but we render them differently, and it's the rendering of a life that is so unique to us.

It is a pleasure to express and articulate the self: there's an erotic dimension to that kind of representation. Indeed I think Freud's theory of the instinct with its source, its aim and its object is an arc

. . . a pure arc . . . without any actual "Other" present in a way. But it's almost a pure arc of the pleasure of representation, because the erotics of the instinct drive is not simply in its final gratification through an object: it's the entire process . . . In order for there to be the reduction of excitation, for there to be pleasure, representation is needed.

My own view is that in the formation of character we similarly have that arc: except I would say that, instead of there being a pure line from source through aim and object, there are many lines that fragment and break, in something like a vast symphonic movement which is, in and of itself, a pleasure. It is not the end point, not what we find at the end, not the objects that reduce the excitation, that constitute the pleasure. The pleasure is in the entire movement: which nonetheless remains something far too complicated and condensed, too thick, to be reduced to a single meaning, or even to two or three meanings, or two or three interpretations.

AM: What about Winnicott's distinction between the optimal progression of an ordinary human life and what he views as the superior development of the creative artist or artistic personality?

CB: I think by "ordinary" he means a return to the unformed existence of an unconscious. Certainly I think psychoanalysis, if it proceeds via the medium of free association, engages the analysand in a process of expression that leads consciousness to realize how extraordinary unconscious life is; in that respect, we must live dangerously, because we do take risks by allowing our unconscious life its freedom. It takes risk to speak what one thinks freely. Therefore, an analysand who is operating within the milieu of free association is living dangerously. And I believe there is a great deal to be gained from that kind of risk: not only is the free-associating analysand creating his analysis, he's creating his life. This is true to the extent that one is not operating through a process of carefully constructed narrative, which then leads the analyst to an equally carefully constructed interpretative narrative, i.e., interpretation of the transference, and so on and so forth. It leads to something more dense and unconscious . . . more frightening, in a way, for both the analyst and analysand, in a sort of pleasurable way . . . One does not often know consciously what to make of this, even though one has quite an acute sense that these movements are essential, intriguing, mysterious, developing. . . .

AM: There was an enormously small word in your last answer of some consequence. You said: "*if* a psychoanalysis proceeds via free association. . . ." That seems to imply that an analysis could proceed differently.

CB: There is a fundamental divergence between analysts or schools who see the analysand's free expression of thought and feeling as a priority, and those who don't. There are, in a certain sense, two paths. Along the first, this fundamental expression would have to take priority over the psychoanalyst's interpretation: without this freedom of mood, of thought, of feeling, without this density, the analysand is not going to issue a license to the unconscious; he or she is not going to find a voice in the context of an analytical situation. For the analyst, this means remaining quiet when he or she can see certain things operating within the transference. The analyst's silence, then, is in the interest of that movement, of that evolution in the analysand which gives rise to meaningful, if limited, self-reflections, to self-generated insights. To insights, mind you, which proceed not only from the psychoanalyst, but from within the patient: insights which over time establish an intriguing relation between the analysand's production of his or her own existence, between the creation of a life through free association and the unconscious movement that informs those insights.

That's one theorization, one path psychoanalysis has taken. On the other path, which is very different but very popular at the present time, is the patient who speaks about his or her life to an analyst, who then translates that speech into a metaphor of the patient's relation to the analyst; or of a part of the patient's self in a here-and-now relation to a part of the analyst. This is something which is not difficult for well-trained psychoanalysts to do, and in my view is also very interesting and meritorious in some ways; but it offers psychoanalysts the opportunity to resolve the ambiguities of a session's unconsciousness through a kind of reliable interpretation of events as they see them taking place. This, I believe, forecloses free association in the analysand, although one could argue that the process is split off within the patient, experienced somewhere but not uttered. Still, the difference between that analysand and the one who's freely speaking is enormous. Well, this difference poses a problem. I have no idea what will happen but, perhaps as time goes on, there will be two substantially distinct traditions in psychoanalysis, and people choosing to have an analysis can have one or the other, and will then know more or less what country they're entering.

AM: It would seem that each of those paths carries with it, perhaps unconsciously, a very different sense of what a psychoanalytic cure would entail.

CB: The highly interpretative analyst is very embracing, and promotes a cure by object relationship, by narrative restructuring. Of course, in the best of times, the interpreting analyst is in fact illuminating important pathological structures, important transferential anxieties: and therefore there is enough truth to his exercise for it to be meaningful for an individual. A lot is gained in this kind of an analysis; if it were a complete waste of time people wouldn't stay with it. They might be drawn to it but wouldn't stay with it for such a long time. But unfortunately, there is as much lost as there is gained in this kind of an analytical procedure. What's lost is something truer to life, because in a life we don't have accompanying us, day-to-day, an interpretative companion. We do not have an analyst alongside us interpreting the interactive meaning of every one of our gestures. And so I don't see how, in the end, that kind of an analysis fits in with a human life. However interactive we are, we're living in a fundamentally solitary space where we will always be generating meanings unconsciously, and only partially understanding ourselves. It is, therefore, the first path of analysis I identified that I believe takes into consideration the full nature of a human life: in that it aims to increase unconscious creativity and to situate unconsciousness, or the interpreting part of the self, in a meaningful but modest relation to creativity; whereas the other form of an analysis operates under a very particular illusion that a partnership, between a purely interpretative self and a purely unconscious self, will exist throughout a human life.

AM: Again on the true self, you write: "A genetically biased set of dispositions, the true self exists before object relating. It is only a potential, however, because it depends on maternal care for its evolution." This could read like an essentialist argument, one that some orthodox Jungians might favor. Was that your intention?

CB: No, though I don't disagree it's an essentialist position. I am arguing that we begin life with an essential core, with a nucleus of logic . . . logical nuclei . . . or, let us say, with "positions" waiting to come into existence, that we somehow have to account for. How can each infant be so different from any other infant? *Forces of Destiny* had on the cover sets of human fingerprints. So what is the psychic correlate of the human fingerprint? I think there is something psychically as irreducibly different about each newborn as the irreducible difference of a fingerprint. And because I don't know where this intuition comes from, I rest back in the area of genetic predisposition. Of course there is a fetal existence, the incredible evolution before birth when the fetus is influenced by the world and engaged in relation to the inside of the mother's body, and to objects beyond the inside of the body. Already then the "something" that we are is in the beginning of a process of fragmentation, of a creative fragmentation that depends on both its own creativity, as well as on the mother's and the father's medium of care: on whether objects are provided for infant and child to use and through which to disseminate themselves.

AM: In what you call a person's "idiom moves," objects in the environment function both as receptors for our projective identifications and structuring agents of the mind. What is the relationship, or perhaps the difference, between these idiomatic expressions of the self and the symbolic elaboration that is the task of *genera*?

CB: I think at any one moment in time, whenever we approach an object, we can say we're either going to use it for its projective potential or for its evocative integrity to structure us differently. There is a different, fundamental orientational attitude in the subject's use of an object. In the process of our own inner unconscious evolutions, we will be using objects either to contain parts of our self or parts of the Other, or in order to break us up via the structuring dimensions that are inherent to the object's integrity. In other words, more to fragment us than to contain the break. In that way, I suppose, where the elaboration of the self is concerned, the movement of *genera* depends upon whether at any moment in time we're deploying the objects in our environment, or whether we ourselves are seeking to be redeployed: whether we're putting ourselves somewhere through the deployment of objects, or whether we ourselves are seeking to be thrown into a new organization.

Any child, then, who is privileged to evolve by virtue of maternal and paternal care will have as an unconscious principle the formation of *genera* and the evolution according to those formations . . . Psychic *genera* cannot emerge within the subject unless there has been substantial support for the evolution of the subject's idiom, which is sort of fundamental paradigm for the *genera* of the self.

AM: In your writing the subjective realm of human experience is paramount, from the womb to the grave. I'm reminded of Victor Turner's etymology of the word *experience*, where he derives it from the Indo-European base *per-*, meaning "to attempt, venture or risk," which also yields the word *peril.* In an essay of Turner's on the anthropology of experience, he identifies the Germanic cognates of *per* in the German words "fare," "fear," and "ferry"; while the Greek *perao* relates experience to "passing through," with all the attendant implications of rites of passage. In your elaboration of the strivings of the self and the workings of *genera*, you seem very much attuned to this tragic quality of much of our existence, as the etymology of the word *experience* indicates.

CB: I like this deconstruction. In a way, the Sophoclean tragic vision is of violent action that breaks things up, followed then by reflection, seeing and sizing up what's occurred. This Sophoclean vision, cast in Oedipal terms, is of devastation, and involves the realization of the unwitting dimensions of the devastation. Put in terms of the Oedipus, we could argue that the entire process is true of the nature of life itself: that consciousness is blind to unconscious development, and that unconscious development is radically destructive.

You could say: 'But what is it destroying?' Perhaps it destroys all mothers and all fathers; perhaps the evolution of any self destroys what was formed for us earlier by the mother, or by the father. Perhaps any evolution is going to break the desires of the Other. It is then that we create our destiny, and live it. There are objects of desire and objects of hate, objects of intimacy and corpses of the expelled; and then, when we look back, in a Sophoclean way, one could say: 'My God, what have I done? Only now I understand it all.' And we see that progression as a tragic one, or as the ordinary way in which life is lived, as something unavoidable. Thus, in the notion of existing, or of experience, are the concepts of a ruthless breaking, of an opening up, of a dissemination, of a perilous venture. And, in addition, of something which borders on a kind of reflective faith: a kind of belief, upon reflection, that what's taken place was unavoidable and essential.

AM: Thinking back at your discussion of the erotics of self-representation and the aesthetics of the self, are these pleasures simply breaks or interludes in the context of this greater tragedy? How do the tragedy and pleasure play off each other?

CB: I think representation is a pleasure; therefore, the representation of Oedipus, the Sophoclean presentation itself, is a pleasure. Whatever the contents of the tale, whatever the story, its telling is always a pleasure. This is why I think, in the end, that Freud's theory of the dream as a wish fulfillment is true: not because the contents of the dream fulfill a precise wish of the dreamer, but because the representation of the dream, its creation, the very act of dreaming, is the fulfillment of the wish. The wish is to represent. So what we do or say is always a pleasure in that sense. Yet the fact that something is pleasing to the subject does not mean that it's good; it doesn't mean that it's going to be morally admirable. The pleasure could be awful, it could be terrible: but it would be, nonetheless, in the service of desire.

AM: Postmodernism contends that "the center does not hold," that the function of narrative–as one way of identifying or cohering around a center–has essentially been lost. Psychoanalysis seems to oscillate between the free-associative dimension you've emphasized and what you're now identifying as the pleasure of the narrative. Still, I've found that a sense of history is missing more and more in the tellings of patients. There seem to be fewer and fewer stories to tell; and the stories people do tell are often altogether devoid of pleasure. This quality, in my experience, almost takes on a pathological dimension. Is this something that you see as a generalized contemporary malady, or is it something that the very nature of psychoanalysis exacerbates?

CB: That's a very interesting question. I've not really heard it put like that before. I agree, there is less pleasure in the historical rendering of the self, or the rendering of the self in history than certainly there was in the past. I'm limited here by my American life, because I lived in the U.S. until I was 30, during the rise of Erik Erikson's work, when the taking of the history and the giving of the history were very important.

Certainly I've understood the phenomenon in terms of the European migrations to America: once one has left one's place of origin for a new country, what one subsequently does becomes in effect a personal account of heroic evolution. The birth of the hero comes with crossing the seas, as Otto Rank might suggest. But the crossing of the ocean, the rebirth on the new continent, and the subsequent evolution of the self, all give rise to a very neat narrative progression, with its emphasis on accomplishment, and so on. A myth, I think, Americans find very palatable. In the world of psychoanalysis and psychotherapy, American clinicians were very very keen to hear the history of the patient, even if the person had been born and raised in the United States. Something of the myth of the hero was an important part of American consciousness. Today in the U.S., that is less the case than it was 20 years ago or so, and I think it no doubt has something to do with the failure to imagine a country capable of giving a new birth to the self, a capacity held to be true in earlier decades. That imaginative possibility has broken down, and therefore a certain relation to the history of the self is now more problematic.

AM: Only occasionally, in your work, is there a mention of Freud's idea of the death instinct, whereas its correlative of the life instinct is given ample press, as evidenced by the emphases on *idiom* and *genera*. How do you envision Freud's grand instinctual dualism? And would you grant it a kind of biological status, or does it serve primarily as a metaphor for the inescapable tensions we all confront?

CB: I think of it as a principle. The death instinct, like the life instinct, articulates or explains certain fundamental attitudes in relation to life itself. That is, if one is going to make use of life, and of all that goes into a life, as an object, we can speak of the life instincts operating; if a person withdraws from life as an object and shuts the self down, then I believe we can talk about a death instinct. Freud's theory of the death instinct, which fundamentally has to do with the decathexis of the object and a retreat into a narcissistic position, is a theory which makes eminent clinical sense to me. One can see it with certain patients who refuse and have retreated from object usage.

However, to give Freud's portrayal of these superordinate moving categories an allegorical power, such that we are driven by life instincts or death instincts, is not something I'm comfortable with. Different from Freud's, Melanie Klein's theory of the death instinct seems more configured around the infant's projection of persecutory factors. Though I find this interesting, I also do not agree with the extent of her allegorization of these two forces in the subject's attitude toward life itself. It's gone too far, and doesn't make sense to me.

AM: You write in *Forces of Destiny* of "a virtually legal imperative to pursue desire, . . . of the ruthless pleasure of the human subject to find joy in the choice and use of the object. Indeed, there is an urge to use objects through which to articulate–and hence be–the true self, and I term this the destiny drive." What do you see, then, as the relationship between Freud's pleasure principle and "the destiny drive"?

CB: I think they are very similar. I think the pleasure principle generates the destiny drive. All that I'm adding to Freud's pleasure principle is an aesthetic dimension, an aesthetic aim. The pleasure of intelligence that forms the link between an urge, the aim of the urge, its object and the gratification of the precise pleasure of the self. That structure, that aesthetic dimension, is a crucial part of the selection and use of an object, which I see as part of the subject's destiny drive.

AM: I imagine it is the case with everyone who practices psychoanalysis that one's own analysis has had profound effects on one's life and obviously on one's thinking. Would you be able to say anything about that?

CB: I had three analysts, the first when I was a student at the University of California. He was a Mexican who, to the best of my knowledge, originally had a Kleinian training and then, after coming to North America, was training classically. My second analyst, during my training period in England, was Pakistani, from the Independent Group, who was analyzed by Winnicott. And my third–one should never say final analysis!–my third analysis was with an Italian. So all three people were from different cultures, with entirely different ways of viewing life, although each one was operating, in his best moments, in a way that conveyed a sense of the universality of psychoanalytical methodology. So I was always, in some ways, in the same place. I was always somehow within the same method, though there were three different drivers, three different people who operated and interpreted.

Obviously one is profoundly affected by one's analyst, but the last person who really knows in what way he or she has been affected is the analysand, precisely because of the nature of the transference and, arguably, because of the need for true unconscious participation to be unconscious. So, I have only glimmers of the ways in which each of these analysts has influenced my way of practicing. And although I was influenced by the best of their work, there are certain ways in which they got me wrong, or said things that were poorly constructed, or took certain positions that I learned from, because I knew they were mistakes. I think I learned from their mistakes as well as from their more creative, technical dimensions.

AM: Is it safe to assume that all three of these people had a language other than English as their mother tongue? I find that rather peculiar.

CB: They all had a language other than English as their mother tongue. I haven't thought about this until your question, but I think each of them also had built into him what I would call a generative hesitation. That is, I was not immediately sensible to any of them, but there was built into their speech, into their form of address, a form of translation which slowed down the process. I think this was enormously helpful to me, because the last thing I needed was quick response, or premature interpretation or precocious comprehension.

And indeed I suppose I was eventually drawn to the Independent group because of the high priority placed on analytical quiet, on the essentials of reverie and the permission not to speak, which was part of that group's technique. My first analyst too, though originally Kleinian, certainly gave me very considerable amounts of time to find myself internally before I spoke, and then to lose my self through speech in ways which were intriguing.

AM: Did it ever happen that because of this intrinsic and fundamental language bridge you had to cross, your own sense of being comprehended was compromised? Was this generative hesitation of theirs paralleled by any hesitation of yours?

CB: Oddly enough, no, I think this may have something to do with the fact that my father is French. His first language was French, his second language was Spanish, and English was his third, no, his fourth language. He knew French, Spanish, Italian and then English. But the three analysts that I was fortunate to have were all intelligent, gifted people who tolerated not knowing, and who gave themselves plenty of time. When they did speak, they all tended to do so with lucidity, putting their thoughts into language in ways I found creative.

Perhaps one of the interesting facets of translating, not consciously but unconsciously, from a mother tongue or a father tongue to a third or fourth language, is that what one says is always going to be rather idiomatic in its expression, always rather inventive, in its arriving in the moment. I quite liked the odd ways, sometimes, in which my analysts put their thoughts. I liked the invention that took place in language. It had a certain sincerity to it, a certain truth, a lack of guile, a kind of refreshing affection.

Any effort of thought into speech, any real effort, is very intense; it's hard work; and when my analysts made their interpretations, what often impressed me was the intensity and concentration, the sheer effort of putting something into language that had not before been put into language until that moment. And the fact that they were not of the same tongue as was I meant that we couldn't have commonly assumed cliches. There wasn't what I'd call the "lazy" element of language. I think I benefited from that; in fact, I know I did.

AM: I'm thinking of your writings, of your acknowledged de-emphasis of interpretation, and your parallel emphasis on nonverbal forms of knowledge, on intuition. To what extent may these attitudes of yours have derived from the experience of your own analyses?

CB: If I were to go back through my books, there's one correction I would like to make, regarding the unnecessary rivalry between verbal and nonverbal, between the uninterpretative and the interpretative. I would want to go back and, in the interest of accuracy, give a higher priority to the function of interpretation than I originally gave in my writings. I think there is a link between language, between speaking and internal inspiration. Whatever one's intuition is, one does not ultimately know what one thinks until one speaks, and therefore interpretation creates perspectives that are intimately linked with the unconscious work taking place inside. I think, regrettably, that I underplayed that aspect of analysis.

AM: Has this shift been reflected in your own clinical practice? Do you find that you interpret more now than you suggest in your writings?

CB: No, I think I always have interpreted more than I was able to bring about in my writing. Actually, it's not that I've interpreted more, but that interpretation was more important to me and to my analysands than I managed to communicate in my written work. Writing in the 1970s about clinical work, I underemphasized interpretation because unfortunately, in Great Britain at the time, it was the view of the Kleinian group in particular, that only through interpretation could one gain access to the patient. So I was inside a political and polemical world at that time, and unfortunately went too far to the other extreme.

AM: I gather from the biographical hints in your own work that you came to psychoanalysis from literature. Could you chart that itinerary?

CB: I came to psychoanalysis when I was an undergraduate at Berkeley, at a point in my life when I was very distressed. I needed help, and so I went to the Student Health Service, and by chance was assigned to see a psychoanalyst. I had been studying history, and had come to read psychoanalysis because I was working on

17th Century New England village life, and was very interested in the Puritan mind. But my introduction to psychoanalysis was really through my own psychotherapy. As an undergraduate, then, I studied with Fred Crews: he invited me to his graduate seminar on literature and psychoanalysis, where I became more interested in the intellectual dimensions of psychoanalysis.

After graduation I worked at the East Bay Activity Center in Oakland, with autistic and schizophrenic children. Working with them I found the mystery of their illnesses so compelling and intellectually challenging that I knew I wanted to continue with that sort of work. I didn't know at the time how I could do it, because I didn't want to study psychology, and I didn't want to study medicine. As I was very keen on literature and wanted to go to the University of Buffalo, I went there to study literature and psychoanalysis. It was through the Department of Psychiatry that I was able to continue with clinical work there; they created a little niche for me, and eventually we helped form together a university program in psychotherapy for people in the humanities. When I had to choose, ultimately, between being a professor of literature and clinical life, there wasn't any difficulty for me. I knew I wanted to train to be an analyst. I wanted to train in Great Britain, where I was accepted for training and came over in 1973.

AM: Sometimes, when I read your work, the words *use of the object* echo with a ring of self-serving ruthlessness, where arguably the self being served is only served at the expense of other human beings, of other selves. Is it your position that your writings are intrinsically divested of ideological, moral or ethical implications? I can't help but wonder if the language itself is somehow a by-product of the "ruthlessness" of the 1980s, and of the social and economic policies of that period. . . .

CB: One of the difficulties in writing about "ruthlessness" was the fact that in the 1980s, the term had a very particular moral significance–and correctly so. It was paradoxical that, at a time when the concept of the id–of that which grasps and takes for ruthless, amoral reasons–had departed psychoanalytical writings and been replaced by too sanitized a language, I was, in a way, reintroducing the idea just as a certain type of greed was operating in a ruthless way in the culture at-large. This is something I was aware of, and was not all that pleasing to me. But nonetheless, I spent a lot of time on those essays, going over and over them to try to make clear what I was writing about. In effect, whether we like it or not, if we cannot be ruthless in the primary, instinctual sense, in the sense of the infant's need to feed, if we cannot follow that early urge . . . I don't believe that the true self, or object usage, will arrive. Indeed much of psychic conflict has to do with different forms of antipathy towards urges and drives and so on. But where ruthlessness is concerned, I address it on purely psychological, and not moral, terms.

AM: A focus of *Being a Character*, already prefigured in *Forces of Destiny*, is your concern with the creative personality; with the fashioning of a life as a work of art. You point out how so much of this effort has to do with the maternal provision of an illusion of creativity in infancy, from which the child secures a sense of somehow engendering the object world. But you also stress repeatedly, albeit in passing, the function of what Peter Blos calls the "pre-oedipal father." What about the infant's generation of and introduction to the object world, via the ministrations and presences of both parents?

CB: We are now having to try to define what we imagine to be the infant's experience of the father. My own imaginings incorporate many of the well-known psychoanalytical views of the place of the father: the father as the embodiment of reality beyond the couple; the father, in the Kleinian sense, as the embodiment of the phallic entry into the mother's body; the father as intergenerational presence, and so on. But to these ideas I would add the "textural" difference of the father from the mother, or the "feel" of the father: the father who embodies a different odor, a different smell, who has a different way of holding, of carrying the child; who has a different way of breathing, of walking, a different tone of voice. Qualities which, for our purposes of discussion, I would say embody the masculine. The father is the embodiment of the masculine, much as the mother is the embodiment of the feminine. And I think, at both a biological, sensual level and at a higher level of imaginative distinction, that the mother and the father are enormously different; and that the infant, therefore, is, as it were, carried by two different persons. Arguably, the presence of agreeable difference–of difference not in the violent sense, not in the sense of having either gender eradicated–is an essential part of the child's development of creative opposition.

AM: Blos talks about the early father's role as being essential developmentally in breaking the symbiotic bond to the mother and instituting that sense of difference. Would you say something similar?

CB: Lacan takes that position as well, I think, in his concept of the Name of the Father, invoked to separate the infant from the mother. Yes, this I think is a widely held European view. I think in European psychoanalysis there is a consensus that the father has an important function in separating the infant from the mother. One could call this a kind of early Oedipal formation based upon the father's desire, as it is imagined by the child. In it, the child, so to speak, imagines the father's entry in order to properly create the separation from the mother later in the Oedipal period.

AM: Before addressing the question of the contemporary fate of our cultural superego, I wonder how you see the origins of the personal superego? Given what you just said, if you take Freud's classic Oedipal conflict on one end, and Klein's much earlier developmental configuration of the superego on the other, how do you see the father's role in the formation of the superego?

CB: I believe Klein and Freud are talking about two different mental structures; though they both use the term "superego," they're not talking about the same mental structure. On the one hand, Freud's idea makes enormous sense: that in identification with the father, the child takes in and psychically transforms the actual Other into an imaginary companion, as part of a tripartite structure between the instinctual urges and the ego-self's presence. It makes sense if we look at it as the first moment, or moments, in the rise of a judicious self-awareness, in which the child is actually weighing up, *in consciousness*, the play of the different elements of the self that get mediated by the ego: of instincts and paternal prohibitions, of paternal views and so on. This theory of the superego, then, has much to do with the arrival of consciousness, of a sort of self-reflectiveness or awareness. But above all else it addresses the child's mediation between the different forces of the mind, the different elements that go into a self.

On the other hand, the Kleinian superego refers to persecutory anxieties the infant projects into the object, which is then imagined to be harmed by those very projections. It has a principle of retaliatory law, an intention to harm the infant. So there is an initial anxiety, perhaps an initial drive, increasing greed and envy in this area, which intensifies the attack on the object and then leads to this kind of projective circle I've just defined. Now, I do believe this is a factor in all infant life, but that it's more decidedly present in infants where there's been a breakdown in the infant-mother relationship. To such a child the persecutory anxieties become more predominant. I do not think this is linked to the father, as such; this is not part of superego formation. This is part of the formation of consciousness, but is not the moment in which self-awareness arrives in the infant. What Freud envisioned, and how he saw the superego played out within the context of the family, is a very different imagining, of a very particular way, that the child has of conceptualizing himself.

AM: Quoting you: "I think that one of the tasks of an analysis is to enable the analysand to come into contact with his destiny, which means the progressive articulation of his true self through many objects." Very simply, how does psychoanalysis accomplish this?

CB: By supporting the patient's right to free association. Through free associating the patient unconsciously selects objects of desire and articulates, through these objects, evolving self experiences. Now, some patients have a very real difficulty free associating: for some initially it's impossible, and therefore the analytical task through interpretation and other means is to try to free this person up so that they can actually speak more freely, so that they can develop a form of unconscious creativity. Once that occurs, once the analysand is freely associating, then he or she is quite naturally picking objects up. We're talking here, of course, of mental objects: of objects that come into mind through which nascent self-states are released into articulation.

AM: Is it free associating, ultimately, that you see as being the curative or reparative factor, even in dealing with the scars that result from the early breakdowns or failures in environmental provision?

CB: I certainly think that the capacity to freely associate is the most important curative dimension of the psychoanalytical treatment. It is the medium, in my view, through which analysands can articulate themselves, reflect on what they mean by what they say, and ultimately develop a good enough intrapsychic relation between the unconscious part of the self–which is ultimately beyond knowing–and consciousness which wishes to know something and to make something out of unconscious processes. This I think happens through the process of free association, which is a kind of intermediary between purely unconscious phenomena and lucidity. In short, free association is the presence of the true self in a session.

AM: In this light, what about the dialectic of transference and countertransference? As forms of knowledge encapsulated outside of words, in the realm of the psyche-soma, how can their dynamics "provide" for destinies to unfold? Could you relate some clinical examples?

CB: As I said a moment ago, it's through free association that the destiny drive has its purest form or path. But patients also use their analysts, or they use part of the analyst's personality, quite unconsciously, I believe, in a way that this usage remains unconscious even for the analyst himself. Through the use of an analyst, the patient can elaborate, or give rise to and articulate, different parts of the self.

This, I think, is where there are very profound differences among patients who do not make a lot of sense when looked at according to psychoanalytical psychodiagnostics. For example, one can be working with a narcissistic analysand or a borderline analysand. The two can have similar pathologies. With the borderline there can be a movement between claustrophobic anxieties and agorophobic anxieties, a back-and-forth oscillation; with a narcissistic patient there can be a kind of autistic, enclosed dimension to his or her object relating. One can see these shifts in both, but with one of these individuals there may be a much greater use of the analyst. For example, one borderline patient might be relatively nonverbal, relatively dead; another might be more verbal, describing different experiences with very different shades of affect that in turn elicit different feelings, different associations, or different responses from and inside the analyst. In the latter situation the psychoanalyst is being used much more complexly; the patient's degree of object use is much richer. Both patients are the same psychodiagnostically, but when it comes to the use of an object, the object is being used very differently.

This kind of transference, which Winnicott only implied in his concept of the use of an object, is not something to be found in the psychoanalytical literature. There one customarily finds references to fairly clear coercions, or fairly clear projective identifications, which have a particular sort of effect upon a clinician: inevitably, the outcome of the pathology. The logical extension of Winnicott's thinking, where the use of an object is concerned, is to look not so much at the pathology of the analysand, but at what outside the area of the illness are the capacities of the personality in relation to the Other. That is, how can this personality use the Other? This makes all the difference in the world so far as the ability to make use of life as an object is concerned.

Thus, we can take a borderline personality like Sylvia Plath, who had a tragic life and committed suicide . . . And yet, at the same time, she wrote some of the world's greatest poetry, with a capacity to relate to her cultural objects that was quite profound. Another borderline personality, not a poet, who was restricted in many areas, might not make use of any objects and would have an even less enriched life. Sylvia Plath was mentally ill, as indeed are all borderline personalities, but unlike some, she also made use of life: which perhaps is one of the reasons why we look to her as such a tragic figure. If her life had been an irremediable write-off, if she had been a total loss to herself and all others, then individuals reading her works and reading about her would not feel such a loss. But it's because she enriched herself and others through her use of the object world that to see her kill herself, we feel an even greater loss. Because this was not a dead soul. There are some patients, unfortunately but true enough, whose lives are so bleak, who are so profoundly without creativity, so unnourished by any part of their life experience, that one can feel in the countertransference that one is not being used as an object, one is not being utilized unconsciously.

With such patients, there's very little life present; whereas in other persons, with similar structural difficulties and with similar pathologies, there is a more complex and enriched use of the self.

AM: You mentioned a type of patient who presents him- or herself as dead, and often stays that way for very long, excruciating lengths of time. Technically, where free association is not within the patient's repertoire, do you just wait out that person, or that self state?

CB: I don't have, as I expect you'll appreciate, categorical, technical moves. Inevitably, my response would rely entirely upon who that particular patient is, where that particular patient was in the analysis, what understanding if any I had of what the aim was of that deadness. There are certain situations in which I will be quiet and say very little, if anything, in an hour, or in the course of days. But there are other occasions in which I will be talking to the patient, telling him or her what I think this means, what is happening. In the best of times, psychoanalysts hopefully find themselves approaching a problem with a particular patient, differently than they would any other patient. Our own technical interventions, I think, are thus part of the unconscious work occurring usually, spontaneously and freely within us.

AM: In your concluding chapter to *Being a Character*, you talk surprisingly about the "necessity" of a false self; how there is something intrinsic to psychic life that seems to require it. You almost seem to suggest that to fully develop the true self, or to elaborate one's idiom, could lead one to the limits of madness. Could you address this idea?

CB: The false self allows each person to construct a ready-made means of negotiating with the conventional object world, while preserving the complicated movements of the true self in the unconscious. I should make a parenthesis here and say this was Winnicott's point to begin with: when he first constructed his theory, he said there was a *necessary* false self in relation to the object world.

AM: Is there an echo here of the conservative nature of the life instinct?

CB: Perhaps there is . . . and certainly there is an echo, really and simply, of going back to Freud's theory of unconscious functioning.

In remaining true to Freud's theory of the unconscious, we operate as highly complex creatures. The simple operation of condensation or displacement in unconscious life is so thick, so obviously beyond consciousness, that were we to be continuously reminded of our complexity, we would be confronted with a form of madness. We forget, we simply forget about that complexity. In a way we forget about ourselves; and in forgetting about ourselves, we allow the self or selves to get on with their own perambulations, evolutions, interests, curiosities, and so on . . . And we benefit from that kind of forgetting.

AM: Much like Lacan, you too seem involved in a "return to Freud" that continually mines his findings to rethink his concepts. There is a vitality, in your writing, that in a way returns the unconscious to ontological status. How does Christopher Bollas understand, or imagine, the unconscious?

CB: When I was re-reading *The Interpretation of Dreams* some years ago, I was struck by the fact that in Chapters 4, 5, and 6, we have the clearest, most lucid charting of the way the unconscious works in psychoanalysis. I was immediately struck by how all of Freud's subsequent theorizings on the unconscious, particularly in Chapter 7 of *The Interpretation of Dreams*, in his metapsychological papers, and then with the structural model, were all much less adequate, much less clear. In those chapters of *The Interpretation of Dreams*, together with his books *Jokes and Their Relation to the Unconscious* and *The Psychopathology of Everyday Life*, Freud indicates how the unconscious works. He shows through examples condensations and displacements, substitutions, assimilations; he illustrates the dense texture that is the unconscious process of an existence.

I was taken by how the dream, as a nighttime representational event, as the mid-point in a total process originating within competing daytime psychic intensities, worked to discharge the excitements and the energies of those very intensities—but without discharging their meaning! I was taken by how, the next day, the breaking up of the dream text occurred, through the process of free association, which in turn breaks open this condensation, and leads to a kind of intense outward movement. That whole arc, that whole evolution, is a remarkable example of how we live unconsciously. It's a process I've verified in my own life, as well as in my work with patients, charting the flows and ruptures of my own psychic intensities.

I came then to believe that Freud's theory of the dream's evolution, of this nighttime event which carries with it the history and experiences of the preceding day, the history of the infant or child, and which brings all this into a text that's broken up through free association . . . I came to believe this entire process takes place on a much smaller scale, one might say on a less unconsciously creative scale, during our every day. This realization led me to imagine self experience in ways which, through re-reading Freud, I feel are closer to the way we truly are: that is, at any one moment, under the influence of our entire history. But then something new occurs. We meet up with an object which evokes an intensity within us: not because the object has some inherently meritorious dimension, but because it has to do with our own self. Something I see walking along a street generates an intense moment for me that it wouldn't for you, or for anyone else.

This reaction, then, obviously has to do with one's subjectivity. But without the object there, without the integrity of *that* object, the reaction is not going to happen. Freud, for example, sees a botanical monogram in a bookstore, an object with quite a powerful evocative capacity to it. At that moment of perception a kind of nucleus is made, and a gravity befalls Freud. We could say this is a type of *genera*, newly formed. Then, for Freud as for us all, upon the moment's being experienced, upon the completion and fruition of that intensity, certain things will come into consciousness and begin to break up that moment, through the trains of thought that had compacted into its evocative quality. We are then off in a thousand different directions, until the next such psychic intensity. Now, I realize this is too schematic, too simplistic. Intensities are occurring inside us all the time. We can remember an intensity from the day before or a few hours before . . . we don't have to be experiencing an actual object for all this to be taking place. But if we can begin to see this phenomenon as a kind of universe of stars . . . as limitless, gravity-laden intensities that somehow endure and convey themselves, then I think we have a rather accurate metaphor of what we are and how we think: a metaphor that makes room for both our conscious and unconscious minds.

AM: Where a pathology or a neurosis is present, would you agree that the number of objects that might evoke these intensities in the course of a human life is somewhat limited? And is there invariably a limit to the number of objects that even a healthy personality can be "intensed" by, so to speak?

CB: That's a good question; I only wish I knew the answer. Individuals who are ill, who are foreclosed for different reasons, will have a narrower range of objects. They will therefore have fewer generative, evocative experiences of the object. It doesn't mean, however, they're going to have fewer psychic intensities: they could have more psychic intensities than another individual. But they will have less generative experiences of the object world. No doubt, in order to protect ourselves against the intrinsic complexity of our capability, we choose to limit the field of the evocative, because otherwise it could be too intense an existence. Certain friends of mine, for example, who are poets, tend to maximize their perceptions of the object world and thus invite quite powerful evocative moments. They live a life of continuous surprise, whereas I myself am too cautious and conservative a person to want to live that stimulated an existence.

AM: Your emphasis on the object's evocative qualities reminded me, indirectly, of Lacan's idea of the signifying chain. What has been his influence on your work? Unlike Wilfred Bion and Winnicott, whose provisions come across as maternal, indeed as transformational objects or transitional spaces, in the course of your oeuvre, when it comes to Lacan I sense a more "ghostly" presence. Why is that?

CB: It's not simply Lacan. I think it's the French, and French psychoanalysis, which I feel very close to. I've read in translation some of Andre Green's works, as well as Pontalis and Smirnoff, but I have a less consciously foregrounded use of French thinking than I do of British thinking. About Lacan, I did not like his work to begin with. I was unsure whether this was a person who was to be "believed." There were grave questions in my mind about whether he was writing in good faith or bad faith, but I benefited from close friends who had studied his work or knew him personally, most importantly Stuart Schneiderman. So I have read Lacan and find him increasingly relevant, but in ways I'm afraid I just don't know.

AM: When I originally asked the question about Lacan, in my notes I had next to the word "ghostly," in parentheses, the word "fatherly," followed by a question mark. When I conceived the question, I didn't know your father was French. . . .

CB: That was immediately how I understood your question, you see! I think that I'm very influenced by my father and his way of thinking, by his whole frame of mind. He thinks, and has lived his life (he's still alive), as a French person does. His world is so much a part of me, so unconsciously absorbed, that it makes the French and their thinking very familiar. I feel in some way as if these are the people from whom one learns. But I don't speak or read French adequately, and that makes for a complex relation to French intellectual tradition. On the one hand, I would like to know more than I do, but I'm restricted by my own inadequacies, as far as the language is concerned.

AM: Your idea of "futures" harkens back to the earlier reference of the postmodern "selves." The plural is one you yourself often use, as the idea of the self's multiplicity has recently been making a lot of noise: Stephen Mitchell and Jane Flax have both written extensively on it, theorizing multiplicities that James Glass, on the other hand, sees as an unwarranted, and indeed pernicious exaltation of the states that inform multiple personality disorders and schizophrenia. What do you mean when you write of "selves"? How do they manifest in the course of a given treatment? And where do you stand in the current debate?

CB: It depends upon how the term's being used, on what we're addressing or attempting to articulate. We are "selves" because in the course of time, of a human lifetime, this self that we are has many representations of itself, along with many representations of the object. In one day alone we go through many different self states, which by itself implies a plurality to our experience of our own being. And it's not an occasional plurality: it's a structure. We're fated to be multiple; to have, in a sense, a multitude of self and object representations. At the same time, I believe that all of us have–if we're fortunate enough–a feeling of unity: a feeling of there being one "self," even if we were to argue against that possibility. In the spirit of your polarization of the argument, I think that both positions are correct. One without the other is either too simplistic or too dangerous: we are both multiple and one at the same time.

So we do have a sense of a self. In an essay from my book *Cracking Up*, I argue that we have within us a sense of a nucleus that gives rise to our particular aesthetic in being. We have a sense of our own self-authorship, of something that is irreducible and that determines us. It is my point, in that essay, that though we may never know what that "something" is–in theology some might say it's "God"–that sense is a kind of organization that somehow determines us, that drives or predisposes us. But I can't say I have a great interest in this particular debate, even though I am sympathetic with those who regard this celebration of multiplicity as too "over-the-top"; I agree that it is, that it's too celebrated as a kind of accomplishment. We seem to go into fashions where there are these polarizations of one side of a binary process, and I think we are now over-privileging the multiple.

AM: You quote Madame de Stael: "The greatest things that man has done, he owes to the painful sense of incompleteness of his destiny." Is there an echo here, of a Lacanian dialectic of desire and "lack"? Or does "the incompleteness we all must endure" refer to something else?

CB: I think it refers to being a psychoanalyst at work with a patient. To the fact that, as a psychoanalyst, one launches the most intense process of self discovery that we have yet fashioned in Western culture, and that this process can be generated and cultivated by two people working together. And yet, at the end of the day, this process raises more questions than it answers. I have to live all the time with my own sense of incompleteness as a psychoanalyst, and my analysands' sense of the incompletion of their own analytical lives . . . I'm now 51, and probably more aware than before of what will inevitably be the incompleteness of a life. One can only know, only see, so much. It's not as if there's not a lot more to be seen or known, even within oneself . . . but we're too unconsciously productive to ever be able to fully grasp ourselves . . . In that sense we can't get hold of ourselves.

AM: Last night I had the occasion to hear an interview with Allen Ginsberg. After starting off by revisiting states or stages of Ginsberg's life that might have been reflected by the poet's changing appearance over the years, the interviewer ended up by asking: 'Who is the real Allen Ginsberg?' To which Ginsberg replied: 'Well, they all are, and none of them are.' He went on to relate his experience as a practitioner of Buddhist meditation, and spoke primarily in terms of a Zen orientation. When Christopher Bollas writes about the true self, is there at any level a correspondence with the self that Zen purports to influence?

CB: If so, it is not intentional. But it certainly has come to my attention, predominantly from people who are Zen Buddhists, that some of what I say resonates with some of their own beliefs. When writing, as in *Being a Character*, about the unconscious as a form of fragmentation, of a psychically intense experience, as a process of deep or thick experience that radiates out and dissolves the intensity, or through which the intensity is dissolved, Zen practitioners have told me that what I'm trying to convey is close to the notion of that which is gained through the dissolution of the ego: a view which, when I first read about in Zen Buddhism in the 1960s, I always thought was nonsense, because I understood it in terms of ego psychology at the time. Nowadays, I understand a little bit more about the idea; that is, that a form of consciousness must dissolve in order for a type of freedom to occur within the subject. In that limited area, then, I reckon there is some overlap between what I'm saying and what Zen Buddhists have maintained and believed for a very, very long time. But, as I'm not versed in Buddhist thought, I'm not in a position to comment on confluences in any depth.

AM: Complementary to your notion of destiny is that of "futures," what you call "imaginary objects that are visions of potential use." "Fated futures," you write, "carry the weight of despair"–where you acknowledge the stifling effects of oppressive socio-cultural contexts alongside customary environmental and parental trauma. Could you reflect for a moment–perhaps much as you have in chapters from *Being a Character* on "The Fascist State of Mind" and "Generational Consciousness"–on the "futures" that inhabit our present socio-cultural, or "postmodern," contexts? What do you see them carrying into the twenty-first century?

CB: For a black child living in Detroit, in a large family without a father present, and with a mother overwhelmed, perhaps on dope, seeing twenty-year-old blacks being killed, and few surviving into their thirties . . . One would say there's very little in that child's future. There's very little in what he or she can imagine about a future that will facilitate the radical imagining of a self: this is essential, in my view, for any person's envisioning or appropriation of a future, and for its use as an object. Among middle class people, each generation violently destroys the previous generation's ideals and objects; it is through this process of destruction, then, that each generation constitutes its own objects, through which to envision its own future. And it is in this respect that a generation gets hold of its future and uses it as an object.

Much of the literature today, on the so-called lost generation, is a literature written by people in mid-life or older, in which there's a kind of anticipatory grief over what today's youth will not get. I'm suspicious of that kind of writing. I think it reflects more of the generational crisis of the baby-boomers themselves, a generation of great ideals that is now facing its demise and having a very hard time dealing with the losses that are part of that evolution. What's happening, I think, is that this group is projecting its own despair over its own mortality, into the next generation; so that the adolescents of today, and those in their early twenties, are unconsciously meant not to have as good a future. I don't believe this will be true. I think that young people today, from what I can see, are generating their own idioms: musically, in fashion, in literature . . . and I see no indications that they are bereft of a capacity to envision their futures. They don't imagine themselves in their futures in the ways we imagined ourselves.

When Sputnik went up in 1957, all Americans thought that they were immediately part of a march into the future, called upon to save their nation twenty years hence. And there was an enormous fuss made over our generation, as the one that could save the generations then in power. This made for an over-investment in the politics of future, and in the future of a self imagined through politics. Today, of course, there is enormous despair in the United States and in other countries amongst people of our generation over the so-called failure of politics.

If my generation is critical of contemporary youth, over how they've lost their ideals, have no political aims, or don't seem particularly interested in "doing" anything, I'd say that criticism is an unfair and inaccurate portrayal of contemporary youth who generally seem to have a more modest idea of what is realizable and can be accomplished in a life. They're not all marching off to Harvard or Yale or looking to get MBAs . . . and I think it's altogether for the better. They're less likely to be materially as well off as our generations were, or so we're told, and so their imaginings of their future seems more modest. But by "modest" I don't mean less creative: it may well be a more creative generation than ours was.

AM: In this context, you end your chapter on the destiny drive with a lovely meditation on the richness of the term "personal effects," and with a mention of the analyst's related work in discerning the analysand's culture. We're back, it seems, in the realm of an anthropology of the person: among objects, structures, and relationships that echo for me Gaston Bachelard's idea of a "poetics of space." Would you comment on this?

CB: I'm pleased you bring Bachelard into this conversation. He is someone whom I read in the late 1960s and was very important in my development. I loved *The Poetics of Space, The Poetics of Reverie* and his other books. I think he's had an effect upon my imagining of psychoanalysis, and on the way I think of people. Roland Barthes was also very important to my way of thinking. Some of his early books were very crucial to the way I imagined my patients, if I think of the ways in which he deconstructs cultural objects to reveal mythopoetic thoughts; I found intriguing, for example, his idea of the way a culture thinks through its commodities. And I believe it's not too difficult to move from his analysis of such phenomena to any patient's discussion of an object in a psychoanalysis. These objects are saturated with private meanings and idiomatic significations.

AM: In your own work you've hinted at some of the "personal effects," at some of the personal and cultural objects that fill "your house," so to speak. What are some of those around which your experience has crystallized?

CB: It's hard for me to know, because I think those individuals whose works influenced me–whether in literature, film, music, or painting–are usually not persons whom I formally turn into objects of prolonged study as such. Ironically, I probably spent more time with certain writers and thinkers whom I believe I should come to terms with, whom I should address or make use of, than those who really and truly affect me. Of these I am less aware. So I have, for example, felt I *should* work with the thoughts and theories of Wilfred Bion. Working with Bion's writings has been important to my own way of thinking, but he's not a pleasure to read. I don't find him such an agreeable spirit, if I can put it like that. His language is, to me, colorless and without poetry, without vitality. But at the same time, he is a profound thinker, and I made a decision that I had to come to terms with him.

Of those people who have really and truly influenced me, most are from outside of psychoanalysis. Some, like Gustav Mahler, or Kant, I cannot even say in what way . . . Mahler has influenced for me a vision of the self, or a vision of life; for several years I listened to his music, read the scores, listening and reading at the same time . . . But I couldn't possibly say how that has affected me. More recently, I saw De Kooning's exhibit in New York three times; the first time was so overwhelming I had to leave halfway through. Then I returned the next day and saw the exhibit through, and then returned again two days after that. I suppose I spent about seven or eight hours at this exhibition; and I know for sure I have not been so moved by an object in a long time.

I think DeKooning's way of painting captures something about the nature of the unconscious; there's something about his expression of textures, of thought and ambition and endeavor, and about the way he erases . . . The way he scrapes off certain lines, certain figurations that are then painted over . . . but the erased lines are still there somewhere . . . Something about his vision, his vision and revision, really spoke to me. What he taught me, in a way similar to Freud's theory of deferred action, is that the unconscious is not just an envisioning, but a re-visioning; and therefore, while one is writing one's self, one also edits and cuts and pastes and reviews, again and again and again. I think this was a very profound "discovery" on DeKooning's part. One has to put it that way. It's in Freud, but DeKooning actually, literally, illustrated the discovery. So in all I've been very affected by this, and seeing that exhibit has changed my whole way of thinking about life. But will I cite DeKooning in my next book? It's unlikely . . . It would seem odd, out of place . . . perhaps even a bit precious . . . And I wouldn't know where to place him.

AM: There were two other influences I thought you would have mentioned. What about Melville, and Henry Moore?

CB: There are writers who have been lifelong companions, and Melville is one of them. Like all American school children, I read his works when I was very young. I grew up by the sea. As an 11-year-old I was once swimming off the coast, about 100 meters off shore, when a very small California gray whale–which didn't seem small to me at the time!–passed right by me. I recall thinking that a reef that had usually been in its place had unrooted itself and was moving toward me . . . So I therefore had a very particular love of whales from that moment on, because I thought my life had been spared. In an analytical vein, when I was later doing my dissertation on Melville, I was unaware of the link to my own boyhood experiences. But Melville's fiction I always found very intriguing. One has in the very early novels, in *Omoo*, or *Typee*, a sort of adventure story, a young person's novelistic moment, novels of travel. In his subsequent novels his writings deepen, as more and more repressed phenomena from his own life start to emerge. And then you get to the profound engagements in works like *Moby Dick* and *Pierre*. The parts of the self have by then shaken him deeply, and writing becomes a means of survival. And to his great credit, mind you, he negotiates and resolves a crisis in such a way that he no longer has to write.

As long as you're asking about whom I've read and has influenced me, I've always read Camus. And there was a period of time when I was very influenced by the plays of Ionesco and Durrenmatt. I loved Ionesco particularly; I loved the surrealistic imagination in his plays. In the early 1970s, in London, I taught Modern European Philosophy to a group of very gifted American undergraduates; I taught Hegel and Heidegger, works like *The Phenomenology of Spirit*, and *Being and Time*. Reading Heidegger was a very important moment in my life, and changed my way of thinking in my 20s. I had been influenced by Heinz Lichtenstein, a psychoanalyst in Buffalo, whose essays were later collected in a book called *The Dilemma of Human Identity*. Lichtenstein had studied with Heidegger, and really had Heidegger in him. And as his own psychoanalytical vision had been informed by Heidegger, when I taught *Being and Time* it was, in a way, Heidegger taught through Lichtenstein.

Henry Moore? I would be hard-pressed to say in what way sculptors like Moore, Gabo or Barbara Hepworth have influenced my vision of life. I actually met Naum Gabo, and learned a lot from his writings about sculpture. I knew Bernard Leach, who was one of Great Britain's great potters. He was a deep and profound man, and any visit with him was a very special occasion.

AM: Let's follow on this train of thought. Freudians aren't wont to speak of myths generally, outside of Oedipus. Yet in Melville you've mentioned one of the greatest modern myth-makers. How has, or what sense of, myth has informed your thinking?

CB: I think anyone who grows up by the sea forms a type of myth about the meanings of his or her childhood, that invariably incorporates the order between two entirely different worlds: the terrestrial world and the sea. Being on the boundary of two very different worlds, to be a participant in both, in different ways, to grow up in that place, naturally lends itself to constructing myths out of if. My schoolmates from Laguna Beach have all, I think, constructed quite powerful myths that involve a kind of story or legend of the self alongside the sea, and of how one carries the sea within. I still am very close to my school friends. We see each other every year . . . I'm now referring to people I was with in elementary school and in high school. I know each of them has that part of their life formed into a myth that is always with them, in one way or another.

AM: You are, after all, an expatriate. Is there something about the sea, for you, that inspires both daring and nostalgia?

CB: I think that anyone going out to sea as a child, or who is part of a culture that goes to sea, lives in an intimate relationship to that which gives life and takes life. I used to assist as a lifeguard during days when there would be a very powerful surf, with very big waves. And of course I would be part of rescuing people who were close to death, close to drowning . . . In that kind of situation you also see people who have drowned. So as a child and an adolescent I saw people who were killed by the sea.

AM: Perhaps one of your most fertile and arguably long-lasting contributions to theory is the idea of the transformational object. How did you come to elaborate the idea, and to what extent was it informed by your clinical work and observation?

CB: I first wrote about it in my notebooks in 1973, and it was a reflection of my own experience of being in analysis for the first time: of what it feels like to speak oneself and then to be understood in a very particular way, and for that understanding to change one's perspective. It was the generative dimension of that ordinary aspect of a psychoanalysis which got me to thinking, among other things, what kind of object accomplishes that? Or, in the sense of an object relationship, who is that? Later, when I first began doing analysis in 1974, as I was very aware that my analysands would be experiencing me as a process of transformation, as well as of the difficulty of an adequate transformation, I then developed a different view of technique, and of the crucial nature of wording persons to themselves.

AM: Following up on this, we talked earlier about the dream, especially where your "own return to Freud" is concerned. You've gone beyond, however, a broad textual revaluation of *The Interpretation of Dreams* and of the theory of the unconscious Freud propounds there. The dreamwork, and the dream space, have become in your work not only metaphors but models for both psychic life and the very dialectic of psychoanalytic practice.What about dreams, dream space, and the dream that we are?

CB: A session is a potential space. As the patient starts to talk, the psychoanalyst associates. Both participants engage in a process of free association along the lines of the dream work as defined by Freud. In this respect, both persons are dreaming each other through the workings of substitution, assimilation, condensation, displacement, etc. They may actually form something like a text, as in the analyst's making of an interpretation. Whether or not it is an inspired interpretation, or an inspired comment, whether it comes out of the dreaming between the two of them or not, always remains to be seen. Very often interpretations are matters of routine; whether transference interpretations or not, they may often recur in the analyst's mind. One could say then that interpretation may not come out of the dreaming: the dreaming continues but it doesn't give rise to the comment.

But sometimes what an analyst says to a patient is actually and distinctly different. It's new, it's inspired, and both patient and analyst know it to be so. And I think both know it to come out of the interplay between them. But perhaps precisely because it's inspired and condensed and overdetermined, this kind of interpretation usually has a short shelf-life. The patient makes use of it quickly, unconsciously, and it's then broken up, disseminated, and like a dream it unravels.

I think the dream is the heart of psychic life, and if our patients didn't dream and remember their dreams, if there weren't the possibility of dreams being told, I don't think there would be a thing called psychoanalysis. We simply wouldn't have it. And I agree with Winnicott that the dream really and truly is the pure unconscious, which makes its presence very important to the kind of work we do.

AM: Would it be correct to say that you view the dream as a locus that replicates, on a daily or nightly basis, the containing function of the mother's unconscious for the infant? You also speak of it as a place where the self is "loosened," deconstructed, as it were, allowing for what you call "a plenitude of selves". . . .

CB: J. B. Pontalis makes this point. And I agree, that the dream space inherits the place in which the mother functions in relation to the infant. So to dream, to bring oneself together in that kind of place, is based on a kind of memory of being brought together by maternal holding and maternal reverie. The process of dreaming is therefore, intrinsically, a recurring, regressive, re-finding of an early type of object relation that was profoundly transformative.

AM: Clinically speaking, if a patient routinely reported nightmares or disturbing dreams, would you see this as an indication of faults or failures in that person's earliest environments?

CB: I think invariably so. It's very interesting that most schizophrenic people find their dreams terrifying. Many schizophrenics report no dreams at all, and have managed to eliminate dream life, or at least any contact with their dream life. We can speculate, then, in an individual for whom dreaming is nightmare, that there has been a breakdown in early maternal holding. This is not to say the mother fails the infant, because many things can go wrong from the infant's side of the equation that make it impossible for any mother to effectively hold the child. But something has gone wrong, and therefore there is not an experience of good-enough reverie in the mother.

AM: What about the place of dreams in clinical practice, in the actual course of a psychoanalysis? Does their unfolding point invariably to the healing effects of treatment, in a somewhat sequential way, or do they function differently, differentially?

CB: I think one can determine psychic change from dreams. That is, one can tell when a patient has changed in and through the dream, or when the dream registers the change. Take, for example, a patient who never dreamt about her children, and for whom her children were of no psychic significance whatsoever because of a profound pathology of a narcissistic type. When she first included one of her children in a dream, this indicated psychic change; and it was evidence of a change in relation to all of her children. She had created room within herself not simply for the child, but for someone whom she could nurture, whereas in most of her dreams she'd been searching for the nurturing Other and unable to hold onto a capacity for nurture. So dreams do register important psychic change. Personally, however, I have never had the luxury to read through the notes of an analysis and systematically study the history of its dreams, in order to be able to comment on whether or not that important private literature is indicative of a very precise kind of evolution and development.

AM: There's a word you use in *Being a Character*, in the essay by the same title, that I wasn't familiar with. "We are inhabited by the *revenants* of the dream work of life . . . " I'm left with echoes of remnants and reverie, of covenants. . . .

CB: What I meant by *revenants* are the phantasmatic, the phantasmagoric residues of our dream works, and so of our life as well. It's a word that carries the outcome of our own private unconscious creations.

AM: When we first contemplated this process several years ago, the lone condition you stipulated was that we record the conversations here in London, in your space, because you needed to provide for what you called "reverie." What is *reverie* for you?

CB: There are always levels of thought, levels of engagement, levels of response to a question, levels of thinking about something. I can think off the top of my head . . . I can provide a certain level of response to what you might be discussing, or to what a patient might be saying to me. But for reverie to take place, I have to be able to drift inside myself. . . in a more associative way . . . in a less quickly reactive manner. I also have to be relaxed within myself for this to take place, and speaking to you here as opposed to speaking to you just after traveling on an airplane allows me to get to a different level of thinking. It's always a frustration for me when I travel to other countries, as I am never able to get to a level of thought that I value very much. I think it's one of the reasons that I love doing psychoanalysis, because it's a real privilege and pleasure to be working with people within a methodology that frequently allows for this experience of reverie.

AM: In another conversation, Marie Coleman Nelson and I explore the possible impacts, on both the unconscious and on psychic development, of the techno-culture in which much of Western consumer culture exists: a culture, for example, where ancestral notions of time and space have practically collapsed, and the fertile confusion of tongues that was Babel is being superseded worldwide by an electronic culture of prefabricated images. What do you see as being in store for our species, as language becomes more and more homogenized, less creative, and as our visual capacity becomes increasingly prominent?

CB: The younger people I see in treatment are indicating a frustration with homogenized imagery and cultural symbols. For example, rap music which is violent, sexist, almost anti-melodic, is exceedingly popular amongst middle-class children all over the world. I take this to be a good sign, a good indication that a revolution of sorts is taking place in consciousness.

These kids do not want to be part of an anodyne world, laundered of the visceral dimensions of an existence. I'm not pessimistic about the cultural future of our civilization. I actually think our generation–I'm speaking now of people in their 40s and 50s–has been less creative than it could have been, and it's ironic because it's an unusually self-preoccupied generation: in the sense of the history of generational consciousness, we've been more aware of ourselves as a generation than other previous generations, but not more creative and, if anything, somewhat less creative. If one looks at music, or to fine art, literature or philosophy . . . if one looks around for very creative people who are in their 40s or 50s, there simply aren't many. This wasn't the case with earlier generations. I believe we have been in a kind of cultural wasteland of our own creation, something our own generation has created with a certain abandon. I don't understand it myself, but it's there to be seen. And I don't think it's going to last very long. I don't see this period of the Miramax world, let's say, of the homogenized, cinematic productions that have had a culturally devastating effect on European film industries, as proving to be the end of Western culture, or of the generation of meaning in Western culture. We've seen bits and pieces of this, but I think there are also signs of ferment and creative destruction amongst younger people.

AM: As you've occasionally tackled questions pertaining to the relationship between psychoanalysis and culture, I was wondering how you view the rabid rise of fierce and violent nationalisms and religious fundamentalisms around the world. Today's news alone highlights the ongoing Bosnia tragedy, Cecenian uprisings, fundamentalist crusades in Algeria and Palestine, and even here in Western Europe the increasing intolerance of immigrants in Western Europe–a topic Julia Kristeva took up in *Strangers to Ourselves*. Is this something psychoanalysis should also be concerning itself with?

CB: I think psychoanalysis should enter public discourse. I think it has a great deal to offer to a public understanding of destructive processes, and it's a great shame that it has been less utilized than it has. I was at a recent reunion of the Free Speech Movement in Berkeley, where seminars and discussions on the 1960s were taking place. One of the noticeable absences, in terms of critical perspective, was the psychoanalytical view of culture and social movements, and of the link or relation between violent destruction and economic deprivation. This is less so in Europe, where people make use of psychoanalysts. I am part of a Labour Party think-tank, in which there are two other psychoanalysts, and ten or twelve social theorists and media thinkers. I think it's important that these circles want to have psychoanalysts present, and want us to be part of the cultural deconstruction of contemporary culture.

But getting to the heart of your question, I think that the world has always been a terrible place in many respects. And it's an unfortunate but essential part of every human life that, unless one is immediately and directly affected by extreme political privations, there's some distance we can put between ourselves and the world. One can go through childhood, adolescence, and youth without being too aware of this. But by middle-life, one becomes more and more aware of the world at-large, of the processes occurring in and around the world, by which one is not immediately and directly affected, and this recognition brings to mind just how disturbed world affairs are. Yet how is the situation in our world now worse than it was in the 19th century or the 18th century? Certainly the capacity for destruction is greater, the ability of groups to destroy their societies has been increased by technological developments, and mass communication makes it possible for a man like Saddam Hussein to dominate a large country because he can control it through the media and communication networks. In the 19th century, arguably, it would have been harder for someone like him to do this. So, in that respect some things are worse; but I don't think that the world is decidedly more venomous, more malicious than it's always been. It's always been awful.

AM: You've suggested that you don't think the world is any more of a horrible place than it's always been. Yet throughout the West there's a growing concern with what is arguably a significant increase in crimes committed by juveniles. Aggression seems more and more unbridled among the young, and in our societies generally: to the point that a sense of evil, which you have written about, seems to have become more pervasive, more concrete, less of a metaphysical concern. . . .

CB: I don't think the young are more violent than they were. What they have now that they didn't have before is access to lethal weapons. Access to guns has made the American adolescent in some cities a more dangerous person than he was before.

Street violence, street aggression is fairly high in Great Britain, which goes contrary to the notion of this being a gentle country. It's not. But English persons tend not to be armed, and guns are quite rare.

AM: Amid the general consensus that violence is on the increase, I've often wondered if a sense of group solidarity, of communal values or ideals, is disappearing. With this in mind, I was wondering if psychoanalysis ought to confront the question of whether our dominant models of the superego (Freud, Klein) need rethinking. Are they too proving inadequate in an age when sexuality, arguably–and I'm not sure you agree–is not the unspeakable culturally repressed force that Freud first unearthed?

CB: I believe that sexuality is still *the* unspeakable repressed force, and I would take the politically correct movement in the United States, and the fate of certain persons who are right now incarcerated because of that oppression, as evidence of my contention. In the United States there is an epidemic of belief in sexual molestation. Persons accused of molestations are in jail, and we now know many of them are innocent; still, they remain in jail. In religiously fundamentalist families, or in their secular equivalents, one finds situations where there is not a high degree of sexual molestation but a great degree of oppression, where sexuality and aggression are concerned. When children from these families reach adolescence, one of the ways they can imagine sexuality and aggression is through fantasies of violence and of sexual perversion. So, taking adolescent girls, for example, one way they can imagine and talk openly in their family about their sexuality is by putting it in someone else and demonizing it. Then it gets attacked but represented at the same time. So, towards the end of the 20th century in the United

States, there is, from my point of view, a resurgence of the hysterical personality, of hysterical complaints and a mood of hysteria. I would say, then, that sexuality, for its oppression to lead to these rather bizarre forms, is still very much a sufficiently dangerous phenomenon. But I think your question had to do with a breakdown in values in the U.S., as this connects with something gone wrong in the formation of the superego. . . .

AM: Thinking back at that marvelous essay of yours "Why Oedipus?" one thing I've noted is that you do seem, in your own reflections on the super-ego within the context of the Oedipus myth, to attribute a shifting but significant power to the *group*, as embodied in Sophocles' play by the chorus. If this is the case, where can we nowadays locate the voice, the principle, the authority, if you will, of the paternal function? In our own social context, where, in what group, can we locate that function?

CB: I think it's crucial here that we keep in mind Winnicott's concept of the superego, which Adam Phillips writes up brilliantly in his book *Winnicott.* Winnicott argues, in essence, that the child's sense of what is right emerges out of its experience of being with the mother and the father; he argues, in essence, that the child has an intrinsic sense of right and wrong. This sense is not something internalized, so to speak, by virtue of a reluctant moral appropriation that results from a pure identification with the father; nor, indeed, is it a begrudging accomplishment of Klein's depressive position: i.e., the achievements of a somewhat expedient requirement to maintain the loved object at the same time that it's discovered to be a hated object. Personally, like Winnicott, I think that the child has his or her own intrinsic sense of right and wrong. This doesn't mean that knowing what's right leads the child to behave correctly: one can, in fact, often see a child acting mischievously, looking carefully at the parents, not because he wants to find out if what he's doing is right or wrong, but in anticipation of a certain censorious response from the parent–precisely because he knows that what he's doing is wrong! In a child's participation in culture, he comprehends pretty quickly what is good behavior and what is bad behavior. This development is a part of human nature, in a very similar way that the experience of anxiety, or the experience of guilt, or the experience of despair are all natural.

The Oedipal period, then, in which the threesome assumes significance, inaugurates the child's negotiating new difficulties with the mother and father. This is the period when a boy will go through his castration complex, or the girl goes through hers, and each negotiates their appearance of mutilation, and all else that goes into this incredible period of a life. My point in "Why Oedipus?" is that there is a stage beyond this, a stage that's always existed but only becomes increasingly apparent with a latency or school-age child. When the child goes to school, and when taking part in the group feels all right, the child is in essence carrying part of the family structure, of the Oedipal structure, inside the self. He or she may in fact be imagining the loving mother and the loving father. And yet their own families are, to their surprise, not powerful or strong enough to sustain the family laws, habits, and idiomatic features away from home; children find that these laws don't always print out onto culture at-large, where they meet a different world. They not only find that the world is different, but that each of their peers at school has different families, and that together they're all part of what is in effect a very large group. It's this participation in the group which radically challenges family structures.

And that actual group, moreover, is coincidental with the arrival of an internal group of objects, where the child's self and object representations of the mother and father, of the self and others, is impressively multiple. And because of this multiplicity of structures this development dissolves the primacy of the dyadic and triadic structures. It does not erase them, however; so that we can and do return in our lives to dyadic and the triadic structures: to the former, for example, by having a relationship, and to the triadic through the creation of a family of one's own. These are, I think, essential transformative retreats from the fact of a human life: from the fact of the actual group, and from the internal group of objects which had earlier dissolved the more simplifying structures. But I think in part we're talking about these issues out of the spirit of your comments regarding the world at-large. Is it not a more dangerous place? Is it not a less culturally generative space? From my point of view, it is simply a realization about what is always beyond our families and our private lives. Out there is a world of a large collection of peoples, of countries, of forces which is beyond our thinking, beyond our organization.

AM: In a different vein, you've spoken often of the "integrity" of an object. What do you mean by an object's "integrity"–a word that itself connotes a certain moral value or quality. What determines an object's integrity?

CB: I simply mean the structure that any one object possesses. Mozart's 40th symphony, as an object, is different from his 25th symphony . . . and it certainly differs from a Bruckner symphony. So that each time one hears that symphony, each time one approaches that object, it has a recognizable integrity to its structure that can't be changed. It can be interpreted differently by different conductors, but there's a reliable, integral feature to it. When we choose an object, we very often pick something that will process us, and the integrity of the object is an important part of the gain to be derived from that object's selection. Psychoanalysis has tended to focus too much on the projective uses of an object, on what we can put into it; it thus has tended to regard objects as sorts of neutral or empty spaces to receive our contents.

For example, in psychoanalysis we speak of the mother and the father as if there were no intrinsic distinctions between mothers and fathers, when of course we know there are enormous distinctions. But we can't make room for those distinctions when it comes to theories of projective and introjective identification. Allow me to correct myself a bit: we can with introjective identification, but we can't so much with projective identification. And we don't need to really: those theories are important and exist in their own right outside of their particular frame of reference. But at the same time, when we make use of objects, when we select a book to read, or a novelist to explore, we're going to be processed by the integrity offered us by that object: namely, by its structure, which differs from that of other objects. That's what I'm really focusing on.

AM: But in a culture where bombarding images mediate, and often condition and define the experience of objects, can we still speak of their integrity? I'm thinking, at a very basic level, of how Madison Avenue manipulates our desire, and through its selling of sex, for instance, can distort, thwart, or even pervert our expectations–indeed, our experience–of the opposite sex. . . .

CB: Our experience and use of objects is always vulnerable to an interpretive appropriation of those objects by powerful movements or authorities outside our realm. So I don't think, for example, that Madison Avenue's interpretation of our sexual objects is more oppressive than the interpretation given to objects by a 17th-century minister in New England, who dominated the village and indicated to all and sundry how they were to interpret their environment, or their sexual objects, and how they were to understand their desires. However, there's already a difference between life in an early 17th-century New England village and life toward the end of that century in a New England village. The difference is not that the people were any less sexual or less sexually specific in the early 17th century, and therefore more liberated in terms of sexual desire in the late 17th century. The difference of course was in the mentality. Toward the end of the 17th century there was a greater degree of toleration of human preferences, and a less effective oppression created by the church. That's where matters were different.

So in contemporary terms, I don't think the oppressiveness we live in will end people's subjectivities. The politically correct movement, combined with the ability of the media to generate a kind of homogenized vision of life, will not stop people from reading, from writing music, from painting. Their forces are not going to stop civilization. But there is a mentality in these forces which makes the quality of our life different, and thus restricts us. This we must oppose . . . Hence the spirit of your questions. In that sense, I agree: there is something to be opposed. But if you're asking me is this the end of culture, my answer then is no. We have been here before, and we will be here again. Hopefully, though, it doesn't have to happen in the lifetime of every generation. But if we could go back through the preceding generations, we might hear how each generation had a similar experience of the world. Again, it has to do, I think, with the sense of decline that takes over each dominant generation, and its surrender of power to the new generation. It's about the sense of failure, the sense of despair, that arrives over what wasn't accomplished.

AM: Looking back at your concept of the evocative object, you make a distinction between what you call a "mnemic" object and a "structural" one. Can you clarify the distinction?

CB: The structural object is close to what I later call the "integral object," which I've written about in *Cracking Up*. The mnemic object is an object that is significant because it has received prior projective identifications on the part of the individual. In *Being a Character*, for example, I pointed to a swing that has particular significance for me. However, a swing is also a structure, it does something . . . This comes close to the concept of what the integrity of the object is, and of how it will have its own particular effect upon my self. So we can use objects both mnemically and structurally. Another example: Schubert's *Unfinished Symphony* was the first symphony I fell in love with as a child, one I'd also purchased through the Columbia Record Club. In that way it's mnemically powerful for me: it brings back memories of my life at that time. At the same time, it has an independent structure to it; it has its own integrity independent of my projections. And I can also appreciate it as a piece of musical composition in its own right, and thus see the difference between it and Schubert's other symphonies. Thus we will sometimes choose objects for their structural capability that may have no mnemic significance for us whatsoever. If I choose, for example, to go sailing or boating, I pick an object that is part of a process that engages me, but is not mnemically significant for me.

AM: In your opening chapter of *Being a Character*, you make a peculiar reference to what you call your "postmodernist cousins." Who are they, and why do you call them "cousins"?

CB: I'm very aware that my own particular development as a psychoanalytical theorist has gone along postmodernist lines in some respects, and I think many of your questions and comments are quite correct in placing me within a certain intellectual tradition. I'm also aware of being influenced by some of the works of Jacques Derrida, for example. And having done my training in literature at the University of Buffalo in the 1960s, where there were many soon-to-become postmodernist thinkers, one couldn't help but be influenced by postmodernist thought. There are, however, some ways in which my thinking is not postmodernist. You pointed out, for example, what you regarded as a certain kind of essentialism in my thinking, with which I would agree. So I see my own positions as a theorist containing substantial contradictions. And although I can understand why I'm seen as a postmodernist writer in some ways, I would also say that I'm an essentialist in others: hence I could not say of Derrida, or of someone such as he, that he is a brother. But I can see that he is a cousin! There are familial connections, although not always direct ones.

AM: Reading your work as an oeuvre that has paid such focussed attention to the subject-object relationship, a flash came to me of the title of a book that was very important in my formation, Martin Buber's *I and Thou*. Is there a space where human objects–be they evocative, or objects of desire–or even the "ordinary" object world, say, of Zen experience–can engage us as subjects, and collapse the dualism of subject and object?

CB: No, I don't think so. I don't think we can be engaged by the human other in such a way that they cease to be an object for us. In our psyche we will always be unconsciously or consciously objectifying them. But the "other," the human other, in particular, does have a profound subjective effect upon us: in the sense that our subjectivity is restructured by their processional effect. I tried to get to that side of the equation of object relations by conceptualizing the other as a process, as a transformational object. And I do have a project to try to delineate and differentiate, among the internal objects we hold in us, those that are fundamentally a result of our own work, and those that might be more fundamentally the work of the other upon our self. But I haven't yet reached that point in my writing.

AM: When you say that objectification of the human other is inevitable, do you mean something more than it can't help but be the recipient of our projections and transferences?

CB: I simply mean that we form the other as a mental object. For however actual, however substantial, however intimately and profoundly sensitive the other is, and for however much they embody the "otherness" of the other, we always destroy that sense through our formation of a mental object: as when we change the other according to our own desire, or our own subjectivity. And it is in that act that we always reconstitute the other inside our self.

AM: And yet you do talk and write about the encounter of unconscious subjectivities in the process of analysis. About how, at the level of the unconscious, we can be subjects to one another. . . .

CB: I understand more precisely your focus now. Both persons affect one another, subject-to-subject, at that unconscious level of inter-affectiveness or interrelating. There really will be direct processional effects . . . one upon the other . . . unconscious to unconscious, according to the laws of unconscious condensation, displacement, substitution and so on. However, each person will at the same time be objectifying that experience: that is, bringing it up into mind both unconsciously and consciously, so that those objectifications of the subjective dimension will always be retranslated and re-formed by the subject. Then as time passes . . . we're not talking about a long period of time, it could be even a matter of minutes . . . there are subsequent re-editings and changes of that initial engagement. That's why I like De Kooning's theory of the unconscious, because I think the initial moment does get erased and changed and then changed again, until the revision itself is changed and edited.

AM: There's a marvelous phrase in *Being a Character* that I'd like you to talk about. In the essay that gives its title to the book you write, apropos the ego-psychological ideal of adaptation to reality : "It seems to me equally valid that as we grow we become more complex, more mysterious to ourselves and less adapted to reality." A sentence like that could drive legions of therapists crazy!

CB: Another way of looking at it would be to say that reality is increasingly less available for adaptation. Apropos of your earlier questions of the disturbing changes in the world, my response in part is that it's not just that the world is changing, but that we're changing too. This is usually the sort of perspective of a person in mid-life, or later; but it's one in which you realize that the world is so complex a place, how could one possibly adapt to it? So, what is reality? Assuming one could even find it how would one adapt to it? I know what ego psychology meant. I know that it was talking about the broad structures of a life: marriage, children, professional life, the ability to manage the problems that come with each phase in a life cycle, and so on. Certainly the concept of adaptation is a useful one, but it's also exceedingly restrictive and, as a view of what takes place in the course of a human life, I think unfortunately and substantially wrong. That is, as we get into mid-life in particular, we enter a phase of the life cycle in which we become increasingly aware of how complex life is; of how in some ways it can't be adequately thought. Life is too complicated to be thought out. And it's not just life as a phenomenon: life, whatever it is, is beyond our thinking. Political affairs are in some ways too complex for a single thinker to think out . . . or to be content with his or her thinkings. Each of our own lives is so complicated. There are so many strands of interest, of convergence and interpretations, that at any one moment in time we ourselves are, as conscious individuals, beyond our own individual efforts of thought.

This, I believe, is humbling. I believe it leads us towards more modest senses of what we can accomplish in life. Another way of looking at this attitude would be to see it as part of an effort to promote a vision of the end of an analysis. What is the frame of mind of an individual towards the end of his or her analysis? I don't think psychoanalysis has offered visions of the self after a psychoanalysis is concluded. It's left us with metaphors like "integration," "adaptation," "depressive position," and so on, which are accurate so far as they go, but in and of themselves are rather meager in comparison to the complexity of a life, and how one looks upon and relates to that complexity.

AM: What are your hopes for psychoanalysis? Are we a dinosaur close to extinction? Or is there room for us not only to survive but to thrive in contemporary society?

CB: Psychoanalysis just has to survive "the psychoanalytic movement." If it survives psychoanalysts and their schools then it will grow and develop. But this remains to be seen.

WORKS CITED

Bachelard, G. (1969). *The Poetics of Space* (tr. by M. Jolas). Boston, Beacon Press.

_____ (1971). *The Poetics of Reverie* (tr. by D. Russell). Boston, Beacon Press.

Buber, M. (1970). *I and Thou* (tr. by W. Kaufmann). New York, Scribner.

Freud, S. (1900). *The Interpretation of Dreams*, in J. Strachey, ed. *The Standard Edition of the Complete Psychological Works of Sigmund Freud*, 24 vols. London, Hogarth, 1953-73, S.E. 4-5.

______ (1901). *The Psychopathology of Everyday Life*, vol. 6.

______ (1905). *Jokes and Their Relation to the Unconscious*, vol. 8.

Hegel, G. W. F. (1977). *The Phenomenology of Spirit* (tr. by A.V. Miller). Oxford, Oxford Univ. Press.

Heidegger, M. (1962). *Being and Time* (tr. by J. Macquarrie and E. Robinson). New York, Harper.

Kristeva, J. (1991). *Strangers to Ourselves* (tr. by L. Roudiez). New York, Columbia Univ. Press.

Lichtenstein, H. (1983). *The Dilemma of Human Identity.* New York, J. Aronson.

Lyotard, J. F. (1984). *The Postmodern Condition*. Minneapolis, University of Minnesota Press.

Melville, H. (1981). *Moby Dick, or, The Whale*. Berkeley, University of California Press.

______ (1969). *Omoo, a Narrative of Adventures in the South Seas*. New York, Hendricks House.

______ (1971). *Pierre, or, The Ambiguities*. Evanston, Northwestern University Press.

______ (1959). *Typee, a Real Romance of the South Sea*. New York, Harper.

Phillips, A. (1988). *Winnicott*. Cambridge, Harvard University Press.

CHRISTOPHER BOLLAS: SELECTED BIBLIOGRAPHY

The New Informants (with D. Sundelson, 1995). Northvale, NJ, Jason Aronson, Inc.

Cracking Up (1995). New York, Farrar, Straus & Giroux.

Being a Character: Psychoanalysis and Self Experience (1992). New York, Farrar, Straus & Giroux.

Forces of Destiny: Psychoanalysis and Human Idiom (1989). Northvale, NJ, Jason Aronson, Inc.

The Shadow of the Object: Psychoanalysis of the Unthought Known (1987). New York, Columbia University Press.

Marie Coleman Nelson

Man must learn with awareness to be many men, and to hold them all together . . . At that point, instead of other men, he will govern his own personalities; and these will have names, so as to be known and ruled. And thus man's greed for dominion will no longer seek out an 'Other' . . . since every one of us will be able to be as many men as one is capable of subjugating.

–Elias Canetti

In the course of recent years, I have had the privilege of working very closely with Marie Coleman Nelson, one of the last of that daring and dying breed of psychoanalysts Freud exalted in his 1926 pamphlet, ***The Question of Lay Analysis****. Best known for her groundbreaking work in what has come to be known as paradigmatic psychotherapy, Ms. Nelson was among the first theorists to propose the idea of a "multiple self," an idea that has gained in intellectual and clinical currency, and has served as an organizing theme for this collection.*

A born storyteller, who even in her eighties continues to thrive on the stories of others, Marie has been a nourishing and refreshing influence on the lives of countless clinicians practicing today. And as I think back over my own development and Ms. Nelson's instrumental role in helping to foster it, I realize how fortunate I've been to have had her as an educator, supervisor and colleague at this stage of her career. For since she returned to the U.S. in 1989, following a ten-year stay in Africa, few have had the opportunity to

[Haworth co-indexing entry note]: "Marie Coleman Nelson." Co-published simultaneously in *The Psychotherapy Patient* (The Haworth Press, Inc.) Vol. 10, No. 1/2, 1997, pp. 61-104; and: *Elaborate Selves: Reflections and Reveries of Christopher Bollas, Michael Eigen, Polly Young-Eisendrath, Samuel and Evelyn Laeuchli and Marie Coleman Nelson* (ed: Anthony Molino) The Haworth Press, Inc., 1997, pp. 61-104. Single or multiple copies of this article are available from The Haworth Document Delivery Service [1-800-342-9678, 9:00 a.m. - 5:00 p.m. (EST). E-mail address: getinfo@haworth.com].

share in and learn from the riches of her many and multifaceted years as a truly unique thinker and clinician.

The interview which follows was conducted over the course of two days, on July 11-12, 1992, and is excerpted from a much longer exercise in which Ms. Nelson's entire life and career were revisited. As it oscillates between the anecdotal and the theoretical, between reflections of memory, practice, and hope, the interview sheds light on the disparate and distinctly idiosyncratic dimensions of a lifetime dedicated to psychoanalysis. In so doing, Ms. Nelson rarely minces her words. Not everybody will like what they find stated: some positions will sound untenable; others, controversial–particularly where women and issues pertaining to a certain kind of feminism are concerned. But for those whose "third ear" is minimally attuned, Ms. Nelson's insights and stories provide a key to the reading of a life whose eros ***and*** *pathos spill onto the page, and spell out her vision for the future and culture of psychotherapy.*

AM: I'd like to start with a quote from a talk you gave several years ago, upon returning from Africa: "I would say, first, that the frontier of therapy must be identified with the living culture, and second, that it must relate to prevailing styles of thought and ideologies of a period." For me, there's something puzzling about the "Americanness" of paradigmatic therapy. You've mentioned shocking several expatriate Viennese colleagues, astounded because it didn't have truth as a central issue; they saw something amoral about the way paradigmatic interventions function. This makes me wonder what, if any, place does truth have in your work? Does it have a creative or healing function, or is it something invariably idiosyncratic?

MCN: One can define truth in all sorts of ways. Just look at the versions the media propound, especially at election time! My particular version of the truth is to ask myself: "Are you willing to do anything that is necessary to heal the patient?" Now, many people operate according to certain prescriptions they learned when they trained. I abandoned that attitude long ago in favor of the notion that truthwise, when one is responsible for healing a person, or when one is selling a product (namely psychological help, and this perhaps is very American), that one must stand behind the product and the product should be as good a product as one can formulate or produce. All paradigmatic styles–and there are many–are characterized by a willingness on the part of the therapist to adopt whatever stance, even whatever personality, that is necessary to be comprehensible to the patient, in order to reach the unconscious.

AM: Isn't there a risk, then, that understanding truth in this way risks limiting truth to a by-product of narcissism? Don't you risk exalting a narcissistic position?

MCN: Any form of therapy can be a vehicle for the gratification of the therapist's narcissism. But the reverse can also be true. If one is obliged, for example, to allow a patient to feel that as a therapist one is very stupid, that's very painful; that's quite a task of endurance for the therapist. Nevertheless, the therapist does it because through that peculiar self-representation, the patient gains courage, in his own self-esteem, to be other than ill.

AM: In that same talk, you commented on your reasons for having left the U.S. for Africa: "I think that I found a lot of things in America crude and unoriginal at this point in history. I'd lost the feeling of identification with much that's American, and in a curious way had to test myself against another setting, to clarify what I am and what's worth being and what isn't. In this sense, my expatriate status was a testing ground and challenge for a lot of analytic theory." If our culture somehow lacks in vitality, in a capacity to bridge past and future, can you still mean that "the frontier of therapy must relate to prevailing styles of thought and ideologies of a period," when we are apparently lacking in both?

MCN: It must relate with awareness. It is the recognition, on the part of the therapist, that the guidelines, the story that psychoanalysis teaches about human behavior (especially the now rather concealed contribution of instinctive traits), is not the only story, because other people hear other voices. People elsewhere hear quite different voices, in many respects, from the voice we think is the only one. There are certainly people, therapists, who are relating to some extremely underprivileged and bizarre types of people. Therapists who are working with street people, for example. They're not necessarily psychoanalysts, but they obviously are able to identify with a much broader range of feeling, affects, and thought than that with which they have been endowed by virtue of class or caste.

AM: You've mentioned having attended *sixteen* different grade schools, and how this foreclosed for you, at a very early age, the possibility of making reliable friends. You've also suggested that this movement contributed to an early development of a sense of life's absurdity. How much was this the result of your own early relationship with your mother and father? I recall your description of your mother as an autocrat of sorts, and of your father as a rambling, adventurous, but rather detached spirit. . . .

MCN: Oh, he was detached all right! My father was a great talker, and when I was very young he would always read dialect stories to us. That was a great pleasure to me. My mother, she generally disapproved of dialects. She was more poetic, and made me memorize Edgar Allan Poe when I was about five. My mother was very particular. I would make a mistake in reciting and would simply correct the word, but she would make me go back to the beginning of the sentence, which I still think has inhibited me as a speaker. It's something I've never overcome, as I always spoke under such duress. My father, though not educated, was a man deeply interested in the world around him. At the age of fourteen he ran away from the family farm and worked on the railroad, as a fireman on the engines. He owned mines at one time, and also had an assay done during the '60s which confirmed the presence of gold in the bed of the Duke River; and it's still there today, because it costs more to extract it than it's worth.

AM: It's striking that someone with a father interested in geology and mining river beds and mountains, should have ended up a psychoanalyst! How did you discover Freud?

MCN: It was after I entered the Air Force, a year before the end of World War II. I found the military interesting as a structure, but it was most enlightening because it was the first time I'd ever lived with unrelated people. It destroyed an illusion that I had, which was that everybody does the best they can at what they're doing. That was my first discovery, you see, soon to be followed by Freud's *Introductory Lectures*. I went to the Post Library, where I remember rooting through stacks of comic books to find at least one serious magazine that would be worth reading. And, lo and behold, I found a paperback of Freud's lectures. It was absolutely pristine; nobody had touched it. It was all clear, clean, neat and *there*, for me to read, when I had never read anything by Freud. I was absolutely overwhelmed by it. And I said, "This explains everything!" When I came out of the Army, I got myself an analyst. I'd never heard of psychoanalysis before.

AM: Throughout the years, you've commented somewhat openly on your analysis with Dr. Hyman Spotnitz. You've talked about an initial year characterized by "reasonable" communication, then followed by two years of silence–which you describe as being characterized by an "artificial feeling," a feeling which, in retrospect, you've also come to extend to the experience of that first year. What was the impact of those early years?

MCN: With reference to the experience of artificiality, I did talk about problems, but I talked about them in a rational, biographical way. I didn't feel, even as I talked about them, that this was all there was. At a certain point, "all there was" began to feel artificial, as if there was a whole indescribable area that I somehow didn't have language for. So I didn't address a lot of things. I never spoke about my feelings for Spotnitz or the great distance I sensed between us. I didn't talk, probably, about doubting him–doubts which maybe weren't conscious at the time. Because what I had at that time must have been a great willingness to hope. I mean, I assumed that my experience of my analyst was similar to the feelings of expectation I nurtured for my father . . . You know, whenever my mother would get a letter from him she'd always downplay the event, muttering something like "promises, promises"–whereas I'd be so happy that a letter had come that I didn't care about the promises. So I guess I was conditioned to wait a long time for something to happen.

But I also had great difficulty talking, in uttering anything. He stopped talking; for two years, he would admit me silently, and after fifty minutes would say the time was up. Then he would discharge me, and that was all. I would stew; I was very uncomfortable; it didn't make me angry, but it put me at sea, and I didn't know how to express myself. Then, after a very long time I began to cry. Why did I cry and where? I cried at Carnegie Hall, listening to *Die Moldau*, by Gustav Mahler, and I just sat there . . . I didn't know that it was so beautiful; I couldn't believe that anything was beautiful enough to make me cry.

AM: Your choice of words is striking. "He admitted me, and then he discharged me." It almost sounds like the language of an asylum, or the Army . . . But there are also echoes, in the word *admission*, of a sense of recognition or truthfulness; and in *discharge*, of a sense of release of affects or energy.

MCN: *(moved)* Yes. I was probably one of Spotnitz' first analysands. My feeling was that he did what was necessary, what was possible, because I also was trying too hard to talk. I also was feeling too defective, and he may have found that whatever he said, I reacted badly to, in a negative way. So he probably felt that nothing he said facilitated anything. You see, I really felt the analysis was my job. Because when my father would leave, I'd be left alone with my mother. I wouldn't know where or when I'd see him again. He'd go off to some other town and say "Take good care of your mother." Those last words left me feeling terribly responsible. So, I took care of my mother.

AM: I get the sense from your account that Spotnitz was groping, or fumbling along. . . .

MCN: That's what I never found out. I didn't succeed in getting Spotnitz to respond to such an inquiry. On one occasion I did press him on the question of his silence. He responded, "You are doing the analysis yourself." I pressed him no further because I took his statement as a compliment, feeling that, like my parents, he approved of hard work, and hence repressed my need for his participation.

AM: This might be a good place to cite an anecdote from the analysis, of a turning point when Spotnitz extended a finger to you. You give five interpretations of the gesture . . .

MCN: It was his interpretation that marked a turning point.

AM: Can we talk about that incident and your readings of it?

MCN: Let me say that I know enough about these things from being an analyst that, very often, after an analysis, both parties want and indeed are encouraged to feel a sense of completion, of success.

I felt so integrated by that analysis; I was so helped by that analysis; through it, I became solid. Consequently, I don't like to communicate anything that suggests that the analysis was not therapeutic because it really did give me a direction in my life. That analysis made me an analyst. I had been an editor, I had been an artist. I could do too many things, and did them all well, and had fun doing them, but everything was so scattered. At a certain point you begin to feel, "I really must settle down and accomplish something." This was particularly necessary for me because I had no higher education. I only went briefly to Columbia after the Army. But as far as the analysis goes, maybe because I'm getting to the age where I can't just pick up and leave everything like I used to, certain things occasionally crop up that make me realize what was not resolved.

I had worked most of the time in my analysis on my difficulty with my mother. I didn't identify it clearly then, but it was a struggle to remain a person, a separate person. She opposed my autonomy very strenuously. Spotnitz functioned mostly as the surrogate mother of whom I was afraid, and he got me over that fear. But I had always, over and over again, wanted Spotnitz to let me hold his hand. Now, I didn't mean that I'd hold it forever; but just once, I wanted to hold it. I felt that if he'd let me take hold of his hand, he would become real to me; and if he was real, I would be able to talk and be more genuine, less artificial. This desire persisted for quite a while, and I must have known, at some level, that it connected with an early image of my father walking ahead of my mother and me when I was very young. I'd run ahead to take his hand, and he would pull it away. For me that was terribly painful; I've never forgotten how painful it was.

Anyway eventually Spotnitz did extend a finger; I held his finger briefly and then let go . . . I had very mixed feelings about the gesture. In a way, I was embarrassed by it, and wondered whether he'd extended it to me as an infant that clutches a finger, or whether he thought that I wanted to hold his penis; or perhaps he thought I was trying to seduce him. I thought of any number of possible interpretations. He then reported on the incident years later, at a very large meeting which I happened to attend, because I was visiting the States from Nairobi. "I want to tell them something about you, Mrs. Nelson." He asked, "Do you mind?" As I didn't, I said no. Then he talked about this being the turning point in my analysis. Now all these years I had thought that the turning point had been symbolized by another event, by a dream I had. . . .

I was in the dentist's chair. The dentist left the room, and left me with all sorts of stuff in my mouth–cotton, a drain, and various other instruments, what I called "hard-boiled" stuff (that was when dentists sterilized instruments by boiling them). As the dentist didn't return, I finally plucked all this hard-boiled stuff out of my mouth myself. I interpreted that dream as emblematic of my breaking through to being able to talk of my feelings, and not simply of my experiences. At the meeting I was rather disappointed, when Spotnitz didn't mention the dream. I felt bad that he ascribed the turning point just to his finger.

AM: Is there a difference, say, between the quality or the experience of your silence with Spotnitz, and how silence makes its presence felt in an analysis today?

MCN: I think mine would be read by the analyst in much the same way now as then, primarily in terms of sexual development. It could also be read legitimately as the experience of any only child with one parent, the mother. The speech inhibition certainly would be attributed to nursing, to the earliest mother-infant dynamics. I don't know how an analyst of today would interpret the absence of a father. I think they would not consider it very important.

AM: There's a connection I'm beginning to envision in that both episodes–the outstretched finger and the dream–involve a manual operation. . . .

MCN: I have enormous material with hands, and am always rather annoyed at the interpretation of masturbation–which is the first thing analysts think of if somebody talks about a hand. But a hand was important to me. My hands drew and they drew well. For the longest time, when I was a political cartoonist, my hands said all the things that I couldn't say with my mouth. Plus I always think of the hands as the frame through which the child first sees the world. It holds up its hands like this . . . *(cups her hands and motions with them to her face and eyes)* The hands are enormously important. They are the primary thing that grasps the world: not just people, but the whole world, and with which the baby plays too.

AM: As you speak, I wonder what role magic played in your formative years. Could you, for instance, talk a bit about the trickster? I recall an article of yours where you say that the trickster demands that the analyst become a liar . . . You also refer to him as "brother sinner," or devil's advocate. What's the trickster's place in your "scheme" of things?

MCN: My model is to use the trick when everything else fails. I once had a patient whose perceptiveness was of the kind that, with an elephant smack in front of her, she would see only to the side, or maybe below or above the elephant, but never the elephant itself! Of course this is an exaggerated cartoon! But I had trouble working with her because of this difficulty, which simply had to be worked through. I could never take a chance with her, as she always had to idealize me, regard me as better . . . Her goal in treatment, her transferential goal, was to be like me. It was impossible.

I knew that until she ceased idealizing me, she could never express anger or irritation or anything else with me. She could only act out her emotions in various ways elsewhere. Then one day she commented on a painting that I had hanging in the elevator hall. It was a tropical painting, very colorful. She came in and she talked about the painting, the birds, the foliage, and so on, when I asked, "What did you think about the elephant?" And she said, "The elephant?" I said, "Yes." "I don't remember seeing an elephant," she said. "You didn't see the elephant?" I exclaimed. "How could you miss the elephant?" And she said, "Did I miss seeing it?" I could see the accommodation of siding with the aggressor, or in this case, with the trickster, sliding into place. I said something like: "You can see it when you leave." I knew that, when she'd get outside, she'd look and look and look for the elephant and of course there would be none! She came back the next session enraged with me and, of course, disenchanted with me as well. Everything I wanted to have happen, happened. As a result of that paradigmatic maneuver, she now knew that she didn't have to swallow me hook, line and sinker.

AM: At the end of his essay "Breaking the Frame, Stopping the World," Michael Eigen, a dear friend and colleague of yours, questions the place of the trickster in contemporary psychoanalysis. He writes: "How far can beneficent trickery take the individual in a time when a lethal mixture of business and show business, the Trickster as fraudulent consciousness par excellence, is a presiding image over all? Can a paradigm of the Trickster break its own framework? Does the creating of such a paradigm imply its self-transcendence, or does it inevitably collude with the evil it mimics?" What about the trickster, now, in this day and age?

MCN: I don't agree with Eigen. The trickster is not a universal in the consciousness of most people. The trickery that's going on today is a cultivated, orchestrated, intentional social or class effort to make the best of a good thing and is tied, in almost every instance, to the economics of milking the market for all its worth. It all boils down to power, to economic aggrandizement. But a true trickster doesn't play that part. A court trickster isn't in it for the money, and does not benefit greatly from being a trickster; he does not gain materially. What he gains is the admiration, the ambivalent interest and attachment of the king. The trickster in folklore is a figure who can do both good and evil in equal measure. He is an admired figure, one used mostly in a rescuing role.

AM: As Eigen himself suggests, the trickster is probably the paradigm par excellence. Still, it remains one among many. From what I've gathered there is a crucial element of selectivity in resorting to a paradigmatic intervention.

MCN: A paradigm is a highly creative technique, and it's a precious technique, to be used preciously and with respect and inspiration. *(fumbling for the right metaphor)* The theory of paradigmatic communication is that multiple layers of attention, multiple concerns are involved; it's like a beautiful floral arrangement . . . it's like . . . , well, it's like aspirin. Nobody knows why but aspirin is good for an awful lot of things. And aspirin can also be useless or even damaging when taken indiscriminately. Just a certain amount of paradigm is appropriate for certain things; and when it's exceeded, the benefit of it vanishes. So, it's like aspirin. It addresses a variety of conditions in the treatment. It should be used only under certain circumstances, when one recognizes an obstacle to the progression of therapy, and has tried more conservative means, and even the most conservative: doing nothing, in the hope that, whatever the problem, it will be spontaneously worked through.

AM: I think of your experience in Africa, and I look at any number of other lay analysts: I look at Christopher Bollas, born in California, transplanted to England; Stuart Schneiderman, the Lacanian from New York, who goes to Paris and spends his formative years there; there's Julia Kristeva, who's Bulgarian but ends up in France. There seems to be some connection between analysis and exile, a connection that perhaps is rooted in Freud's own history as a Jew; and of course there's the further development of psychoanalysis via the post-war emigration of European analysts to this country. In sum, this thread seems to weave its way through any number of personal analytic histories and orientations, as well as through the history of the profession. How do the themes of exile and alienation pertain to your own work?

MCN: Fundamentally, some of the notions of togetherness that permeate analytic discourse, the notion of therapeutic dialogue for example, carry with them a momentum of their own, and pursue a course which is inseparable from the duality of the dialogue's very origin. Consequently, unilateral definitions or understandings of such phenomena are impossible, because there is no single origin. That duality creates a new story, which involves the embrace of a paradox. All of this is true, all of this is also not true. . . . The analyst can never be completely engaged, can never fuse entirely with the patient; part of the analyst must always stand aside . . . though not necessarily aside the patient! A patient can be quite overcome with ideation and affect, to the point where the analyst is even forgotten for the moment; then the patient's discourse earmarks a regression or narcissistic transference, at least until they rise from the couch and say: "For a while I forgot you were there." Therefore, I don't believe that one ever loses oneself, though I do believe that the result of this particular kind of standing aside does in fact create an abyss. For from the time one has been immersed in analysis, an analyst can never interact the same way again, the experience of the world is always going to be different. Everything one hears, everything that's said, every meeting and transaction, in the analyst's experience, will be marked by an element of absence.

AM: Of absence, or what Lacan calls the "lack" that is intrinsic to our very being and condition. But you've sidestepped my question. Do you see the analytic encounter, as such, as reproducing the cultural exile and alienation that has marked the transplantations of lives and experience in the hundred-year history of the profession?

MCN: Well, no. I see it involving a split, whether voluntary or involuntary, or even compulsory perhaps. It's a split that involves a commitment to perceiving one's experience in the world. I'm talking about the idea that an author can't see anything happening without translating it, to some extent, into a written piece in his head.

AM: In a delightful 1985 interview called "Analysts at Work: A Talk with Marie Coleman Nelson," you mention having been kept in one place for thirty-four years thanks to analysis. You say: "Given the temptations of the world, and my bent for adventure" (your father's influence, again, I suppose) "that's no small thing." What about the paradox of restlessness and stability? I wonder how you have lived or played out these tensions in your life, considering that analysis is a priesthood of sorts that requires fidelity, stability, and a good degree of renunciation, not only of the sexual kind?

MCN: Well, one of the ways I've lived it out is in foregoing a lot of things that feel I would have done very well, not the least of which is writing more, even in my own field. That's one way I'd be relieved of the feeling of the divided self. If I ever do isolate myself sufficiently to write, I will write about this divided self. There are many things I should have written and haven't, and that I may never write. And the knowledge of this pains me. Another way I've dealt with the tension was by starting the center in Nairobi, which somebody told me was the first psychoanalytically oriented training center, even the first therapeutic training center, in Africa. This enterprise, though, didn't involve an abandonment on my part, nor was it an adventure in the classic sense.

AM: Your own training was at the Institute of the National Psychological Association of Psychoanalysis, which was founded by Theodor Reik: a man you found to be powerfully narcissistic. Could you talk about your introduction to NPAP, and about the early seminars there? You refer to the school as an intellectual home.

MCN: I wasn't working yet as an analyst, but got to attend the meetings where Reik lectured. NPAP was just being formed, and I was told by one of the now-deceased Viennese founders that my application for admission had caused the first split in this organization, because I didn't have any degrees. However, I'd written and been published in the field, and was working as a research assistant to a noted analyst in the association. I was also in analysis. So after not knowing whether to throw my application out or give it house room, they apparently decided to keep me around. That's when I heard Reik lecture. Now, at that time I was really an intellectual snob. I never could understand why Reik came to all his insights via literary allegories and allusions. I thought that was pretty strange, because I could arrive at the same conclusions just by hearing the question posed, without going through all these highways and byways of his. I later came to realize that if you really have a love of analysis, then you have also to love other paths to analytic insight—and people do take and ruminate over different paths.

AM: The actual work of analysis takes place in a pretty unique space, one that's both codified and ritualized, and at times highly personal. What is the importance of space and place for you?

MCN: I've had so many offices. An office is an office. At least in my work, I don't feel bound to any space. But I did feel bound to the space of my first few years, in West Virginia. I remember crying for that space as a young child, when I was still with both my parents . . . I'd cried because West Virginia had been meaningful in the sense that Searles talks about space and the surround, the non-human surround to which one becomes as attached as one does to people. I never really loved another space until I went to Africa . . . the bellybutton of the world: the Leakey dig at Olduvai Gorge, I wanted to stay right there, in Kenya. And I eventually moved there; for how often can one be a tourist? You don't really grasp anything about the people, except the hotel waiters. . . .

AM: Some theoretical considerations, if you will. Analysts hold different opinions about constructing a personal space, which you've already said isn't that much of an issue . . . But do you carry with you anything that marks the space as distinctly yours?

MCN: My pictures. My paintings. Which are African. And my books. If I move, it's a very systematic exercise. I make a diagram. I put the furniture exactly where it's going to be. I know beforehand, and just put it there. But the first thing I do is to hang my pictures.

AM: In the interview "Analysts at Work," you remark about old age. You say: "I have a horror of growing old, senile, and pretending that I hear my patients when I really don't. So at sixty-five I decided it was time for a change." Now that you've been to Africa, now that you've made that change and grown even older, has that horror been mitigated?

MCN: I was cured of a lot of things in Africa. And I think I was cured of that horror. I was cured of that horror because I absorbed something of the African linear view of life; that is, the way generations interact. Without even knowing it, I absorbed it. The African culture I knew is a reconciled one . . . its people are immersed . . . Whatever they proclaim themselves in terms of Western society, they have a way of dissipating that horror: for one thing by the emotional and spiritual investment of having family. Generations of the family are invested in its being perpetuated; so that a child is always a welcome thing . . . And a welcomed child will really want to have children. This helped me, without even knowing it or thinking about it, to begin to see life as something that wasn't so discontinuous. Life, then, and especially growing old, doesn't seem so horrible.

AM: In the same interview you counter one of the main criticisms against the paradigmatic approach, that it interferes with the transference. To quote you: "I say that it's much more effective if you get in there and amplify the transference, play it back to the patient so that he sees it in all its absurdity and distortion." Can you just elaborate on your understanding of the role the transference plays in treatment? One might get the impression that the paradigmatic technique could explode the transference prematurely, abort its evolution, or even seek to resolve it with a vengeance. . . .

MCN: Well, that's because I speak so dramatically about it! Actually it can be a very laid-back thing. It doesn't have to manifest with fireworks. A very calculated type of response extended over a period of time, under certain circumstances, can be very effective. It's extremely difficult to cure obsessional and compulsive people, for example; but when you can get an obsessional to laugh at the obsessions, you've got a cured patient on your hands; maybe not yet, but on the way. If you're sometimes absurd in your recommendations, which you don't actually expect anybody to follow, you're often able to push people off the cusp, off that static point. People have to be aware of their inconsistency as well as of their rigidity; by the same token, a patient has to become aware of the absurdity of the path that he's following. But there are also patients with whom such interventions are absolutely contraindicated. With a psychotic patient who's totally fragmented, you want to create a very consistent atmosphere. . . .

Eventually, in any therapy, you have to explode what Searles has described as the transference of idealization, which corresponds to a certain developmental stage. You can do that, not by talking about it, but by deviating from what the patient comes to think is a consistent way of your being in the office. You see? It's not an interpretation, but then again, it is: the interpretation being that things aren't always the same here.

AM: In an autobiographical essay of yours, "Getting from There and Then to Here and Now," you write: "At fifteen I escaped my mother and became a left wing activist, working as an organizer, a journalist, a syndicated political cartoonist and an editor." I get the sense somehow that your work as a cartoonist is still present in your work as an analyst. And you've mentioned absurdity so many times that I wonder if existentialists like Camus and Sartre influenced your work at all?

MCN: Well, let's say that my work is existentialist until it becomes absurd. Many of the images I get with patients take the form of a cartoon strip, several frames that play out in a certain way. When I drive, for example, I amuse myself with cartoons that I think of and involuntarily create . . . even with punchlines under them! It's the way my imagination works, and I find this very helpful; this may sound very callous, but the fact is that I can keep myself out of non-therapeutic countertransferences by resorting to such imagery. It happens automatically, and in sessions is not necessarily transmitted to the patient; but it keeps me alert with patients who might bore and bog down other therapists. I may act down, you see, or I may go silent, but I'm not bored. I never cease to be actively interested in ideation, whether the patient's or my own.

AM: But getting back to the existentialists and their influence . . .

MCN: Yes. I was at that time not impressed by the existentialist school of psychoanalysis, primarily on the basis of Binswanger's famous case of Ellen. She was a bulimic, who died. In a book called *Existence*, there's a long documentation of Ellen's life and treatment, a kind of philosophical summation of her way of "being in the world." Yet there was nothing in the case that sounded alive to me, no comments on efforts to keep Ellen alive, or on the failure to keep her alive . . . I was very much defended against, and offended by the existentialist rationalization that this was a model treatment presented as a true account of how existentialists worked. It just seemed horrendous to me. And why pick somebody who dies in the end? What does it tell you? To let such patients die?

AM: In this regard, there's a comment of yours, from your article "Getting from There and Then to Here and Now," that I've always found impressive: "What I have come to realize is that *true* allegiance to any established theoretical or procedural system is, for me, equivalent to a declaration of faith felt as confinement . . . that perpetuating the stance in the face of other options is clearly a self-imposed confinement." Can you elaborate on this?

MCN: There was a time when I so lacked social insight that I imagined people wanted to be free, and in the course of my life, I discovered how this is far from the desire of many people. People want comfort; people want security: security *and* comfort, if possible, but mainly security, for which they will put up with all sorts of deprivations and degradations against their freedom. What's interesting now is that whereas people once derived a sense of security from the fact that America was built on the notion of freedom, today they're not so sure that that freedom exists either. They're becoming increasingly uncomfortable with the recognition that our world is shrinking from the size we dreamt it to be. People are now beginning to question whether security and comfort are natural bedfellows after all. At any rate, in therapy, I don't believe that's the case.

AM: What do you make, then, of the degree of orthodoxy and conformity that many psychoanalytic circles seem to generate, inspire and at times actually demand?

MCN: I could simply say that this is the story of the primal family: you have a leader, lieutenants, and people who are basically trying to attain some security and comfort through the hierarchy. But I also believe the phenomenon has a lot to do with the comfort one gains through repetition. Don Juan emphasizes this to Castaneda when, in *The Teachings of Don Juan*, he asks: "When you are alone, what do you think?" And Castaneda answers: "I always think the same things." Don Juan calls his attention to this, when he says: "Yes, you endlessly repeat yourself." It's what people do; they endlessly repeat themselves. Partly because they don't realize they're doing it, partly because it makes them feel good.

AM: This is a theme you sound repeatedly. For example, again in "Getting from There and Then to Here and Now," you write: "Perhaps because of my solitary childhood I shall never cease to marvel at the ease with which many of my peers navigate in this sea of collective transference, and even thrive on it." What's it like to have been at the edge, or at the margins, of the entire fleet?

MCN: *(devilishly)* Well, partly it's a sense of humor, you see. If you have the reactions of a comic you are able to see the absurdity of this, and of course if you're a trickster with some evil in you, you easily see how little it takes to rock the boat. And when the boat rocks, everybody becomes like rats leaving a sinking ship. They don't know what to do with themselves, and they all scurry around . . . Suddenly, with their security threatened, people's dignity takes a back seat, and it's lots of fun to see that happen!

AM: Connecting to this is a great quote from Mailer's 1964 *Presidential Papers,* which you cite: "The great shadow is that there is a plan for everybody now in our country who is willing to live the way others want him to, to talk the way others want him to, with one big new thick verbiage. Yes, there is a place for everybody now in the American scene, except for those who want to find the limits of their growth by a life which is ready to welcome a little danger as part of the divine cocktail."

MCN: Yes, I like that. I like a little danger as part of the divine cocktail.

AM: The quote echoes your early and apparently very resilient anti-fascist sentiments. It also brings into focus a different kind of fascism, one more pervasive and less clamorous, but that makes for so much of the conformity and homogeneity in our society today. How does Mailer's quote reflect your own thinking, especially in light of our American mythology which exalts the cult of the individual, while what we may actually be witnessing is the death of the individual?

MCN: Oh, do I believe that the death of the individual is imminent. I think it's kept in a state of imminence. I don't envision very much change, unless it arises out of the kind of misery that can't be ignored, like the misery that defined the Great Depression. The federal programs were the result of people first marching to their local store and shouting, "Credit, credit; we need credit!" And the storekeepers saying. "I'm sorry, I can't extend any more credit. You'll have to go to the town hall." And the people went to the town hall, and the town hall complained to the state, and the people said, "We'll march to the state capitol if we have to, but look, we can't stay home and die of starvation." People have to be desperate in order to do anything. That sounds terrible, and fascistic in itself. But this country remains immersed in the feeling that "Big Daddy" is going to make everything all right. The truth is that we may be creeping towards the same kind of ferment that was the aftermath of the Depression.

AM: When Mailer writes about "the divine cocktail," my immediate association is the Christian plea: "Lord take this cup away from me." Today that plea rings alien, maybe because we've done away with so much of the concept, let alone the experience, of *passion.* What can psychoanalysis do to restore a sense of passion in people's lives?

MCN: Psychoanalysis isn't prepared to deal with anything like this. Except for the French. French psychoanalysis knew what to do with it. Psychoanalysis really developed in France for the first time during the '60s, in conjunction with the strikes; Sherry Turkle has written about it, in a book called *Psychoanalytic Politics: Freud's*

French Revolution. At that time in France there was a general awareness of the way things were, economically and in the culture, that combined with an awareness of self.

AM: But while France can reverberate with the kind of theoretical and intellectual criticism that a Lacan might stir, why did the politics of psychoanalytic thinkers like Erich Fromm and Herbert Marcuse, whom you seem to echo, fail to flourish here?

MCN: Throughout most of this century, everything in this country has been geared to an action system. I'm inclined to agree with what Robert Jay Lifton says, that once the frontier was gone and the atomic bomb dropped, people had no other place to dream of going to, and could no longer harbor the fantasy of the perpetuity of the race. After that, no generation could be born without the knowledge that it might be wiped out. That's a terrible knowledge, one I think we're all deeply in reaction against.

AM: In the article "Psychoanalysis and Sorcery," you address the analogy between Don Juan's tutelage of Castaneda and the relationship between analyst and analysand. You also mention how Castaneda's apprenticeship recapitulates the life cycle, and the hero myth. This idea prompts me to wonder if the analyses we conduct today can still encapsulate a sense of a *life* cycle, of a singular experience over time which nevertheless unfolds according to a mythical blueprint of sorts . . . As *postmoderns*, can we still talk fruitfully and benefit from a sense of historical development in which myths are operative and come alive?

MCN: What interests me is the manner in which the analysis itself enables the patient to create, or revise a myth of his or her development–a myth that has to grow. Why do I call it a myth? Because that myth may or may not correspond at all to anything that the analyst hypothesizes. But there comes a point where the analyst realizes that myth is providing a framework for a new self image–where the patient's myth is inscribed, in a way, like the hero's journey. And this involves the patient's own interpretation of what he's been talking about; and because the story is transcendent, you mustn't mess with it. You don't demolish it because you don't know how it's going to turn out; you can't anticipate whether it's going to remain static, or whether it's going to build further and constitute a resolution of some sort, a coming to terms, a freeing of the old, repetitive self definitions. A laying of the ghosts of Christmas past.

AM: Much of our work involves the telling, elaboration and re-envisioning of stories. In a book entitled *The Call of Stories*, Robert Coles stresses the healing value of storytelling. As a clinician, do you attribute a greater healing function to the telling of a story than to the verbalization of any other thought? Or is there a difference between stories, as systematized narratives, and what we call "saying anything"?

MCN: When it comes to building a story, I must see value in it. Remember, my father would come home and delight us with stories. But in and of itself, weaving a story isn't always something valuable. For example, a patient I treated had had ten years of prior analysis with another analyst. Ostensibly she improved a great deal, but I was very leery about the story she was evolving. I considered her story very reductionist, obsessive and static: storytelling as congealment, a foreclosure, a mammoth resistance. She was one of the patients I terminated when I moved to Africa. At that time she became ritualistically involved with a small group devoted to astrology and crystals, and she still wasn't able to sustain herself economically, but paid no attention to this. Something was clearly amiss in the therapy, considering the time that I'd treated her. She was content and no longer an isolate. I was not content, but I kept this to myself; it was better than nothing, and in any case I had to go. You see? And her story involved fixating on a childhood experience with her father in play. He would hold a pillow over her face and she'd feel she was suffocating, which afterwards she took to be the ultimate cause of all her miseries. But I didn't believe it. I never feel happy with reductionist myths. It's like rationalizing the child's difficulties by saying he fell on his head when he was a baby.

AM: There seem to be so many patients today who can't tell their story, sometimes out of reluctance or difficulty, but very often because they simply see no value whatsoever in telling any kind of story, of narrating themselves. These patients move about in a sea of everyday indifference, attributing little or no importance to anything that's either happened in their past or that's happening around them. When I see this, I don't think of the phenomenon merely as a question of denial or repression, or of some schizoid self-presentation. I sense, instead, that people nowadays really don't enjoy telling stories: not everyone has a sense of reconstructing a life, or having their identity constructed through and invested in, a personal and familial mythology or history. Are these people any less amenable to analysis?

MCN: Sure they're less amenable. There are very few stories they can tell that are as evocative of identifications as the stories received, say, through the media of film. I don't care how good one's stories are or how interesting: they can't help but pale before the torrent of murder and mayhem around us. And I've heard some hairy tales from the couch, but I must say they weren't as insistently lurid as today's movies.

AM: As a culture then, or maybe even as a species, are we losing the capacity to tell stories? And, if so, what does that say about the future of analysis?

MCN: Well, I do think we're getting incapable of listening to long stories. As I've already suggested, I think recounting one's personal story is discouraged in the face of the plethora of imagery and dramatization always available on TV and movie screens. Patients even compare their occasional high-points to the screen: "It was like a movie." Life becomes an imitation of film, not vice-versa.

AM: In an accelerated and future-oriented culture like ours, can people learn to revalue the past?

MCN: The past can become so far past people don't even know it happened . . . There is no past. People act as if there is no past.

AM: Are we losing, then, a sense of vital myths? There are many Jungians who say that science is a new myth, but science isn't going to involve or engage everybody.

MCN: No, but science fiction is getting better and better. In today's lifestyle, everything already can be furnished and accomplished remotely. I started to read science fiction out of curiosity. Much science fiction is devoted to life in the galaxies, life in the future, where life is very remote. Most of the people whom one meets in these tales are born in the galaxy, while the earth is nothing but a sad story of decrepitude. Science fiction creates the myth of a future. I read it and I think about what it would be like in a galaxy, and whether I'd like to live there. I'm being very frank. I'm interested in what kind of thoughts the stories generate: of the domes under which future generations live, with vegetation transported from dying earth, and of how bleak and horrible it is outside this enclosure. To live underground and under the dome: it's all very conceivable.

AM: Getting back to your article on Castaneda. You mention in your postscript that, had Castenada lived a century earlier, he might have relied on someone like Kierkegaard as a paradigm or paragon: that same Kierkegaard who in turn had based his work on Socrates' example. Who would Castenada turn to today? Underlying my question is the sense that Don Juan, and later Don Genaro, fulfill for Castaneda a fatherly function, presenting again the mythical dimension of the relationship alongside its developmental necessity. But in societies like our own, where families are more and more intrinsically dysfunctional, where traditional parental roles have been exploded, and one or both parents are virtually or actually absent, what do you see as the therapeutic range of analysis when the paradigms of mother or father, which have carried the burden of the species from its conception up until today, suddenly, within the space of two generations, no longer carry the same weight and meaning?

MCN: A great deal of those representations would probably be carried on in sibling-style relationships. There's also a hint of this, especially among lesbian-paired women, who don't do a lot sexually, but do drink a lot of tea together and talk about themselves! The health food and exercise preoccupation, the focus on the physical body, comradeship supplanting courtship and romanticism: this emphasis softened up the Athenians, who began to contemplate their navels, and were finally overrun and destroyed by the Stoics, a race of squares who believed in abstinence, discipline, and weathering hardship!

AM: I'd like now to discuss two articles by your late husband, Benjamin Nelson, that seem to have provided the groundwork for your conceptualization of paradigmatic psychotherapy. As co-editor of your book *Roles and Paradigms in Psychotherapy*, Ben contributed two important articles to the volume: "The Psychoanalyst as Mediator and Double Agent," and the "Historical Roots of Paradigmatic Psychotherapy," written in collaboration with Herbert Strean. In the first, which dates back to 1965, he cites the "critical sociological dimensions of the analytic situation," suggesting that the analyst serves as both mediator and double agent. He speaks of analysis as a kind of litigation, where roles change but–and here he refers to Kafka–the centrality of the experience of a trial in human existence is consistently maintained. Do you think that metaphor is still a relevant one?

MCN: Definitely, absolutely. I think it's still relevant, but that people who maintain these structures of guilt, social guilt or personal guilt, are not prepared to fight with their demons in the same way as people once were. There is a much greater tendency to justify whatever defects people feel they have, psychologically, and they have more self-indulgent ways of dealing with their dissatisfactions and disturbances. In the past, people were more inclined to project their anger onto objects and the social structure.

AM: Are you suggesting that guilt itself is less pervasive, or has it simply been transformed?

MCN: I would say transformed. Circumstances in the social fabric, notably in religious structures since the time of the Reformation, have permitted the externalization of guilt onto different objects, with different explanatory rationalizations. Before, guilt was mostly personified with population growth and the diffusion of ethnic enclaves; now, guilt is projected onto "others," so that there's a rambling political agenda that doesn't find expression in pure politics but finds voice and justification in personal grievances.

AM: You seem to imply a need to revise Freud's structural model and our conception of the superego. Are we today working with a different kind of superego, and if so what does that say about Freud's tripartite structure?

MCN: It seems to me that all of Freud's structural formulations need revision in light of profound changes in cultural patterns. The superego is no exception. The superego is the territory of sanction, and according to Freud it originates primarily in the relationship with father in the oedipal stage. As you've pointed out, our century has witnessed and experienced the erosion of the traditional family structure. The models that justify the particular quality of Freud's superego have shifted from family structures to social imperatives. The idea of the family has become more ideal than reality, whereas previously it was experientially substantiated by paternalistic arrangements in the structure of society. As a result, I think that the representations in the superego are profoundly altered. When you have so unequal a balance between the maternal representation and the paternal representation, so that one or the other is blighted by negative perceptions or depictions (a simple example is the necessarily working mother interpreted or portrayed as neglectful), then you will have a much more severe, or discordant, split in the superego. That representation, then, becomes a consistent message to its bearer on the basis of principles and beliefs that, by necessity, will be very differently colored throughout the culture.

AM: Are you suggesting that we may be moving from a developmental sequence in a cultural pattern which made for a somewhat "natural" and shared sense of right and wrong (derived from the dynamics of the Oedipus complex), to a very labile, free-floating construction where there is no shared understanding for right and wrong?

MCN: That's right. There is another aspect of this that contributes to what I feel, and that is I do not believe in a true self or a false self. I believe in *selves*. I had always had the impression that any self representation is going to be "true" when it represents itself; when it presents itself, it is true, and when it doesn't, it's false . . . but only false or gone until the next time. In our society we are now confronted with many options, many models of self-definition, models which do influence us and render us far less predictable than we were in simpler, preindustrial times, when the family structure really dominated people's way of being in the world, and there were only two options: either to go along with the dominant model, consciously or unconsciously; or to deviate from it. And when you deviated, the deviation was usually so visible in the life, and made such demands, that you either lived up to the new model and ideal, or renounced it. But nowadays there are enormous options for denial and acceptance in the very substructure of the superego.

AM: In Ben's article, "Historical Roots of Paradigmatic Psychotherapy," he seems to side with the ego psychologists in justifying their amalgam of psychoanalysis into an American mainstream where optimism and adaptation were of primary concern and influence. Yet ego psychology seems galaxies removed from the world of Kafka. What do you make of Ben's apparent contradiction?

MCN: Ben was both far more optimistic than I was, and far more adapted to conventional systems of thought. Originally he was a medieval historian. And Ben was apolitical, while I had always been active, and have always had a profound desire, when there is any sort of social conflict that I regard as important, to really "DO SOMETHING" . . . Where I sought to really participate in a conflict, Ben would remain aloof. Consequently, he could be optimistic; Ben could perceive the newer ego psychology as extremely constructive; he knew the limitations of Freud's perceptions, especially where the social milieu was concerned: for example, he was attuned to the influence of the media on a child's development long before it was defined. But he was also resigned emotionally and rather pessimistic, and in fact, had two extremely severe depressions: one before I met him and one in later life. So what you have is clearly a complex personality, capable of identifying with Kafka and also the brighter side of life.

AM: In that same article, Ben contends that in the convergence of social science and psychoanalysis which you fostered together, paradigmatic psychotherapy acknowledged its debt to ego psychology. The post-war transplantation of psychoanalysis to the U.S. is also mentioned, in the context of America's "optimistic belief in the rational, progressive perfectibility of man in society." One gathers, then, that Ben is arguing in favor of the plasticity of psychoanalysis and its adaptability to meet the ever-changing demands posed by social and psychological factors. He also mentions the peculiar historical malaise that gave birth to existentialism, while heightening the social awareness of meaninglessness in the '50s and '60s. Now, it seems to me improbable that ego psychology and existentialism can somehow be reconciled and integrated in this optimistic and extremely plastic understanding of psychoanalysis. Am I reading the article incorrectly or is there, again, a contradiction or a paradox that may have escaped Ben?

MCN: Ben would always say that he was never amazed at the extent of the disorder in society. He said what really amazed him was that anything ever got done. You can see in this attitude the flip side of pessimism. I suppose, looking back, that I first reacted with enthusiasm that revisions of Freud's narrow reading of superego and ego functions were at last admissible, despite the ego psychologists' turgid and pedantic literary style. Their thinking was a breath of fresh air. While I scoffed at their thesis of "neutralized" ego energy, their work encouraged analysts to extend and deepen the understanding of mental function and process, which previously had been regarded as heresy. Now, of course, Hartmann has also become archaic in turn, of interest only to analytic historians and metapsychologists. As for Ben, he passionately believed that any discipline has to be orderly and progressive, it has to move along. For him, these were signs that psychoanalysis was moving along.

AM: Whatever the contradictions in Ben's writing, I've found a much more flagrant one, I believe, in your own position. You've suggested to me that the paradigmatic notion of discontinuous selves finds an echo in Lacan's uncompromising critique of ego psychology. In fact, you and Lacan both refer to the notion of the ego as a *fiction*: you penned that very idea years ago, and it still constitutes the essence of Lacan's critique. So how can a clinical orientation which openly acknowledges its debt to ego psychology be so plastic as to announce, twenty-five years later, that it now finds itself in accord with the very theory that aims to explode the tenets of ego psychology and debunk it altogether? You, too, can't have it both ways!

MCN: Nothing can be debunked that hasn't existed. One of the reasons that ego psychology has so fallen out of discussion is the tediousness of the way in which it was described, and the difficulty in reading Hartmann, Kris and Lowenstein. You'd read it and think, "I must be very stupid; I don't understand this." So you'd read it again. And still it is obscure, with virtually no relevance to actual clinical practice. In fact, it carries the practitioner still farther away from the emotional reality of treatment. The theory was so detached it would slip out of your head!

Anyhow, I think ego psychology was a necessary stage in the recognition of a truth that Freud did not see, or did not deal with. However, one doesn't need to be stuck with the theory of ego psychology. The fragmentation of perception now, both in patients and in the media, in the whole culture, the plastic quality of representation makes for a very disintegrating experience, and the analyst has to acknowledge and resonate with its impact. Now, at this time, in this historic place, I feel that what I see before me is not the false self, or the true self–it is *selves*. And behind the selves lie the major developmental elements, the experiences, and the dominant feelings that these selves have generated, whatever they were, with whomever and in whatever order or sequence they appeared, in terms of black and white, in terms of good and bad, in terms of horrible and wonderful. So it's not necessarily true that a person is a cohesive self, or in possession of a true or false self: a person is a self rendered into selves that are capable of accommodating to various situations. That doesn't mean healthy; that just means capable of engagement.

AM: Is there a difference between your position and Lacan's, even though you both have this sense of the unified self, or ego, as a fiction?

MCN: I think of these selves as a harp, which is a vertical concept somewhat like Lacan's. Some things, some experiences which may be intrapsychically generated, or generated from the outside, strike certain chords, themes, or stances on this harp, and that is what you hear.

AM: To the extent that it will take psychoanalysis–like any social science–time to analyze, understand, and integrate newly evolving social factors and transformations, are analytic theory and practice fated to lag behind these new developments? Is there a risk that psychoanalysis will always be antiquated at the moment of its application in the clinical setting?

MCN: The very material of traditional psychoanalysis is the study of regressive forces. You may say, "but one gets an image of progressive forces in the patient too." Of course you do. But you're not jousting with the transcendent forces; it's the regressive forces with which one has to cope strategically in order to create or facilitate any change in the patient. When you have something that deals with and explores the past, as Freudian analysis does, then it necessarily generates a conservatism because its inherent movement is a movement into the past. In Jung, that movement is mythologized. In Freud, it's mythologized too, but in a more individual way. That's why you have this spate of belief systems, temporary and transient, in which people are encouraged to look into the future, and be preoccupied with all sorts of things which add up to rebirth, reincarnation, longevity and survival. So, I don't think it's possible, when you are dealing with material of the past, to even focus on the future, because to focus on the future requires all sorts of hortatory prescriptions before one has even understood the symptoms. And a competent analyst doesn't do that. A competent analyst may encourage the patient under certain circumstances, but would not give prescriptions for living.

AM: How do you reconcile, in your clinical practice, the retrospective nature of analysis with the needs of a generation whose myths and focus, whose very *selves*, are often so distinctly future-oriented?

MCN: That's an issue that has to do with affect. There are certainly people with a great deal more psychic energy than others. Now, psychic energy is a very funny thing. It has to find its discharge in ideas, in thoughts, and a future-oriented person is one who wants to create, who wants to participate in creation, and finds routines tedious because they don't provide this sense of mental expenditure. It feels like standing still. Bollas addresses this with his idea of *psychic genera*. Such people can't bear to stew around in their own juice of ideas, fantasies, and functional repetition. They have to do something with these things or they go crazy. So I certainly feel that future-orientation may be linked to affect pattern, to biological givens and even body image.

AM: That leads me to your own writings about paradigmatic work, and back to your book *Roles and Paradigms*. A good way to start would be to clarify the difference between *nuclear* and *ambient* paradigms.

MCN: Mostly one conceptualizes the paradigmatic maneuver in terms of an inability to deal with an issue in a more conservative way. With some patients, one has to recognize a ground-note of difficulty that doesn't always manifest clearly; this way the therapist is enabled to address the difficulty through the use of fantasy, or a bright idea of what to say. The problem is usually a pervasive, long-lasting, but inexpressible one, or one that's even unfelt by the patient; at most he or she may mention that something "feels wrong." It is a deep problem of identity. I would call such a difficulty *nuclear*, requiring from the therapist a similar response, not clear-cut but fuzzy, spacy: like the vague suggestion of a mood, of a feeling rather than a thought.

I once had this patient who was "schizophrenic," who defined himself this way. He had been seen by many therapists, and still felt fragile, afraid. The feeling was a chronic one, and it tortured him. I know that until that's somehow mitigated, he's going to be paralyzed in all his dealings with the world. He is constantly in a fixed stance of fear, which he cannot define except in terms of his infantilization by his mother: an infantilization which continues to this day because he still can't work, though he says he was once able to. But then he entered an analysis which, he claims, destroyed him, because the analyst put a Freudian interpretation on everything. That's what I call a nuclear problem. With him this means there is nothing I can do in the course of treatment where I can elude this reality . . . that whatever happens, I must always bear in mind that this fear has somehow to be mitigated, at least in his relationship with me. But our relationship is of the very type that he claims destroyed him in the past . . . He also invested every communication with analytic undercurrents, and was adamantly humorless. So we couldn't simply have fun together.

AM: A nuclear paradigm, then, would be any maneuver aimed at mitigating or alleviating the crippling effects of a central or core issue that pervades a person's life. What about the ambient paradigm?

MCN: The best example that comes to me is that of an obsessive compulsive patient who often teetered on the brink of decision, but could never make one. For example, a patient whom I had taken at a reduced fee couldn't decide what to do with a raise that he got in his job, and this went on for weeks. Finally, I said cheerfully, "Well, give it all to me. I can use it, since it's nothing but a worry to you." Immediately, the very next session, he came in saying he had decided what he would do with the raise. You see? This is what I call an ambient paradigm. It addresses a symptom, a high level symptom. It's not aimed at something that's deeply, deeply ingrained.

AM: But couldn't one argue that the specific ambient symptom is reflective of the more entrenched nuclear pathology which characterizes an obsessive compulsive?

MCN: Strictly speaking, obsessive compulsive traits have more to do with the way the child is treated in the toilet training period. I frankly believe that an infant doesn't have enough organized mental process to develop obsessive compulsive traits. Infants may manifest symptoms, such as those resultant from anxieties a mother may transmit, but obsessive compulsive traits have to do, I think, more with the vicissitudes of toilet-training. That's a pretty classical notion; nothing original in that. At any rate, when you are able to help an obsessive-compulsive patient to laugh at the symptoms, as the patient did when I invited him to give the money to me, you're on your way.

Anyway, a funny kind of encounter over these issues can help the patient to laugh at the symptom. When he can laugh at the symptom, he can resolve the compulsion, and learn to laugh at the character trait as well. You can kill with laughter; you can kill a trait off by laughing at it. You learn to see its absurdity, and when you see yourself in such an absurd way, when you feel the absurdity as a belly laugh, you've conquered it.

AM: Arnold Bernstein, in his introduction to the 1981 issue of the journal *Modern Psychoanalysis* that was dedicated to you and your work, mentions a paradigmatic behavior studies seminar. With you and Ben, Bernstein, Murray Sherman, Herbert Strean, Robert De-Neergaard and Arthur Blatt. What was this seminar? How did it evolve, and how long did it last?

MCN: I was teaching at NPAP and was a functionary there; I saw these colleagues as supervisees or students in training there. It was a wonderful group; just a scintillating group. We presented patients and also discussed theory. Forty years before "self" became a hot issue, the whole notion of the self, of the "varieties" of self became very central in our discussion. Another area that we were extremely interested in was the different styles in which we utilized these paradigmatic interventions.

AM: Your remark about analysts' individual styles reminds me of the difficulties and struggles inherent in the development of a personal style, especially when we all can't help but be influenced by the style of our own analysts.

MCN: Developing a style is very difficult. It took me many years, or what feels like many years, to realize that one didn't remain silent all the time, and that some patients certainly couldn't tolerate silence . . . and had to be talked with. I think once I realized that, I became much more at ease with my patients. I've often thought about my own analyst and how terrible it must have been for him to keep quiet; it must have been awful to remain silent for that long . . . Five times a week for two years. It's difficult for people to remain silent five minutes, for heaven's sake!

AM: What do you see as the function or responsibility of a training program, in helping a trainee to individuate? Or is that just going to be a natural process that will or won't happen according to a trainee's own abilities and personality?

MCN: Well, it's really an individual question, not so much in a purely personal sense, but in the cultivated need to identify with some particular theoretical position or advocated technique that is favored at a certain period. I think there are people who retain an allegiance to be "true to themselves" forever; then there are also people who replicate their own analysts, for a time, and then move on to something else. Then there are others who are more eclectic, who experiment. I've often thought that had I been more intentionally innovative, I might have gravitated toward a different type of therapeutic group, one less orthodox than my own parent organization had been in earlier days. One more receptive to self-study and the examination of countertransference than even our paradigmatic seminar. One principal deterrent to this was my editorship of

NPAP's quarterly, *The Psychoanalytic Review*, for seventeen years. I simply loved it. When nothing else held me, the *Review* did.

AM: One or two more questions about the article on paradigms. You state there that both nuclear and ambient paradigms are intended "to energize the treatment and to initiate movement of some kind." For the Western mind, this seems to beg the issue of linearity. What is the movement towards? What is your own personal philosophy regarding the goals and aims of a psychoanalysis?

MCN: Well, the selves, such as they are, need to become a unitary body: a peaceful federation of selves. So I conceive of analysis as a means to achieving a bond between these different selves, so that each self knows that the others exist, and so that each can lock in when it's appropriate and bow out when it's appropriate. The analyst, then, shouldn't have as a goal some specific ideal of how this patient should or shouldn't evolve through treatment: because all the different aspects of the person represent a creative evolved coping with what the outside world has laid on it. And when this bond is accomplished, there's not the confusion or rigidity that bespeaks pathology; there's no ingestion of the indigestible, to use Fairbairn's notion of indigestible objects, which otherwise have to be expelled in dysfunctional ways in order for the patient to feel real.

AM: Would you say, then, that this "fraternization" of the different selves equates somehow with what Lacan calls the recognition and realization of one's *desire*: or with his understanding of what ought to constitute the aim of an analysis?

MCN: I wouldn't argue that it doesn't. It's a nice way of putting it, and I guess it's very French.

AM: You once pointed out to me that only a Frenchman could come up with the idea of the mirror stage, given the French propensity for appreciating the aesthetics of reflection, and for giving the kind of importance they do to the body.

MCN: France is and was very big on mirrors. The French have a longstanding historic preoccupation with appearance, with etiquette and subtle sensuality. Maybe that's why they tolerate and can toy with ambiguities better than Americans. I also wonder about Africans, who often own no mirror: in which case–and I believe this to be true of all people–the child first sees other bodies, then discovers its own limbs because they can do what other people's do. Especially hands and arms, which show up and get discovered before feet! There's something else, though, about mirrors. Check out the Manichaean, or Gnostic creation myth, in which the evil forces of earth and darkness sought to lure God (light) down from the heavens by creating a mirror, expecting he would be drawn to his own image.

AM: God as Narcissus!

MCN: Exactly. God didn't have a high IQ rating in those days!

AM: Back to your book on paradigms. In one essay, "Therapeutic Redirection of Energy and Affect," you make passing reference to the early controversy surrounding Freud's concept of the death instinct, and the general aversion to the concept that persists up until this day. How do you read and utilize the concept, if at all? Does it have a place and value in your work today, when so many people disavow it?

MCN: I don't disavow it, but it doesn't really have a place in my work, unless I'm working with a very deathly person, in which case, it could hardly be justified as an instinct; I'd call it a position, an obsessional reification of the idea of death. I imagine people who work a lot with severe depressives are acutely aware of it. And I certainly acknowledge that particular idea when I encounter people who work with geriatric patients, the dying patients. I feel that in those clinicians, there must certainly be a parallel ideation of death because I couldn't imagine really feeling gratified by helping dying patients face death more cheerfully. I always think of my function as involving the preservation and enhancement of life, and if I can't feel I'm doing that, if I felt that all I am helping someone to do is die, that would be terrible. I realize this sounds highly unethical, cruel, heartless, monstrous even, but it's my true feeling. I want to work with life as long as I'm alive. As an old woman, though, I often realize that people who are very put off by my age, are themselves afraid of dying. So if possible they project the fear onto me. In that case I become a useful person; they can project all their fears of dying onto me, and not bother about their own death. Which reminds me: do you know of Paul Goodman's little prescription for what a child needs to complete a personality? Oh, its beautiful! It's in *The Dead of Spring*, in what is possibly his first monograph, published in 1950. It's an allegorical story, where he scorns the familial triangle as inadequate to create a complete person. He says the child needs, if I recall correctly, twenty-two people, of which I can only remember a few: he needs one object to introduce him into the life of sex, one to contain the mystery of life, and so forth. Finally, one is required to initiate a person into the mystery and acceptance of death. Goodman lists a whole host of people, then exclaims, "So many people to create one person." Very nice!

AM: Earlier you mentioned some reservations that arose from your collaboration with the Spotnitz group, with whom you've otherwise remained on very friendly and collegial terms. Can you talk more specifically about the similarities and divergences between the paradigmatic and Modern schools as they've developed over time?

MCN: Modern Psychoanalysis and Spotnitz leave out of consideration many cultural factors, many truths. Modern analysis does not truly deal with the notion of introjection, but believes that people are what they are because of what happened to them in the pre-oedipal period. If asked, the modern analyst might rationalize that societal and cultural factors are transmitted first by the parents. But this begs the question. Each generation represents its own experience in time, which is in many respects different from that of the parents. Consequently the child embodies vestiges of parental heritage plus the *x* factor of its time. I believe that all hope for anything good, alongside the species' sadly remarkable capacity for evil as well as for good, is tied to man's deep capacity for change and for introjecting all kinds of models.

AM: You don't believe, then, that introjects occur or are replicated on the basis of a given set of fundamental preoedipal ones. . . .

MCN: *(definitively)* I don't believe it; I simply don't believe it. Especially now, when there's such an impact by the media–of ideas, of enactments–in constituting the imaginary life of the child, who starts out seeing things that in a million years hadn't appeared before the eyes of the entire species. Just imagine the enormous effect this has. It creates a totally different emotional structure, for one thing: a structure of extremes, of monstrous things. Before, children perceived monstrous things from fairy tales and picture books; now, instead, they see real people routinely committing monstrous acts. The structuralization of the imagination can't help but be very different, much more kaleidoscopic.

AM: Are you suggesting that the greater receptivity or plasticity with regard to introjection is a historical phenomenon of rather recent development?

MCN: Absolutely, absolutely. Though the occurrence itself is not a first in the life of the history of the species. Consider the frenetic seizures that gripped communities during the Middle Ages, as depicted by Peter Breughel, for example. Or the licentious revolt of Moses' followers while he attended the summit conferences with God. In much the same way as Johan Huizinga's introductory contrast, in *The Waning of the Middle Ages*, of the occasional ringing of church bells across the field of a thinly populated countryside to the emergent hubbub of the city-state.

AM: So even as early as a generation ago, people weren't as predisposed to a lifetime of introjective processes?

MCN: That's right; and the time may come when that predisposition will recede, when–as appears now to be happening–deterrent legislation attempts to regulate even the most intimate, and formally private arrangements. Freedom of decision may close down again, and the next generations may be kept oblivious to certain realities, just as happened under communism and fascism. A culture raises its children with the images that prevail in the culture. There's nothing novel or exceptional about this idea, as there is an undeniable connection between primary experience and social experience. The Moderns, for all their vaunted modernity, don't pay attention to that in a theoretical way, they don't deal with it. Spotnitz, for example, never addresses this dimension.

AM: How then do you react today to Arnold Bernstein's contention of a decade ago that paradigmatic psychotherapy is simply another aspect of Modern Psychoanalysis? He seems to subsume your work under the greater rubric of Spotnitz's. . . .

MCN: Paradigmatic psychotherapy is but one dimension in a broader movement to cultivate psychoanalysis and define it in a modern setting. I think that clinically Modern Psychoanalysis is nevertheless very helpful.

AM: A major interest of mine revolves around the disappearance of the father in much contemporary theory. Obviously, there are societal correlates which point increasingly to the so-called "absent father," or to the father whose own identity as a figure of male authority has been reconfigured, if not actually undermined. Do you think there's a correspondence between the disappearance of the father, and his vanishing from prevailing modes of psychoanalytic discourse? Whatever happened to Oedipus?

MCN: *(wryly)* Oedipus is around. He's around for some people, but not for everybody. You see, practically all of psychoanalysis has immersed itself in preoedipal theory, and all of the attention is on the mothers. That's going to change, and is already changing. When you read the book reviews, of both biography and fiction, you see that authors and their characters are calling the father back. Bollas, for instance, in his *Being a Character,* he also calls the father back. I find he's articulating and writing about a number of arguments and ideas I've maintained for a long time. What he calls psychic *genera*, for example, or the idea of the multiplicity of selves. Even his reading of the Oedipus myth, which I heard delivered at a conference before it appeared in the book, I find very "ego-syntonic."

AM: This leads me to want to consider some influences on your work, either openly acknowledged or deserving of recognition. Your writings leave me with two distinct impressions regarding apparent influences. One is that a truly Freudian spirit of exploration, of discovery and new frontiers, seems always to be present in your work; and that for all of your deviance, your work in some way does stand as an homage to Freud—whatever the charges of the orthodox.

MCN: Yes, I feel very empathetic with Freud. I feel that I understand Freud's spirit in an emotional way, not through some formal endorsement of what he believed. He cites many emotional experiences, many psychological experiences, that I can resonate with. But he was also very narcissistic and intolerant of those who dared to be free, and that's been an important lesson to me: to listen very carefully when somebody tells of some other therapeutic persuasion. I want to know, I don't want to emulate Freud in this respect. Also, I've never hungered for the kind of sybaritic adulation that Freud generated. I think it's very hard to be authentic when that happens.

AM: The second influence I note is Winnicott, who seems to streamline your writings. Can you comment on your own intellectual development in light of his work?

MCN: Only now do I fully appreciate Winnicott's work. When his writings first began to appear, I was very much influenced by the classical analysts who considered him full of nonsense and all wrong. Today people recognize intent in his playfulness, and meaning in the clinical phenomena he observed. The way he'd watch the child alone and with the mother was amazing, and yielded a whole body of data that classical analysts didn't get.

AM: In our teaching together you've often privileged a notion of play that seems central and indeed crucial to your work, and to the successful outcome of any analysis. Is the arena in which you play similar to Winnicott's? And is it one of the analyst's functions to teach the patient to play?

MCN: I do sometimes play, yes, and then the play gets worked through. This part I find interesting, because the patient becomes the judgmental parent and ends up objecting to the playfulness. Then I can manifest indignation and say, "Well, have we any agreement here that I can't play if I feel like it?" He admits, "No, of course there's no such agreement." Then I may ask, "Should we make such an agreement?" Or perhaps I'll suggest: "Well, I'll tell you, we're both free here to say what we please. That's the bottom line. I can say what I please; you can say what you please; and right now I please to play." I'll "play" according to whatever seems appropriate for a particular personality.

AM: You take a great amount of pleasure in your work.

MCN: *(proudly)* Yes. And I want to. And even if this a no-no, since we're not supposed to desire emulation, I'm always hoping that some of this courage will rub off on the patient.

AM: What about Searles? You cite his *Collected Papers on Schizophrenia and Related Subjects* as the lone book you'd save from a fire!

MCN: I admire Searles; first of all, he was interested in treating very ill patients, and I am too. That takes a terrible lot of courage and patience, and I have that. And I find treating these people very interesting, in terms of studying and exploring the languages they use. When you have people who speak a different language, or very little of one's own language, the word becomes important; every word these patients utter is representative of all the things they're not saying, so you pay more attention than with a verbal, less disturbed patient.

Searles also stresses transferences to the surround, and not just to people, but to a cat, to a tree. This is a very African notion by the way: working with the capacity to endow all things with the concept of life, to attribute everything with sentient, and not just vegetative, life. When Searles wrote about these things in his first book, *The Nonhuman Environment in Normal Development and in Schizophrenia*, I understood him immediately, and felt very strongly about him. After my husband died, I didn't go to see Spotnitz; I went to see Searles once in Washington. In that lone visit with Searles, I was able to weep. I mean, I couldn't help but weep. I couldn't have done it with Spotnitz.

AM: Why not?

MCN: He was not self-revealing with me: colleagues of mine who have kept working with him over many years say he was or has become very verbal and open, but with me he was extremely noncommittal. I couldn't have talked to him. I would have had an empty echo. Against this disappointment was the reality: I'd had six years of intensive analysis. I did—and still do—consider it successful. I was, and remain grateful. And I was grateful that he endured the years when I couldn't talk at all. Towards the end of my treatment, I wanted very much to talk about these and other things, but he would not respond on a one-on-one basis, so I gave up trying. I'm not a martyr. Why he wouldn't talk to me is still a mystery, but I don't think much about it. With Searles, though, I got the feeling that he was willing, or able, or disposed, to feel along with me. Not to cry, but to feel bad with me about what had happened to me with Ben's death.

AM: There's one more name that generates all sorts of rabid feelings in the psychoanalytic community, and that's Masud Khan. His own renegade spirit and supposed escapades are pretty notorious, and yet you admire his work.

MCN: Yes. One thing that horrified people was that, in *The Long Wait*, the last book he wrote before dying, he tells openly about attacking a patient who was a Jew. But I didn't feel that it was all that terrible. I thought that maybe he did it deliberately, intentionally, and did not simply act out as he was accused of having done. It sounds terrible, but perhaps he had a reason for doing it, a reason he didn't rationalize in the writing sufficiently, or clearly, or justifiably. Maybe he was working from the position of a recognized parallelism in their respective lives: just as the patient was "fated" to be Jewish, so was Khan "fated" to be a prince, with all the characterological baggage that goes with a prince's upbringing. The man was, you know, fiercely criticized for his princely, some say arrogant, manner. But maybe such a thing can't be rationalized; one can say something to patients that, no matter how you explain it, would never wash with the reader.

AM: Here's a list: Spotnitz, Searles, Winnicott, Bollas, Khan. No women.

MCN: I know no women. I don't seem capable of admiring women. And by-and-large women aren't crazy about me. "Sicklied o'er" by an authoritarian mother. I have some good friends, I've lost some good friends. They've just died on me. But, I didn't bond to any of these people the way I did with Searles. Some women can speak of a woman friend that way; they can feel they've been enriched. I can't think of a single woman that I've felt emotionally enriched by, even though I have been enriched situationally, and professionally, by several women. This lacuna about women may partly result from the endless search for the lost father. I enjoy being with men, in sex, in edifying discourse–and a happy combination is best of all!

AM: When I first conceived of our interview, one intention was to revisit and explore the age-old question of lay analysis. In this context, Arnold Bernstein refers to you as "one of an almost vanished breed of analysts who come to the field from other professions." How do you see the field of lay psychoanalysis evolving today, and what place, if any, do you see for lay analysts today?

MCN: I think the apprentice category everywhere is vanishing because people have constantly and endlessly to validate themselves with certificates of attendance somewhere. I think it's all very sad, and goes along with the intolerance for a certain kind of across-the-board eccentricities. People used to be tolerant of eccentrics. These people lived there and were part of the local scene, part of the social fabric. Now, in every category of life in this society, people have to be validated. Everything requires some sort of certification. Today, if you slip through the cracks, it's a miracle. A miracle of achievement, of deviance.

AM: Speaking of apprenticeships: there seems to be so little recognition these days of the need and the richness of learning from an elder. It's as if wisdom were passé. And yet your mention of apprenticeships brings to mind the fact that psychoanalysis might be one of the last remaining "medieval," guild-like occupations.

MCN: That's true. But now, authentication is beginning to become a requirement so extreme that there's very little freedom to move about and find someone whom you'd really want to work with over a period of time. And moving about, say from one supervisor to another, has become very suspect, as has moving about from one school to another. It is suspect; and I was fortunate not to have that problem. I have also dealt with and supervised some people who have a history of moving back and forth: the trouble they face is usually connected with the difficulties in staking some claim to independence, to some degree of independent thought, and it's very sad. Even where the safeguards of analysis are concerned–namely, that people be well-trained, and continue their analysis and case supervision–even this process has become so hedged in that it ceases to reflect and inspire a freedom of choice.

AM: Along these lines, you make light of your own organizational accomplishments. And yet, while in Kenya, you initiated the first psychoanalytically inspired training program in Africa!

MCN: Yes. I wasn't there long before I noticed that missionaries were high on samaritanism and low on training. Psychology itself was virtually an unknown discipline, and the psychiatrists, through training and necessity, relied on pharmaceutical interventions.

AM: In a review of yours which appeared in the journal *Voices*, on I. Sow's book *Anthropological Structures of Madness in Black Africa*, you write: "The focus on narcissism within Freud's developmental framework has led 20th century psychoanalysis in a retrograde, even a medieval direction, with a hypothesis that schizophrenic illness derives from defective mothering in the earliest phase of infancy. Perhaps the witch mother theory should occasion no surprise." Can you elaborate?

MCN: Overwork, understaffing, and the siren song of perks by the pharmaceutical houses conspire to discourage Kenyan psychiatrists from theoretical formulations. Even if they are drawn to such ideas, psychiatrists cannot devote blocks of time to individual patients. But I was accorded the privilege of treating patients, and found them highly responsive to psychotherapy despite the fact that I was white and an outsider. There are, of course, significant cultural differences one has to bear in mind. First, the extended family; secondly, the different handling of the neonate and young infant by the mother; third–and this is true especially for boys–a child's position in the birth order; fourth, the fact that African cultures are still overwhelmingly patriarchal.

Also, I found while I was there that Africans didn't need what we'd call paradigmatic interventions. They benefited greatly from exploring their dreams, which they were culturally disposed to respect in the first place; plus they have a built-in respect for the senior age group to which I belong. So they took treatment seriously, despite a latent reservation about "white" medicine.

AM: Did this experience mark a change in your understanding of the effectiveness of paradigmatic techniques?

MCN: I have generally used paradigmatic interventions less as time goes on. Partly because the paradigmatic addresses both the cognitive and the feeling levels; partly because there is now, thank goodness, a dawning awareness (both in my own field and in the experiential field of social contagion) of the fact that people everywhere are exposed and succumb to enactment, to auditory and visual imagery, to affective issues, which was not true in our culture during the mid-Fifties. One could introduce a sophisticated paradigm to which the patient would resonate, but now it's just another stimulus, nuttiness which in some ways parallels the media and other external social stimuli. It may sound strange, maybe even unpredictable, but survival itself is less predictable–expectations of what will happen in therapy are not the same as the expectations of earlier patients. Just as Africans cannot, in general, tolerate the high levels of medication consumed in the West, here you have a kind of shutting down, an immunity, to the effects of a paradigm, and to other communications as well.

AM: I'm wondering if what we're all seeing is a diminished sense of the existential reality of what it means to suffer in the course of a human life. People now want quick fixes and, as Americans, we believe in perfectibility, while denying the crude realities of aging and death. There's a prevailing sense that regards suffering as something that ought to be banished from the realm of human experience.

MCN: Exactly. Patients want to be made to feel better, and you didn't have that exclusive demand in the past. Of course people then wanted to feel better too, but they wanted to feel better via understanding, and that's no longer the case. Most people nowadays don't have a passion for understanding, which again I attribute very specifically to the hypnotic and dysjunctive effect of the media.

AM: If the demand, then, that patients are putting upon analysts is for little more than an emotional bandaid, does analysis risk running into a dead end if it doesn't find a way–and here I'm being facetious–to not only alleviate but obliterate human suffering?

MCN: Well, of course that's not possible, by any means . . . by any means whatsoever.

AM: So how can analysis hope to work fruitfully with patients whose nominal goal or aim, and whose culturally determined goal or aim, is to see their suffering removed?

MCN: Well, it can't work, nothing can work, because the premise is a false one: that suffering can be obliterated.

AM: Then how do we keep patients in treatment and stop them from going on an endless merry-go-round in search of a fountain of youth, or for a way to obliterate the suffering? Is there a didactic element to our work?

MCN: Then you hold the patient in treatment via the transference, and the patients improve because they see you're surviving. You exemplify cognitive and emotional techniques, and you teach them–I'm sorry to say this–a certain stoicism.

AM: You're sorry to say?

MCN: Yes, because I don't particularly admire stoicism. I mean, it's too bad stoicism is a learned trait. It's not natural. It's a pity that people can't achieve desire, but that they have to fall in love with desire itself, specifically with the desire for transcendence.

AM: You surprise me. I've never sensed a Dionysian element at work in your personality. I know it's in your theory, but I never recognized it before in you!

MCN: You don't know how fierce I am. Let's say that I do the best I can to help keep my patients on the ground and to help them become good drivers. But if I can't do that, then by all means, they should learn to fly! I think that if people are able to create a bond between their own selves, they will endure, and not only endure, but endure with a kind of verve and pleasure in the very fact of their endurance. A quality of endurance that signifies transcendence.

WORKS CITED

Bollas, C. (1992). *Being a Character: Psychoanalysis and Self Experience*. New York, Hill and Wang.

Castaneda, C. (1969). *The Teachings of Don Juan: A Yaqui Way to Knowledge*. New York, Ballantine Books.

Coles, R. (1989). *The Call of Stories*. Boston, Houghton Mifflin.

Eigen, M. (1981). "Breaking the Frame, Stopping the World," in *Paradigmatic Theory and Technique: A Tribute to Marie Coleman Nelson*. Modern Psychoanalysis, 6:1.

Freud, S. (1916-17). *Introductory Lectures on Psychoanalysis*, in J. Strachey, ed. *The Standard Edition of the Complete Psychological Works of Sigmund Freud*, 24 vols. London, Hogarth, 1953-73, S.E. 15.

Goodman, P. (1959). "The Dead of Spring," in *The Empire City*. New York, Bobbs-Merrill.

Huizinga, J. (1985). *The Waning of the Middle Ages*. New York, St. Martin's Press.

Khan, M. M. R. (1989). *The Long Wait*. New York, Summit Books.

Mailer, N. (1964). *The Presidential Papers*. London, Andre Deutsch.

May, R., ed. (1958). *Existence*. New York, Basic Books.

Nelson, M. C. (1985). "Getting from There and Then to Here and Now," *Voices*, 21:1.

______ (1976). "Paths of Power: Psychoanalysis and Sorcery," *Psychoanalytic Review*, 63:3.

______ (1981). *(book review)*: of I. Sow's *Anthropological Structures of Madness in Black Africa*. Voices, 16:4.

Searles, H. (1965). *Collected Papers on Schizophrenia and Related Subjects*. New York, International Universities Press.

______ (1960). *The Nonhuman Environment in Normal Development and in Schizophrenia*. New York, International Universities Press.

Turkle, S. (1992). *Psychoanalytic Politics: Jacques Lacan and Freud's French Revolution*. New York, Guilford.

MARIE COLEMAN NELSON: SELECTED BIBLIOGRAPHY

Evil, Self, and Culture (ed., with M. Eigen, 1984). New York, Human Sciences Press.

Paradigmatic Theory and Technique: A Tribute to Marie Coleman Nelson. Special issue of *Modern Psychoanalysis*, 6:1.

The Narcissistic Conditon (ed., 1977). New York, Human Sciences Press.

Roles and Paradigms in Psychotherapy, (ed., with B. Nelson, M. H. Sherman, H. Strean, 1968). New York, Grune and Stratton.

Transference and Trial Adaptation (with J. Meerloo, 1965). Springfield, Charles C. Thomas.

Films in Psychiatry, Psychology and Mental Health (with A. Nichtenhauser and D. S. Ruhe, 1953). New York, Health Education Council.

Michael Eigen

And it shall come to pass, that before they call, I will answer, and while they are yet speaking, I will hear. The wolf and the lamb shall feed together, and the lion shall eat straw like the bullock, and dust shall be the serpent's meat. They shall not hurt or destroy in all my holy mountain. . . .

–Isaiah, 65:24-25

Something about Michael Eigen makes for a stream of oxymorons. Maybe it has to do with what he calls the distinction/union structure *that characterizes human thought and experience, something he talks about at length in these pages. "In the beginning there was both separation and union, or distinction and union . . . ," he says at one point, explaining his own take on the Creation myth. Maybe that's why, when I think of him, phrases come to mind like "eased awkwardness," or "befuddled clarity." Phrases that describe his bodily expressions as well as the arching breaths and insights of his words and thought. Earthbound and visionary, Eigen goes against the grain, struggling to articulate the spiritual gropings of today's patients, while also tugging at the blinders of those who insist that Freud, on the matter of the "oceanic feeling," did indeed speak the last word.*

When I think back at my first encounter with Mike years ago, my memories are of a shy, self-effacing man, dressed totally in black, perhaps even wearing dark sunglasses, talking about Bion and death at a Modern Freudian training institute. Had he come with a

---

[Haworth co-indexing entry note]: "Michael Eigen." Co-published simultaneously in *The Psychotherapy Patient* (The Haworth Press, Inc.) Vol. 10, No. 1/2, 1997, pp. 105-141; and: *Elaborate Selves: Reflections and Reveries of Christopher Bollas, Michael Eigen, Polly Young-Eisendrath, Samuel and Evelyn Laeuchli and Marie Coleman Nelson* (ed: Anthony Molino) The Haworth Press, Inc., 1997, pp. 105-141. Single or multiple copies of this article are available from The Haworth Document Delivery Service [1-800-342-9678, 9:00 a.m. - 5:00 p.m. (EST). E-mail address: getinfo@haworth.com].

guitar, there'd be no mistaking him for Roy Orbison. Already then, I sensed, this man's comfort zone was on the fringes: of psychoanalysis and mysticism, perhaps, but more importantly, on the fringes of an embracing, radical "otherness." And indeed, as you'll note in these pages, Eigen does walk, or jog, or step, or dance, to the beat of a different drummer; what you won't find him doing, though, is marching. It's simply too rigid a posture, for a man who knows that there are as many drummers as there are patients, and as many beats as there are lives and fears, tears and trembling hopes.

A funny thing about this interview is that Mike cheerfully swears he never wore black, let alone appearing publicly as my feeble memory, or elaborate fantasy, would have him. Even the sunglasses are the result of my dreamwork! But so be it. One thing he did do, however, in the course of our talk, will forever remain imprinted on my mind. You see, Mike squints a lot; in fact, throughout the entire five-hour interview, only once did he fully open his eyes. We were about halfway through our work, when I asked him how he imagined an infant's experience of the mother's face. Then, all of a sudden, his eyes opened. First widely, slowly, then, almost wildly, as they both wandered up and far to the right, as if following a penlight an ophthalmologist might wield. Then, as he began to answer, "Well, there is the eye-to-eye contact, where the eyes are shining or dull or a shade in-between . . . ," his eyes refocused, and settled, and met my eyes for the duration of his answer. Or maybe, I should say, of his meditation. A word, we should remember, that like "medicine" comes from the Latin mederi, *"to heal."*

The interview which follows was conducted over the course of two days, on December 3-4, 1994, in Mike's home in Brooklyn, during Hannukah, the Jewish Season of Lights. The topics discussed prefigure the theme of his recent book, ***Reshaping the Self****, not yet published at the time.*

AM: As a starting point, I was wondering if you could comment and elaborate on a statement you once made: "Freud is right to think of psychoanalysis as wounding the Western ego, although it does not create the wound so much as grow out of it." What is this wound and how do you conceptualize the Western ego?

ME: I don't know. In terms of the wound, of psychoanalysis wounding Western narcissism, Freud had in mind the three great revolutions which kept decentering the human being, so that the human being was no longer the center of existence, nor the ego the center of human existence. In a way Freud's psychoanalysis presents a series of wounds, a series of trauma, a series of woundings, from birth trauma to abandonment anxiety, annihilation anxiety, castration anxiety . . . There's a catalog of anxieties, a catalog of catastrophic states that the infant and child go through, that the human being goes through. It's sort of an anthology of catastrophes. In Freud's informal presentations he depicts these as humiliations, humiliations that the ego goes through, humiliations to self-esteem . . . blows, blows to the ego . . . and he means "blows" literally, not just metaphorically: like a stab to the heart or a blow to the face, the way a poet might mean it. So that his picture of the human being is of the human being going from one wound to the other, and of how the personality congeals, grows, displaces itself around wounds.

When I was in the Nevada desert, a guide told me a cactus would grow straight forever, would grow forever straight if it didn't get wounded, and that the branches of the cactus grow out at the place where it's traumatized, at the place where it's wounded. Freud depicts the personality in the same way, displacing itself, or deforming itself, around the point of impact, of wounding impact. Hit the psyche, and it displaces the self like ripples or waves, it deforms itself around the points of wounding. And Freud describes those woundings in so many different ways, in terms of different developmental phases. But the wounding Freud talks about has always to do with displacements: with how the self-importance, or the self-centeredness, of the human being, the amazing arrogance of the ego, keeps getting wounded by re-centering itself in a larger existence. Psychoanalysis is part of this revolutionary decentering process, another in a long history of ways of placing or replacing the self in a larger context, while breaking the relation to being a big fish in a small pond.

AM: If we somehow conceive of re-centering or decentering the self, there still persists the *idea* of a "center." Do you have an operative idea of a center when you talk about decentering or re-centering?

ME: The first nub, of course, is the seed. There's just the seed of a self . . . But I nevertheless do feel a sense of the value of the idea, in spite of deconstructionism. In certain exercises, for example, I feel more centered. But what that center is, or how to describe it, I wouldn't know. It's not an idea I have an investment in. I wouldn't fight a holy war for one picture of it over another.

AM: I'd like to address what I see as a confusion that surrounds a set of concepts invariably central to psychoanalytic theorizing. How do you understand the terms *ego, self* and *subject,* all three of which appear prominently throughout your writings?

ME: I have never thought these things through, basically. I've thought about them at different points of my life, or through different theoretical systems: for example, what the subject is for Lacan, what the self or ego is for Jung or for self psychology or for ego psychology, or for the British school or Sullivan. What the self or ego is, or what the subject is, shifts in meaning. It is partly a matter of context: what seems to be subject in one context can be object in another. It could be like a Chinese box, or a shell game . . . For Freud the ego is a kind of "I" subject, but it's also a system of functions, it's also the love object of the id. So in a sense it's subject in one context, the system of autonomous functions in another context, a personal "I" in another context, and an object in yet another. So that even in Freud's work, the meaning of ego keeps shifting according to how it's used. I wouldn't want to go to bat for pinning down a single meaning, because it's really dependent on context.

AM: Your own use of the term *self* is very elastic and multi-faceted. You don't hesitate, for example, to resort to the plural notion of "selves"; you speak of a "body self" and a "mental self"; frequently, of the "growth" of self, and the "gift" of self. Sometimes the word *self* is preceded by the article "the," sometimes not. Can you clarify and expound on your own usage and understanding of such terms, both theoretically and clinically?

ME: Maybe I've used the word *self* at different times, at different points in my life, for different growth purposes. So maybe the term has meant different things to me at different crises, at different junctures. Sometimes I think I've held onto the word "self" as an organizing principle, to make me feel more whole. At other times I use the word to give a context or horizon, a vantage point outside of the smaller ego. Sometimes I've used the word "self" because it refers to a feeling of own-ness: a kind of feeling of my own, something very personal. But I don't know that I would be intellectually equipped—or that anyone is especially intellectually equipped—to pin down the many meanings of the word. My use of the word *self*, at this time in my life, isn't quite the same as it was when I was 20. I think our capacities generally involve some mixture of how we experience ourselves: on the one hand there's a personal, warm and immediate experience; on the other hand, there's an awareness of being given to ourselves as pretty anonymous, as pretty impersonal. What we do, then, with what's personal at one moment and what freaks us out as anonymous, or as standing against us from within ourselves in another moment, can vary. I don't know whether I can add anything to the subject in terms of intellectual clarity. It's a matter, I think, of informal use and what mileage one gets from a term like *self* at a given point in one's life.

AM: Would you feel comfortable providing some anecdotal sense of the kind of crises you mentioned, that may have distinguished a shift in your own personal understanding of what "self" might have meant at any given time?

ME: I can think back at when I was in my 20s, on a bus, being in extreme agony. I just suddenly lost consciousness and dipped into this sense of agony, and stayed with an agony that seemed to be located in my chest. It was a terrible psychological pain, not a physical pain so much as a horrendous emotional pain, that I imagined and felt in my chest area. I went further and further into it, and I doubled over on the bus, and then all of a sudden, quite surprised—not having any mental frame of reference for what was happening—the pain opened up and became radiant light. Where before there was just agony and horrendous pain, without my knowing what had happened, suddenly there was bliss . . . It turned into a terrific light that left me wishing it would never end. Of course, the pain didn't go away, but the bliss has never left me either.

AM: In your "Afterword" to *The Electrified Tightrope*, you write: "There is much pressure not to hear oneself (or selves)." Clearly, the idea of the self's potential multiplicity is present in your thinking and experience. First put forth, arguably, by one of your early teachers, Marie Coleman Nelson, it's an idea that's been taken up recently by the likes of Stephen Mitchell, Jane Flax, even Christopher Bollas. How is the concept present in your thinking and, more importantly, how does the idea of multiple selves bear on your practice of psychoanalysis?

ME: I guess I came into contact with the idea first through literature rather than through psychology. In psychology, my first contact with it was through an early book by Erich Fromm, *The Forgotten Language*, and through Jung's writings, when I was still a teenager. How it finally translated for me personally was when I came to be amazed by, or thrown by, or utterly flabbergasted by, the changes of state that one can go through in a single day: the amazing changes of state of which the psalmist writes, how we go to bed crying and wake up laughing . . . How that happens is astonishing, is amazing. Freud wrote about how the very fact that we dream is a signal that it might be possible to cure psychosis. Because if we can dream, if we are plastic enough, elastic enough, to go through such amazing changes of consciousness from normal waking to dreaming states and back again, then why shouldn't it be possible to cure psychosis? The idea of multiple selves, that we are all these things, the actual concrete, immediate experience of change of state, is problematic: what does one do with that? Is one different people when going through these different states? William Blake talks about states, all states, every state being eternal: how all states, once experienced, are forever . . . Or we have to try to picture a unified personality identifying with different states, going through different states. Jung depicted an archipelago of selves. But I don't think either vision is necessarily comprehensive. I think the crucial thing, now, is the debate about multiple personalities or dissociated personalities. I think it's really quite useful, quite wonderful, because it brings the problem out. Perhaps it makes the problem of multiplicity sound strange or unusual, but I don't think it is very strange or unusual at all . . . What do we do with the amazing plasticity and range of states that we actually go through in a day? from feeling more in one's body, more out of one's body, more mystical, more realistic . . . more in love . . . Isaac Bashevis Singer somewhere writes about how all human beings, how even an idiot, is a millionaire in emotions . . . It's a fantastic gift, a gift and liability we're given, to have this extravagant experiential capacity. And it's not at all clear that we know what to do with it as yet. One of the amazing things about going through all these states, for me, is the fact that I'm going through them at all, that I can feel so differently in so many different contexts. It's not a different self that's going through them; it's sort of, how can I be all that? But it's still me being "it"; it's not a different self, or a multiple self necessarily. It's me. It's me being other to myself too. But how is that? How can I be other to myself? How is that possible? It's mind-boggling. The kind of beings we are is really mind boggling. That we are somehow other to ourselves; that it's "not me"; hey, it's not me!

AM: Then what's the difference between Michael Eigen saying this to me now, and what you've explored and experienced clinically with so-called multiple personalities or in dissociative states?

ME: I think one of the big differences, is that I'm more used to it. Someone else, a patient, may not be able to make the links, may not be able to stomach the multiplicity, or take it in and digest it in some psychic way . . . A patient might not be able to say: "Hey, that's me . . . Oh! hey that's not me!" There's not always a place big enough, in a patient's psyche, a house big enough, to make space for these different rooms . . . Someone comes upon another room in the house, and imagines being completely in entirely different territory. They might not realize: "Hey, I've just moved from here to there . . . that the link between. . . ."

AM: What provides that link?

ME: That's what we're working on, at the cutting edge of psychoanalytic praxis. Winnicott's whole career was a testament to the fact that depersonalization, not feeling real to oneself, is the central clinical problem. I believe the link, then, lies in those conditions that make it possible to feel real to oneself.

AM: Depersonalization, or what you refer to in your present writings as psychic deadness. . . .

ME: The sense of a life not having meaning is a phenomenon that's struck me. Nowadays, more and more people come in and actually say that they don't feel alive. It's experienced by many of them as a very painful situation. Now that's a good prognostic sign, because if they were not experiencing this as painful, the situation would be even worse . . . Somehow, these people know what it's like to be alive, if the absence of vitality so troubles them. It's becoming more and more common to get people in practice who feel dead and who want to come back. . . .

AM: What are the factors behind this pervasive sense of psychic deadness?

ME: The most obvious, I would imagine, is the general degree of over-stimulation. A patient comes to mind who had a massive dose of over-stimulation all at once. He pins down his dying to a time when he was about eighteen, to an evening when he, his mother and his father were sitting having dinner. The father went into an unusually pitched rage at him and walked out of the restaurant screaming. The boy felt himself collapse at that moment, and die out, and he's been dead ever since. It was a massive shock that he felt, and it made me think that in some way or other so many people are numbed out or shocked or put in a state of shock by a kind of massive implosion, or massive impact . . . almost like a scream, or someone screaming at them . . . it's almost as if there were a silent scream that is deafening people, who can no longer hear themselves, and are thrown out of balance. . . .

AM: You mentioned wanting to substitute the idea of "multiple states of being" for "multiple selves." That very distinction is, to a large extent, at the crux of the postmodern debate on the self. James Glass, for instance, in a book entitled *Shattered Selves*, is highly critical of the seductiveness of the postmodern exaltation of multiplicity. Conversely, Jane Flax talks about "fluid subjectivities" as a defining characteristic of this postmodern epoch, and seems to be suggesting something along the lines of what you're talking about: a condition where these fluid states do not necessarily involve fragmentation. What is your understanding of postmodernism and its distinguishing features? How has psychoanalysis and your own practice been influenced by a supposed postmodern turn?

ME: I've liked parts of what I've read of Derrida; I've heard him talk a few times. Still, I can't always figure him out, because a lot of the results of his work seem to reflect what we as therapists were doing clinically. I'm sure I haven't grasped the depths of his writings, but I haven't learned anything new yet. What I like is the analysis. I like the poetry of the analysis in the people I've read. I've been entranced by some of the poetry of the prose, which is breathtaking. But clinically postmodernism hasn't added all that much for me. What it's confirmed, though, is that one can transcend almost any clinical situation, and look for another way to handle it: so that whatever lock, whatever impasse is created by the patient and therapist together, one knows in one's being, as well as theoretically, that one can always be doing and being something else. One gets to know that it's always possible to pick another loose end to organize oneself around, to costume oneself in; it's always possible to pour oneself into another mold, and come at a situation from another way so that one always recognizes and utilizes the plasticity of the materials at hand. One doesn't have to be resigned to being boxed in. There is, I suppose, a certain transcendental element in how free one is or can be with any particular patient . . . so that one can imagine becoming someone else, can become another self, or another part of the self, or enter into another state that might yield a different effect on the clinical situation.

AM: There's a section in *The Psychotic Core* entitled "The Point of No Return." There you write: "Many patients complain of an endless sense of aloneness. They do not find a social milieu in which they can feel they really belong. The usual categories of connection such as family, race, nation, work, various subgroups and friends do not work for them . . . (F)or an increasing number, nothing can truly palliate the nagging sense of being different and not quite connecting. In some basic sense, one is not understood and does not understand oneself. One has nowhere to go. One is on one's own." Looking at this, I couldn't help but think of it in cultural and historical terms. Is this aloneness somehow different, say, from the angst of the heyday of existentialism?

ME: I don't know whether it is or isn't. I think it's like a blind man having each hand on a different part of the elephant, or like the same echo at a different point of time, the same wave at a different point in space. When I wrote that, the person in particular, and the people in general, that I had in mind were totally disconnected. They had no place, were off the map, completely had no hope. They had no hope of ever making a connection they would regard as being on the map. And yet it really was miraculous that some of the people I was thinking about at the time did manage to become part of the tapestry of life, without compromising in some essential way the alone self that had been hopeless, that had earlier been hopeless to connect up. Now, how that did happen is rather baffling: persistence, staying with it, staying with the aloneness, making room for the aloneness.

I think that in that passage I was being a therapist to the alone self. I was trying to establish a context for it, for that alone self to be, to be validated and valorized. I remember certain people I've met in my life, like Winnicott, Allen Ginsburg, or the rebbe Menachem Schneerson. When I was with them, I felt it was okay to be the sort of person I am. With them it was okay for me to be somehow off the map, beyond the map; it was okay for there to be in life such a person as I was. In that passage, then, I was trying to encode, for whomever it would reach, something like a message in a bottle. Floating on the sea it might then reach some people, who would hear the message that it's okay for them to be the sort of alone person they are. And by some miracle, by making room for such a message, some of these people, through the course of years, have tentacled out, have tapestried out. They've found themselves situated in a larger tapestry that makes room for the sorts of being they were and are, whereas earlier there didn't seem to be any place for them. Now, how did that happen? How was room made for them, a space for life to begin? . . . It's miraculous, making room for the multiple selves . . . Again, I'm not so sure I like the term "multiple selves" . . . I suppose it's comforting, in a way. And I don't know that "multiple states" is much better. But the idea of making room for this alterability, or multiplicity, or self/non-self, self/otherness that one is, is one of the functions of therapy.

AM: Is this what you mean perhaps when you write about a "friendship of self"?

ME: Make friends, yes. And it's okay to be your own enemy, to be adversarial and antagonistic too. It's okay to be your own worst enemy. It's inevitable. I think the idea of normality can be horrendous, because one carries around this picture that normal people aren't insomniacs, or normal people aren't so hyper-nervous, or they don't obsess, etcetera . . . So you have this picture of what normal people are, but then . . . where are all these people? If you find them, they're probably driving someone else crazy. What's normal is that there is a background radiation of the universe with different, molecular densities that different worlds issue from, and we are part of that universe.

AM: Within a historical moment that either privileges or generates an excess of psychic disconnection and dislocation, and makes of geographic dislocation a basic experience, can psychoanalysis somehow confront the economic and social structures that generate this surplus of social fragmentation?

ME: I'm more Buddhist there. I don't know that it's my job to, or that I can. To think about doing that, on a small level analysts should be less frightened of speaking out publicly about public issues. For example, it is becoming more commonplace to see how so much of political discourse hinges on winning lies, so that a one-up/one-down structure, or an adversarial structure, is becoming increasingly prevalent. Take, for example, the Clarence Thomas/Anita Hill hearings, where from one vantage point you could see so many different political maneuverings to gain the upper hand. It was less important to determine the truth than it was to see which lie would win, or which spin would win; or how best to appear as the more aggressive, the clearest, the one who could knock the other person more efficiently. The premium was not so much on truth as on who could present the clearest, most aggressive and effective image. The choice being offered was rather sickening . . . Within the same arena, one of the things I like about Clinton is that whatever is wrong with him, or whatever the problems with him, he at least makes vacillation, or oscillation or indecision, part of the public milieu. Part, and only a small part, of the reasons he's come into so much trouble is not because of what he's done or not done, but how he's appeared. He hasn't been able to cosmeticize his vacillation or oscillation, or his unsurety, in the public domain, and he hasn't been able to present an effective one-sided, me-against-you, adversarial, axe-man approach. He hasn't been able to develop a winning-enough lie to stand by, with which to knock others down. Personally, and without any delusions about my effectiveness, I like to feel that if I make a public appearance, I'm a spokesman for ambiguity, or a spokesman for oscillation.

AM: In the epilogue to *The Psychotic Core* you specifically address the deforming effects of television and what you call "the collective brainwashing inherent in the maneuvers of contemporary political campaigning." For you who have written so extensively about psychosis, to what extent do these phenomena play a part in its genesis?

ME: I don't know if the media plays a role in promoting psychosis, though it certainly can. I think psychosis and the media are different branches of a deeper, more pervasive tendency toward madness in the human in general. I think madness pervades so many human dimensions, that it is not so uncommon at all. What's uncommon is unmadness. It would be rather unusual to find something happening that isn't quite crazy. But the fact that human beings have invested so much in one-upmanship and territoriality and economic riches . . . me-against-you, me-above-you . . . this has a madness to it. It's kind of crazy in a way . . . but I suppose not doing it would be mad too. I think that our tendency to live a dream, to live according to a fantasy . . . a fantasy of what one would like to be like, and of what life is like, that tendency is rather widespread, and madness is not a rare thing at all.

AM: The polarized debate of the "singular" versus the "multiple" self seems to fit within a dialectical structure that is elemental to your thinking. You've written: "For practical purposes, I posited a *distinction/union structure* that characterizes the self at all of its developmental levels." I was wondering it you can elaborate on this idea, even in terms of its acknowledged antecedents in the work of Federn, Mahler, Winnicott, Grotstein. . . .

ME: Since I now have to use words, and not just grunts, let me say that it's along the lines of what Winnicott has in mind, when he portrays the psyche as being essentially paradoxical on all levels of development. To use words like distinction/union, to become united with this double capacity, runs through the human psyche at all levels: cognitive, emotional, relational, and social. And we don't really know how to conceptualize this capacity except to point to it, and say something seems to be there . . . "I am," but I am in a context, in an intersubjective context . . . I'm you, you're me . . . but I'm not you and you're not me . . . It's a matter of what one can come up with, what one creates with that dichotomy . . . In this sense, I think psychoanalysis today is a kind of poetry. Nowadays, I think of psychoanalysis as an aesthetic, as a form of poetry . . . You have all these psychoanalytic singers and poets trying to express their aesthetic experience: of a session, of the emotional content of a session, or of the impact a patient generates in session . . . It's all portrayed as a cultural microcosm. We have all these wonderful and moving psychoanalytic singers opening up worlds of experience, and it's a matter of whether someone moves you along at a certain point, promotes your own growth towards openness.

AM: When you talk about this "distinction/union structure that characterizes the self at all its developmental levels," I get the impression that you're not talking simply or only about the Freudian developmental schema, of oral, anal, phallic, genital stages. I get a sense that you have implied a different, or at least a complementary, idea of what it means for the human being to develop. Could you illustrate that idea?

ME: Well, it originally grew out of my early work with regression, with so-called "primitive" patients. I was very influenced early on by the British school, where there were a number of people working who seemed to see a positive, regenerative value in what used to be called regression . . . I remember noting at the time how different theories seemed to suggest that one could regress as far back as to a symbiotic state, or to an autistic state; but if that were true, then regression would be extremely dangerous, and the farther back one went, the more isolated or the more fused or the more self-less, in a negative sense, one might become. So, instead of regression being regenerative, it would have to be destructive, and the best thing to do would be to build up defenses against regression. Nevertheless, my clinical finding was that so-called regression or opening up of the self or letting down the boundaries, could be extremely fruitful

. . . This seemed more wholesome, in common sense, and healthful to presuppose . . . My myth, my story was: "In the beginning there was both separation and union, or distinction and union . . . ," so that one doesn't have to be frightened of going all the way . . . that, as far as one can go, whatever world one enters into, you'll be both self and other in various forms of relationship and non-relationship, and that one doesn't have to make a decision, doesn't have to decide whether to be simply alone or simply with others. It's more fun, and less frightening, to be and allow for all of these possibilities: to just glide along, or be able to flow from one state to another. Or to be in mixed states at different times, without prejudging: "Oh my God, I shouldn't be this now," or, "I can only be this now!"

AM: I was wondering whether your emphasis on psychic structure and polarities of experience was somehow influenced by the work of Levi Strauss. I haven't seen him mentioned in your writings, but I'm reminded of a book of his called *Totemism*. . . .

ME: Well, I never got as immersed in Levi Strauss as I did, say, in Bion or Winnicott or Lacan. It's just a matter of luck, a throw of the dice, what authors I got immersed in at an earlier age, and he wasn't one of them. But when I did read him later, I found his work fascinating. The connection, for instance, in my mind and lots of other people's minds, between structure and process, is truly baffling. Years ago, I think it was Gene Gendlin, in a book called *Experiencing and the Creation of Meaning*, who saw an enormous difference between process and structure. I don't understand how he derived the idea, of structure as something more solid and fixed, and process as something more fluid and moving. . . . *(thinking out loud)* Gestalt psychology, I think, suggests that bones, for example, are the results of slower, more fixed processes . . . but it's not like bones are process-free . . . they're made up of slower, relatively stabler patternings . . . The bones of the system on which the flesh and nerves all hang, that's all process too . . . I don't understand the difference between structure and process. I've never felt the need to posit a difference. Just talking about structure is a very creative thing because one picks how one's going to slice it, you know . . . One is always selecting the processes that one's going to talk about, and in what form. . . .

AM: In elaborating this idea of the structure/process, you hint at what could be called an originary matrix of being, at what you call the "living experience of union and distinction out of which the self arises." Your own contribution in this sense is unique, in that there seems to be a "maternal" dimension of the infant's originary experience that somehow goes beyond object relations and even predates the relational embodiments and personhoods of mother and child. Again, we're stuck with words: but you seem to suggest a living experience of this union/distinction structure that actually predates the self, as well as the personhood of mother and/or child. . . .

ME: I think that's right . . . Something that both mother and infant get situated within, though I'm not sure what to say about it. The age-old folklore that we're children of God before we're children of our parents probably hasn't been tapped as well as it might in psychoanalytic thinking, where we're always children of our parents first . . . It actually may take quite some time for an infant to de-infinitize . . . where the infant may go through different states, now more finite, now more up against the solid, real facts of things, and at other times be more and more in an infinite field or infinite horizon . . . To actually come into the realization that I have to be where my body is, that my body is this bounded packet, really takes quite some time and quite some sophistication. Some people feel that schizophrenics resist this development, or that certain sorts of schizophrenics resist packeting themselves that way, or have an inability to tolerate the physical limitations of embodiment. It can't be taken for granted that the sense of infinity or of the emotionally infinite doesn't somehow antedate the experience of the mother or even of the infant.

AM: You seem to be reclaiming for psychoanalysis an actual, experiential dimension of mystery, of the infinite, of the immaterial: words that have always suffered the weight of Freud's "oceanic feeling. . . ."

ME: Well, I've felt the oceanic feeling. The term itself has unfortunately watered down psychoanalytic discussions of mysticism because mystics themselves, while enjoying oceanic feelings, sometimes were often brought upshore and left terrified by the onset of a numinous awakening. They were overturned, and shaken to their core. The prophets, whenever God or an angel appears, get the dickens scared out of them, they get scared stiff, and it's terror, terror . . . So God has to say, "grab your balls and stand up like a man, let's get down to work," because there's such a terrifying impact of the uncontainable, and it's not all peaches and cream and oceanic bliss . . . That's the way it is with mystical experiences, or encounters with the divine. They can be too much for the human equipment at a certain time. Flannery O'Connor, in her short stories, depicts this over and over, where even religious, fundamentalist Protestants are broken by the discovery that what they were preaching actually has reality, and so they become shattered by the actual experience of what they had only been rehearsing. Over and over, her characters are shaken by a divine or demonic happening that makes real what before were only words. It's like the experience of a child, who is intensely wishing or praying for something. In the absence of the desired object, that kind of wishing can make for an altered state. Even as a child, one gets a sense of being different than one imagined one could be, and that sense can grow. It can even have a biography: the sense of the infinite can have a biography.

AM: All your writing is imbued with a deeply charged sense of religiosity, of mystery and wonder. There is throughout the evident sensibility of a mystic. You speak of Bion as a mystic; you often cite Buber's *I and Thou*, and speak of the co-union or communion, not only of self and other, but of self and God . . . You've written on evil and often mention the devil . . . You talk comfortably of both prayer and Buddha. In your epilogue to *The Electrified Tightrope*, you astonish a reader with ideas like: "From the depths of one's being it is as easy to get to God as libido. For Freud libido seeks an ideal imago in traditional terms, ultimately God. The unconscious does not do away with God so much as provide a privileged point of contact with the unknowable." Later, you mention your father's death, and your subsequent immersion into the roots of Jewish mysticism. You then continue: "I used aspects of Oriental and Roman Catholic teachings to organize my mystical propensities. The paradoxical, dialectical, dialogical way of listening/speaking that marks clinical practice mitigated against religious orthodoxy, but my encounter with Judaism made me a richer and better person.

The flow between divinity and libido is so much freer now." This kind of language, this kind of revelation, if you will, in both senses of the word, is courageous on the part of an analyst. Beyond the oceanic feeling, I'd like to invite some free-flowing reflections of yours on psychoanalysis and religion, from both your clinical experience and your own life history.

ME: Well, at the risk of sounding utterly trite and trivial, so be it. From the first session I've ever had with anyone, I've always felt a sacred element in psychoanalytic psychotherapeutic work, and I've never quite understood the animosity so many analysts have had against the seemingly oceanic feeling. I'm astonished, for example, that as terrific a worker as André Green tried to argue it with me. I was astonished that, in his reading of Bion, Green played down or totally parenthesized, nullified, actually, Bion's use and reference to faith. He emphasized almost exclusively what Bion called *k*, or knowledge, or the scientific approach to knowledge, and was convinced that Bion too thought as he did. But as Bion's work evolved, he more and more transcended the primacy of *k*, or the lust for knowledge, or the search for and use of knowledge, within a faith context, and as a matter of fact, he proceeded to almost define the psychoanalytic attitude as an act of faith. And he uses those words . . . Now I think Green is a terrific analyst and thinker, but this blanket statement, with regard to an enormously important part, the climactic part of Bion's work, is astonishing. I take that incident to be a paradigmatic example of how, even with the most imaginative and generative people in the field, there seems to be a strong animosity against the faith freaks. Why faith is played down, though, is puzzling. Maybe there's the threat of fanaticism, or of losing scientific ground; but I think one can be a fanatic in the other direction as well. One can deplete experience in different ways. One can be too realistic, one can be too fantastic, one can be too scientistic, one can be overly fanatical and zealous . . . Rather than have a war between all these different dimensions of experience, it's much more fruitful to keep open the possibility that each have a voice, that each have a say in the play of voices, and to see what happens . . . But whatever faith is, Bion associates it with opening, with the propensity to become open. To go in the other direction, towards *k*, would be a premature exclusion of one voice in favor of another, as opposed to a plurality and balance of voices.

Jung has his funny things too. I can certainly imagine a Jungian saying I'm wrong, but in my reading of Jung, there's so much that is devastating if one takes it to heart. For example, his attitude toward dependency can be shocking at times. He puts down certain neurotics as mother's boys and addresses them with a certain contempt. There's a contempt for dependency and weakness that runs through his writings, which is kind of odd, because he seems to really have generated a lot of positive transference, and then from that position seems to have a contempt for weakness. So there's a kind of double bind that I imagine Jung put a lot of patients in: "you must worship me, but if you do I have contempt for you." It's a funny thing. Now Jung, of course, feels he pulled himself up by his own bootstraps. As a neurotic or psychotic adolescent, he felt he'd strengthened himself and deliberately conquered his weakness, transcended his weakness, by hard work and creative endeavor. And so he developed a certain mistrust of people who can't do that. He may have made his living off of people who can't do that, but he nevertheless seemed to look down at affliction and adversity. So while Jung had a certain depth that few people reached in psychological writings before him, there was an attitudinal problem I recognized. So I tended to gravitate toward the British school partly because, for the first time in psychiatric writings, and in a consistent way, there didn't seem to be a contempt for weakness or a contempt for dependency. It seemed like dependency was now getting its due or valorized as being a legitimate part of life, that ought not to be precociously short-circuited or treated abruptly . . . or dealt with by just tugging at your bootstraps and acting bigger or stronger again. The emphasis in the British school is on staying with the dependent streak until the growth process can come about. It was that different attitude toward human weakness that appealed to me, I think. In practice, the British school also did a lot of goosing into independence, pretty much as Jung did in his own way; so the dependency business does get rather scary with the tendency, even in the British school, to perpetuate it. Nevertheless, there is an attitudinal shift, away from Jung's contempt for weakness, that is evidenced at least in Winnicott's writings.

AM: You've written about faith as you see it in the work of Bion, Winnicott and Lacan. What is faith for Michael Eigen?

ME: Different things at different times. I guess there's spiritual faith and there's natural faith. I place a great deal of weight on natural faith. I've nothing against spiritual or mystical faith . . . but there's an awful lot of faith that springs simply from sensory experience, from how good it feels to be able to walk down a street and move one's limbs and not be in prison . . . It brings up a feeling inside that, while it might be stretching things to call "faith," I really do have to call it that . . . It makes one feel good to be alive, it makes one feel that life is good . . . The body seems to have this faith . . . Very often I've been astonished by how a dying animal seems to not know it's dying, by how it acts in the face of death, and seems to live, to be moving or trying to move or live to the last ounce . . . It just keeps going to the end . . . Or even when it stops moving and gets into a dying position, it doesn't seem to be angry or yelling about its imminent end. Somehow there seems to be an acquiescence, a simple ebbing of energy in the direction of death. It's a kind of body faith, a faith the body has. I suppose one could talk about an affective faith or an emotional faith: the "ouch!" and "yum!" of things . . . "Ouch! That hurt!" . . . or "Yum! That was worth it!" So it's more than pleasure and pain, I think. When one talks about a pleasure principle or a pain principle, one's de-animated it, because it's not simply bad or good, it's heavenly, it's heavenly . . . It's wonderful! . . . it feels yummy all through . . . You know, one would have to be totally mad not to have a secular or ironical self and see the limits of things, but I rather like siding with this feeling of "good to the last drop" in psychoanalysis . . . like a bug that never stops moving . . . There's just a sense of never giving up . . . never giving up on a case . . . not giving up on anyone . . . Who knows better? . . .

AM: All this begs another question. What does Michael Eigen mean by God?

ME: God only knows! I think I have to be honest to say I mean a biblical God, the God of Abraham, Isaac and Jacob . . . But having said that I can step back and say: "Hey, well, what I mean by God could be anything, because I don't know . . . " In a sense God is a total unknown, and yet in others the very notion ties the so-called biblical, personal God closer to me than I am to myself . . . And then there are times one can just lift up one's hands and say, "Wow, all this out of nothingness!". . . which feels wonderful . . . to blank oneself out and be totally open to whatever currents pulse this way or that . . . whether you're into body, or emotions . . . Taoist or Buddhist, whatever, it feels good.

You know, in the Kabala, God has . . . is . . . goes beyond names . . . the *Ein Sof*, the infinite of infinites, the great unknown, the "I-itself" . . . By the time God gets named! . . .

AM: I had a patient once who, in the midst of a fierce negative transference, blurted out loud "I am that I am," without any apparent sense of the phrase's biblical echo. The woman was stating her difference and uniqueness in a rather common-sensical sort of way, but the sheer power of her words was unmistakable.

ME: That's wonderful. I think Ben, in my book *Coming through the Whirlwind*, does something like that at one point. It's what we're doing all the time: we're "am"-ing . . . and we're "am"-ing each other too . . . we're enabling each other *to am*.

AM: In getting back to that early "am," you seem to have supplanted the centrality, for psychoanalysis, of both the real and the metaphorical breast in the early life of the infant, with what you imagine to be the infant's formative relationship to the face. The face almost becomes as important, if not more important, than the breast. In a way, the face takes on a mythic quality in your work. . . .

ME: Well, that comes again from a Winnicottian sense of paradox, from the idea that we shouldn't ever favor only one element of a dichotomy. Why should psychoanalysis have opted for a primacy of the tactile and diminished the visual? Why oughtn't both grow about together in a mutually constitutive way, feeding what everyone calls mind, or self, or being . . . Bion can be quite funny sometimes when he talks about *common* sense, or getting the senses to work together . . . which can't always be taken for granted, you know . . . In an autistic state, for example, a child can be pulled one way by one sense and another way by another sense . . . We oughtn't to need, in theory or in practice, or even in our personal lives, to compromise the multiplicity of the senses, and the different information they provide. But there's more! The different senses don't just give information. They give different worlds, or different qualities of worlds, or different textures to live in, not just information to process, but different tastes, different ways the world tastes through touch, or through the other sensory organs. Or there can be harmony, at various times, between distance senses and closeness senses, a paradoxical interplay again between near and far. It seems quite limiting to say we are primarily near-creatures or that we're primarily far-creatures, or touch-oriented, or vision-oriented . . . In other words, and this seems obvious, as Freud already noted and Derrida points out in "Freud and the Scene of Writing," there is a primacy of multiplicity.

AM: This is the first answer where you've privileged a theoretical reply as opposed to an experiential one. Since so much of psychoanalytic theorizing about the breast involves the writer's fantasies of what the infant experiences or "phantasizes" at the breast, what does Michael Eigen imagine the infant's experience of the face to be? What does the face do to and for an infant?

ME: Well, there is the eye-to-eye contact, where the eyes are shining or dull or a shade in-between . . . The eye-to-eye contact, together with the skin-to-skin contact, generates, so to speak, different sets of feelings, currents and subcurrents of feelings. From eye-to-eye and skin-to-skin, there are currents and subcurrents, some antagonistic, some harmonious. But part of the fate of eye-to-eye contact or face-to-face contact is to enclose worlds, worlds of experience. The face does shine, you know! So I can get a double faith . . . I can get a faith from the breast and faith from the face. Normally, now, that's not the case; normally, they very often tear each other apart, with fights for the upper over the lower; fights for the lower over the upper . . . Normally, there's probably a state of war between capacities; but optimally, that may not be necessary.

AM: A few more things about the early developmental stages. Is there an echo of Lacan's mirror stage in any of this?

ME: I love Lacan, but I twisted him out of shape for my papers, for my writings on faith . . . because face for him, Lacanians insist, really has to do with seduction. The face for Lacan is part of a seductive enterprise, as it also might be for Sartre. On the other hand, for Winnicott the face can be the center of an experiential movement that goes beyond seduction, that connects up with Levinas' sense of the face as infinite. It strikes me both viewpoints are right, and there is much to say about each. We *do* seduce each other through our looks, as well as through much else. One can't localize seduction. Seduction is everywhere. Nor can one localize faith . . . You can have breast faith and face faith. One could have breast faith and not have face faith; and one could have a face faith and not have breast faith. There is faith sliding into Klein's or Lacan's early paranoid, aggressive play of desires, a seductive, demanding faith, enticing-ruling, being enticed by-ruled by the desire of the Other. Levinas writes about the face as it evokes the infinite, or as part of the experience of the infinite, of infinity, of opening infinity. How could one decide between Lacan and Levinas? Why should one have to?

AM: I have a few more questions on issues concerning postmodernism. . . .

ME: Those are funny terms, aren't they? Postmodernism . . . modernism . . . I sort of picture dinosaurs walking around . . . It's funny . . . bit names. . . .

AM: There's another passage from *The Psychotic Core* where you evidence a clear awareness of what might be termed a postmodern sensibility: "Writers today emphasize how present-oriented, episodic, and fragmented our experience is. We no longer simply gain identity from well-defined social roles and institutions." Similarly, in *If on a Winter's Night a Traveler*, Italo Calvino writes: " . . . (L)ong novels written today are perhaps a contradiction: the dimension of time has been shattered, we cannot live or think except in fragments of time, each of which goes off along its own trajectory and immediately disappears. We can rediscover the continuity of time only in the novels of that period when time no longer seemed stopped and did not yet seem to have exploded . . . " If what Calvino says is true in some way, if time and space have been compressed, or if our experience of time and space is different than it might have been twenty or a hundred years ago, how does that experience now unfold in the analytic situation?

ME: I'm intimidated by questions like that because they're so broad . . . though I love descriptions like the one you read because they're so fun! From early on in my writings, I've been drawn to particular portrayals of time worlds for people, and of time worlds in analysis. In an early paper called "The Recoil on Having Another Person," I write about the importance of time experience in the constitution of self. It's about how temporal meanings of the Other, dimensions of time in the experience of the Other, relate to approach-avoidance patterns, to two people being drawn to each other or repelled by each other. The exploration of the concept of time has a long history, in philosophy, literature, and in human experience . . . Condensing time, or exploding time . . . Erik Erikson or Alfred North Whitehead portray a kind of emotional time, or an affective time, or time in terms of pulsations . . . how long, for example, it takes for an experience to develop and be seen through.

By implication, I think of John Dewey's work, *Art as Experience*, where he talks about how an experience has its own particular build-up time, development time, shifts around, comes to a climax and denouement. The question, perhaps, is how is it possible to help people allow this process to happen, and not short-circuit seeing an experience through . . . or how can we enable them to sustain the tensions necessary to fully go through and not thwart an experience? . . . Even the question is hard to organize, because time is such an intimate part, in analytic work, of allowing time to be, of allowing an experience to be.

AM: Has there been, in your clinical work, an experience of time shattered or subverted that was fully shared with a patient?

ME: In general, the so-called borderline personality presents the problem of not giving time a chance, of not giving the analyst or analysis a chance. It's all tooth and nail . . . Time gets eaten up, gets eaten away, gobbled up by the patient in analysis. Let's relax into giving time a chance to develop its own flow, and allow that there should be a "later" . . . or a "then," or enough room or enough of a gap, so that some kind of approach, of movement from here to there is possible. So that analysis can be possible, and develop over time. So that development, over time, can take place. In this sense, you might want to help a person view therapy as a kind of psychic gymnasium, to help build up tolerance, at certain times, for just seeing a moment through . . . for the patient to know, "ah, look, something was just about to happen between us, but it got short-circuited. Where did that moment go? It looked to me like you were about to feel afraid or angry, and suddenly it's gone!" . . . or maybe, "You suddenly felt relaxed here . . . you relaxed here because I wasn't bugging you about anything. All of a sudden . . . Where did it go?" Therapy as a strategy to outflank the thing that kills off or short-circuits the possibility of experience, of letting a moment grow. . . .

AM: What about space?

ME: I love space. But I've come to have the odd view that there's a primacy of time in analytic experience. I know that most of the literature is concerned with analytic space and preserving the integrity of analytic space. But I think there comes a moment . . . a time . . . when space dissolves, but time keeps going . . . a kind of timeless time, where the person becomes, gets dropped into, gets immersed or in touch with some unfolding of affective nuance, of affective resonance. And space, for that time, seems to dissolve, while a kind of pulse time . . . a kind of psychical artery time keeps on going. It's as though one discovers time by losing space at a certain point . . . a kind of timeless time. . . .

AM: The inverse phenomenon of the spaceless space where time dissolves?

ME: I've experienced many patients overly obsessed with space, who have no playful space whatsoever. What they have, actually, is not so much a playground as a coliseum, where there's a battle for survival going on: a territorial battle over who's going to survive in space. These patients inhabit a corrupted space, a violent TV-like space, where the emphasis is on who's blowing away whom; where the violence makes for one explosion after another. So the session itself becomes a kind of explosive or violent space. It becomes an annihilating space, a space that eats up, where the obsession with space again blows away the possibility for time to develop.

It's a void space, in a way, or a big-bang space, or a black-hole space that seems to foreclose the possibility of letting something unfold. Just as something's unfolding, a violent enactment blows it away, so that the experience doesn't get a chance–in and of itself–to come to a conclusion. You never get a chance to find out what the experience could be because the sort of space it occupies nullifies it. It nullifies the experience, blows it away before it has a chance to complete itself. Clinically, then, the problem is one where negative space eats away at the possibility of letting an experience be. It's a very violent, Pac-Man, black-hole kind of space that explodes the possibility of giving people a time to complete any particular trajectory of experience.

AM: Would that scenario preclude or diminish an essential capacity like introjection?

ME: I think that's certainly true. But the problem is even more pervasive, because it precludes the possibility of completing a perception. On a sensory level or a perceptual level, you can't even perceive or see what the world would look like without something blowing the experience away before it has a chance to build. So, it wouldn't be a matter of just precluding introjection or projection. It's a matter of stopping actual innate capacities from having a chance to operate.

AM: Regarding those "innate capacities," one of the writers you address extensively in *The Psychotic Core* is Federn. You talk about his concept of "I-feeling," and his radical contention that mental ego-feeling (and not the ego-feeling related to the body) is the first to be experienced by the child. This seems to have provided a springboard for your own ideas. I was wondering if you could comment on this, and on how our sense of the psyche gets spatialized within us?

ME: Wow! I seized on the Federn business because it was pretty unique. I mean, no psychoanalyst before him had theorized in that way. For the general psychoanalyst, the ego is first and foremost the so-called "body ego," and it was kind of stunning to see that, for Federn, the psyche is first a mental ego. How did he get to that? Probably because he read Husserl. He was a student not only of Freud but of Husserl; so that a Husserlian-kind of phenomenology of consciousness informed his work. As a result, even while he was a staunch Freudian and remained in Freud's camp throughout his career, Federn wasn't able to begin his account of the ego's origins as a body ego. Now, that's an amazing position for an analyst to take!

It also occurs to me, in working with psychotics, and if we think of how psychotics describe their own experience, that Federn's descriptions fit certain sorts of psychosis: with regard to how the body ego can fade away, while an I-feeling still remains. Of course, this I-feeling can be lost too, in more dire states of depersonalization; or the I-feeling itself can persist, but feel unreal. One could also have the I-feeling without any quality of its being warm or immediate or real . . . or a sense of painful estrangement from the I-feeling, that the "I" is going on but I can't experience it. One can have even further I-losses . . . But Federn, in any case, has this range of experience of working-through with psychotics, where he can have the body feeling unreal, or the "I" going on after the body drops out . . . And there's a long tradition in esoteric religious thinking that also fits Federn's descriptions. One sees this, for example, in the esoteric Gnostic tradition, where you have ideas of one existing prior to the materialization of the body.

In a way, the Freudian enterprise implicitly has to do with getting the mind into the body. Freud's whole oral, anal, phallic thing is about ways the mind is incarnating, or a way the spirit incarnates. It's about phases of incarnation, or a development of incarnation. Whereas Federn's question, in working with psychosis, is: "Well, what if I don't incarnate? What happens then?" It's not like R. D. Laing's question, which is more: "How did I get out of the body?" For Federn, the question is: "How do I get into it?" What happens if I don't want to get into it, or if the body isn't sufficiently inviting for me to want to be a part of it? Or if the body subjects me to too much horror?

You know, in the Gnostic myths, the soul has to be enticed or seduced or fooled or tricked into going from the dry domain into the wet . . . Contrary to so much analytic thinking, the first fall isn't from womb to birth. The great catastrophe isn't in going through the womb to getting born. The great catastrophe is going from heaven into the womb. I think that's a worthwhile distinction to remember, especially as experimental psychology is now finally catching up with Gnosticism. We now know that the womb is not such a very perfect place at all. The fetus has traumas in the womb too, and maybe so does the embryo . . . Can you imagine what it must feel like, if there are things like feelings at so early a stage, to go through such momentous upheavals or growths, one after another? It's more titanic and cataclysmic than the unfolding of geological ages on the earth, with its cyclones and earthquakes and climatic changes and ice ages! I mean, what the embryo undergoes in a short period of time is monumental . . . And should anyone be there experiencing it, God knows what sort of experience it must be!

AM: About Federn's notion you write: "Primordial I-feeling drenches the entire cosmos . . . Original I-feeling is infinite." Through your reading of Federn, there's a mystical quality in his work that seems just as radical as his argument for the primacy of a mental ego. I'm wondering if this was something that you were aware of or sensed an affinity to. . . .

ME: Well, I have my own tongue-in-cheek love of that kind of thing, because in the way Federn presents his ideas, the question becomes: "How do we all, who begin life as mystics, become anti-mystical?" How do we develop anti-mystical properties as our ego contracts into our body and into the spatial world filled with the objects that we know and love and hate. The so-called "I"–whatever that is–begins as a bigger I, as a bigger, more cosmic I, and then contracts through coming up against the hard facts of life. It develops a contraction, and we then develop a smaller, more realistic "I" that maps out the spatial realities we have to deal with. The problem then becomes: what happens to the big "I"? What happens to the cosmic "I"? Does it get funneled through the smaller "I"? Does the smaller "I" draw nourishment from the bigger "I"? Are they at war with each other? Do they battle for supremacy? Is one psychotic when one meets the cosmic "I" and delusional when one gets to the smaller "I"? If a developmental statement such as Federn's has anything to it at all, what kind of relationship can be worked out between larger and smaller "I" states? How do we get along? Can we make a playground big enough to accommodate the bigger and smaller states?

AM: Again in *The Psychotic Core*, in writing about Federn, you state: "The subject often encounters pain when he acts on his sense of boundlessness. He meets the resistance of spatial realities and other I centers." It's the notion of I centers I'd like to explore. Is this somehow an early prefiguration of the idea of a multiple self, or what you call multiple self states?

ME: Well, I think of the joke about the guru who convinces his disciple that he's God. Years later the guru meets the disciple, and finds him limping along, all crippled and bandaged up. So the guru asks: "What happened?" And the disciple says "Well, this guy riding his elephant was in my way, and I kept thinking and telling him 'I am God, I am God' . . . and he ran right over me." And the guru says: "Schmuck, he's God too!" An entire range of phenomenological and existential and philosophical literatures have explored different phases, or different aspects, of what it means to be a being who sees himself through the eyes of another, a being who sees by displacement, where I see you through me, or you see me through visions of a free-floating "I," or through the "eye," the organ of sight, that floats freely . . . A free-floating "I" that in any particular moment presents any number of vantage points. That's partly what can fuel resistance from a good borderline patient . . . this "anything" that anyone says, anyone could have said something else . . . any "I" could have acted differently, at any given time.

So a good borderline patient can always say, "Well, why should I listen to what you're telling me . . . it is after all *you* telling me." But there can be an impact between patient and analyst, through which I, the analyst, develop a truth of the moment, a truth which grows out of the impact, that I somehow select and through which I become aware, in an aesthetic way, of the impact's growth . . . I become aware, then, of what it might feel like for the patient to be impacting on me in this way. And I'll develop trains of words or images that grow from the aesthetic nucleus of the impact which, without functioning as a definitive truth or perspective, can still give rise to an infinite number of other possible perspectives . . . Then the one truth, the one perspective I select and present to the patient, becomes a poem, my song of the patient at that moment: and through it, I can access the patient's feeling states. We impact each other with our momentary dream presentations.

AM: You've written of yourself: "From the outset it seemed clear that I could never be a strictly orthodox analyst." It's uncommon to find an analyst truly free of the shackles of schools and doctrine, one able to embrace–and I mean the term "embrace" rather literally–figures as diverse and far-reaching as Freud and Jung, Lacan and Kohut, Winnicott and Bion. What is the process, what is the attitude that allows for your incessant efforts at synthesis, and how have those efforts been accepted in the greater and often rivalrous communities of psychoanalysis?

ME: From early on, it was never a theoretical or technical matter. It was desperation. It was a hunger, a need, a personal need that I met, in reading each of these people at a given time. In an inner sense, I was reconstituting an aspect of myself or area of myself. If I read Jung, or Freud, or Winnicott, I felt that some other part of me was coming into being, or was being mediated into life through these various midwives. So it was, in essence, a salvation quest . . . or a matter of integrity as a person, getting more of myself into being and developing more of a life for myself. I gravitated towards the people who, at different phases of my life, seemed to be midwifing what needed to be midwifed at that particular time . . . And as I have a sense of loyalty, I remain loyal to all my various loves from those different phases of my life. I read Jung before Freud. For some reason I didn't understand Freud when I was younger. I tried and tried and tried to read him, but it was too painful and didn't make much sense. But Jung was easy to read, Erich Fromm was easy to read, and I devoured their writings in my late teens and early twenties . . . So in a way I did it backwards. I evolved into a Freudian later . . . I was a Jungian before a Freudian, instead of the reverse, which ought to be the case, developmentally, according to Jung. Of course, I couldn't be a Freudian either because of Freud's anthropology and reductionist picture of what particular fantasies were important. Not being a formal theorist, it wasn't much of a problem to go through these different so-called schools or theoreticians. It was actually a matter of dire need . . . It wasn't a theoretical matter, it was a concrete personal matter involving the constitution of the self . . . of my own self.

How has it played out in the field at-large? I really don't know. I don't know what position I have, I don't really see myself in the field at-large . . . This much is somewhat clear to me at any rate. When I was in graduate school and going through training, and I stumbled across people like Searles or Winnicott or Marion Milner, I felt inwardly very much like William Carlos Williams describes himself in medical school . . . He said that writing poetry got him through medical school. My having fallen upon people like Searles and Winnicott very early on, long before they were popular, got me through graduate school . . . They got me through training. It's as if discovering them made me feel it was okay for a guy like me to exist, because it was hard for me to get that kind of validation, in the formal training that existed at the time. I like to feel that I've encoded, in my writings, the message that it's okay for people to be and develop in their own way: that we mutants are very real and have a very real contribution to make, and that the world would be poorer without us. We have a right to walk around in the sunlight and to stretch and to play our music and to sing and dance . . . And maybe it's okay for grown-up children, for analysts like us, to help keep the balance, to help keep things afloat. I have, thank God, gotten confirmation from diverse sources: from many good souls who've read my writing and have been deeply stirred or affected by it. I've gotten numerous calls or letters or invitations from people who have had the experience, in reading my writings, of hearing their own voices in a deeper way, of feeling they had a right to be in their own particular way. . . .

AM: Of these influences, Bion and Winnicott seem to stand out as being particularly dear to you. You've studied both for decades, and Bion you knew personally. Can you say something about these two men?

ME: Two great mutant men! Winnicott, I suppose, one wouldn't ordinarily think of as a mutant because he had this myth of normalcy about himself. But, you know, in his writings, especially in his writings about Jung, in his "splitting headache" dream related to reviewing Jung as well as in his actual review of Jung's autobiography, Winnicott talked about having been somewhat liberated, of having been able to achieve a degree of madness in his work. Whereas I don't think Bion had to go through that process of apology for his madness. I think he worked more explicitly with and from his madness pretty much from the onset. I got the impression from his biography that he probably knew quite early that he was quite mad and didn't know what to do with his madness. At a time when people weren't all that concerned with problems of madness and the role of madness in human life, Bion, especially, offered some of the most stunning portrayals ever of the mad dimensions of life.

Winnicott? I visited him in 1968, I think, when I was in London. I was having a terrible time in graduate school, especially with one clinical teacher who'd wonder how I would come up with the things I'd come up with. She would always feel they were right, but didn't know how I got them. So she was put off by me because she didn't get my methodology, even though she seemed to agree with the results. So during this horrible time in graduate school, I go to meet Winnicott, and he greets me at the door saying: "Hello, Dr. Eigen. I'm sorry I haven't read your work." He greeted me as if I were someone. I was quite thrown because my experience of my life in New York didn't exactly convince me that I was someone or, for that matter, anyone. So, here I am, being treated like a king by this old man, who seemed very gentle and sweet, who offered me sherry and then went on trying to convey to me something about the sort of work he did. In the meantime, he felt free to move about the room, or sat at the end of his couch in a corkscrew kind of way, which seemed rather awkward . . . He didn't seem shy, so much as awkward . . . What would it mean to be awkward without being shy? His was a kind of awkward intensity, in which he was digging, digging for the experience that he wanted to convey and the way he wanted to convey it, the way that he could feel it could be conveyed to me. And as I looked at him all corkscrewed up in this awkward, intense way, I found he looked very much like an old woman, in his old age . . . So here he was, screwed up in this awkward intensity, when I had this feeling and thought: "Oh my God, he's sort of like me!" . . . that somehow we shared this awkward intensity in our attempts to get at something, in trying to get at the thing itself and find a way of conveying it. I wouldn't be so delusional as to put the two of us on the same plane, but it was a freeing moment for me . . . It was as if he was not afraid *to be*–in this unsmooth, rough-hewn way, in order to try to get at something . . . Ultimately, something about him conveyed permission. It's as if his message was: "If I can be Winnicott, you can be Eigen!" It was a beautiful moment. . . .

It was a different experience entirely when I went to have consultations with Bion. I walked in, and the first thing I felt, that took me quite by surprise, is I felt he looked like a bug . . . He looked like a bug! . . . He looked frightened . . . like a frightened bug. It's as though he were putting himself under me somehow, in order to understand . . . He was putting himself below me, and I felt for that moment empowered. It's as though he were empowering my narcissism by operating from a position of dread. As the session went on a lot of his pronouncements seemed to me oracular, or orphic, and I felt he could be talking to anybody. I felt that I, as a person, didn't exist for him, and I felt very uncomfortable with that. I found him rather joyless, and began telling him how joyless he was. Then, as things went on, we talked about Plato, and he talked about his analyses with Rickman and Klein, of how his earlier contact with Rickman helped save him from Klein. Then out of the blue he started talking about the Kabala, asking me if I'd read it. I told him yes, I had, but not very much. And he was quick to say that he too hadn't read it much. But it dawned on me as the session went on that he was implying . . . that he was talking to me at a level that I wasn't used to being talked to. I write about it in the afterword of *The Electrified Tightrope*, actually, how he anticipated my development by almost a decade. Anyhow, by the time I left him after the session, again I had a parallel feeling, though not at all like the one I got from Winnicott, because Bion was more bug-like with me, more cryptic . . . But again I had the feeling that if it was okay for him to be Bion, if he could do his thing with me the way he did, then perhaps I could discover a way of finding out what my thing is and to do it with a sense of freedom. Both men had this capacity, I felt, to give permission, to give permission to be different, to be in one's own way.

AM: Were your consultations with either man anything like a traditional analytic or supervisory relationship?

ME: I only saw Bion when he was here in New York at the IPTAR Seminars, and everyone was presenting cases to him. I figured I would try to get the most out of the situation, so I presented myself as a case. He told me to get married, and to stop psychoanalysis. He told me I had been overanalyzed, that I'd been in analysis long enough; that I should break away, and get on with the nasty business of finding my own self. In retrospect it's touching and odd and uncanny and inspiring, uplifting, that many of the ingredients of the conversations we had, while he was here in New York, about Plato, about Klein, about the Kabala, about the weirdness of one's own idiosyncratic nature . . . that many of these ingredients turn out to be generative bits and pieces of my own inner world. It's as if the riches that he spontaneously shared about his own life matched a few gold pieces in my own treasure chest. His words, then, hadn't been random; he wasn't talking only about himself. His own unconscious mind was making selections that resonated with treasures buried in my own being, treasures that our sessions helped animate. It was something like psychic acupuncture, where he was getting to certain nerves, certain pressure points that could be stimulated.

AM: There are two other figures who seem to have left their mark on your work and life. I'm thinking of Marion Milner, with whom I understand you've corresponded for years; and of your first analyst, Henry Elkin. Your admiration for Elkin seems filled with generosity and gratitude, and yet, you write that your analysis with him did not end well.

ME: Henry had a strong destructive side, in terms of being intuitively dogmatic. But he had depth and weight, and I had a very deep attachment to him. Implicit in our contract was the sense that something would come of this attachment. And as I began seeing him when I was quite young and quite hopeful, when he left New York I found myself feeling abandoned, looking, perhaps, for a way I was going to survive without this relationship, to carry on without a dependency that had seen me through some decades. How does one resolve a transference of this nature? I don't know. It's not all that clear to me even now.

Milner? I originally loved her appendix to *On Not Being Able to Paint*. I taught it in my seminars for many years. My reading of Milner was, again, like the other people I'd read, really for my own life. It wasn't, however, her concept of undifferentiation that helped me to reconstitute myself in any way. It's when she couched her findings in terms of a paradoxical formulation, in an "I-yet-not-I" kind of structure or dynamic or process, that I felt moved along. It was the "I-yet-not-I" feeling I got from her formulations that led to the first article I wrote about her work. It was one of the first major articles published on her work, and I thought it was a positive article, a helpful article. Pinchus Noy wrote me from Israel at the time saying how helped he was by it. He told me I'd put my finger on elements of Milner's work that had bothered him, that he couldn't grasp, so that he now felt released to assimilate what he had always loved about her in a more undiluted way. That was the effect I had hoped for, generally. My article on Milner's work, however, apparently precipitated antagonism from Margaret Little who, unbeknownst to me at that time, had used the concept of undifferentiation to couch an awful lot of her own work. Apparently, she felt that I had hurt Marion with this paper. I felt badly about that, because I was trying to help midwife a process, help catalyze a process further. Marion and I had written to each other, and her surprise baffled me, since I'd already sent her my review of *On Not Being Able to Paint*, which contained some of the main ideas spelled out by my longer paper. So I explained to her that what I wrote was the result of a process for me, and that it seemed, from the letters I'd received, to have had some use, at least for other people. So I had, then, to simply find a way of standing by my own reality, by my own experience, while at the same time tolerating, or finding a way to go through the flak, and all that it precipitated.

Well, Marion and I kept writing back and forth for quite some time over the matter. Then, much later, she wrote to me saying I was right in what I'd said; that she felt the article had also been helpful to her, in that I had actually freed her from a dead language that wasn't necessary for the experience she was trying to convey. I think that our love for each other survived whatever it was that momentarily came between us. Our love and what we get from one another survived the viscissitudes of that time. I think in a way that's a good model for therapy, and for living . . . that we lived through the pain and agony of a broken union. We very much value our contact with each other.

AM: One striking aspect of your work, already present in *The Electrified Tightrope* and, more recently, in *Coming Through the*

Whirlwind, is the candor with which you convey your own history and inner realities. In your books you highlight elements of biography, early experiences of religion, family, sexuality, college. In *Whirlwind* you portray the rich world of the analyst's internal struggles with two tremendously engaging patients. Were these kind of revelations difficult for you, or did they issue very naturally? It's not common for analysts to write about themselves so frankly and openly: especially, for example, about their erotic reactions to a patient, as you document in your *Whirlwind* case study of Cynthia.

ME: What's more difficult is how much I haven't done. I would be happier if I could do more of it. Each time another shell is shed and I come out of the closet a little more, I get so much more out of it myself, and so do my patients. Therapy, I suppose, has not simply been a profession, it's been . . . it is my life. Therapy has been less of an external, professional process than it's been an internal birthing process. I wonder if more therapists wouldn't benefit from being more open about how much they get from their patients.

I think we get an awful lot from our patients that helps us grow; our patients help organize us, and we grow an awful lot through the work we do . . . or at least I and certain other people that I know do. Therapy can be unlike other professions in that there's less of a separation between what one does and what one gets out of it. For example, I've seen writings in the literature about therapist burnout, and I'm wondering what it means for a therapist to burn out. Perhaps the person was using the wrong model for therapy, was trying to be more external with patients to make the work more of a "profession," like a lawyer would make it. I get many lawyers who come in and hate what they do, who feel unreal about the ways they have to make themselves function in the external world. A therapist has a chance to have much more of a connection with the work that he's doing . . . Part of doing therapy is that one is always in therapy, one's always in one birth process or another, or is evolving in a deep, inner way in connection with other people. As I can see so far from the effect on others and on myself, the more openness of a certain sort the better, I would think.

AM: You write in *The Electrified Tightrope:* "In the long run my work as a patient is what made me an analyst." Can you talk about that experience, and about that dimension of "the work"? Of the work that is intrinsic to any authentic therapy, and to the fashioning of a life through the interweaving or marriages of our many selves?

ME: Jung said a long time ago that a great psychologist doesn't have much of a choice: that his only choice, so to speak, is whether to spend his life inside a mental hospital as a doctor or a patient. That's kind of tongue-in-cheek, I would think, but the truth is that, for the therapist who lives and "professes" his work inwardly, being a therapist is being a patient in a way. One is always engaged in this kind of evolutionary experience, always working on oneself, and that doesn't make for much of a distinction. The distinction between patient and therapist fades away. Of course, I have to do something for the patients in order to feel justified for earning money for my work. But very often I'll take money from a person and thank them for it, and wonder what I did to earn it: because I probably got at least as much from the experience of being with them as they may have gotten from me.

Actually, as I become a little less frightened of being open, I become more and more aware of how I grow with certain people, and how interacting, especially with so-called "difficult" patients, promotes my own development. For example, if there's a person I cannot help, for whom anything I do strikes out, that person is forcing me, if I'm going to help them, to find a way of being with them that I hadn't exercised before. And if I fail to find it, it will be a failed treatment . . . In a way, it's like a baby bird pecking at the mother, pecking the mother into developing the maternal urge to feed . . . Well, there are certain patients who have to keep pecking away at the therapeutic field until, somewhere along the line, the field develops the capacity to help this particular set of birds develop. And when one of them arrives in the office and you cannot help them, when you can feel their anger or their drive to get help pecking away at you, it's not always easy to recognize that we've yet to evolve a corresponding capacity to respond to their particular kind of pecking. But if one does stick with the process for a long enough time, whether it's ten years, five years, two hundred years or a thousand years, sooner or later, that capacity will evolve or get pecked into existence by the bird's own persistence. By not giving up, that bird, somewhere on this earth, will evoke the particular set of responses that it requires and is looking for. And when that actually happens with a patient, after weeks or months of being stuck, it's marvelous! When all of a sudden, because of an internal shift in one's own being, the case moves on: because the therapist's being has actually changed, and has entered another phase of living, in response to getting pecked at in a way never experienced before.

AM: Thanks for letting yourself be pecked at.

ME: You're welcome, I'm sure!

WORKS CITED

Buber, M. (1970). *I and Thou* (tr. by W. Kaufmann). New York, Scribner.

Calvino, I. (1981). *If on a Winters Night a Traveler* (tr. by W. Weaver). New York, Harcourt Brace Jovanovich.

Derrida, J. (1978). "Freud and the Scene of Writing," in *Writing and Difference* (tr. Alan Bass). Chicago, University of Chicago Press.

Dewey, J. (1959). *Art as Experience*. New York, Capricorn Books.

Fromm, E. (1957). *The Forgotten Language*. New York, Grove Press.

Gendlin, E. T. (1962). *Experiencing and the Creation of Meaning*. New York, Free Press of Glencoe.

Glass, J. (1993). *Shattered Selves: Multiple Personality in a Postmodern World*. Ithaca, Cornell University Press.

Levi-Strauss, C. (1963). *Totemism* (tr. by R. Needham). Boston, Beacon Press.

Milner, M. B. (1979). *On Not Being Able to Paint*. New York, International Universities Press.

MICHAEL EIGEN: SELECTED BIBLIOGRAPHY

Psychic Deadness (1996), Northvale, NJ, Jason Aronson, Inc.

Reshaping the Self (1995), New York, Psychosocial Press.

The Electrified Tightrope (1993), Northvale, NJ, Jason Aronson, Inc.

Coming through the Whirlwind (1992), Wilmette, Illinois, Chiron Publications.

The Psychotic Core (1986), Northvale, NJ, Jason Aronson, Inc.

Samuel and Evelyn Laeuchli

> I want to dream myself into priests and wanderers, female cooks and murderers, children and animals, and more than anything else, birds and trees; that is necessary, I want it, I need it so I can go on living. . . .
>
> –Herman Hesse, *Wandering*

Imagine the embodiment, and then the human marriage, of the living forms of two of this century's greatest sculptors. Imagine a Giacometti, the angst and energy of wire; the mute, shrieking tension between man and God, between human presence and divine silence. Memory, ***memoria*** *of the species. The convulsions of history. Job. The ashes of Auschwitz . . . Then see the deep concave recesses, the lush, embracing folds, of one of Henry Moore's women. The very essence of matter.* ***Mater.*** *Womb and mother. I have known Sam Laeuchli for fifteen years now; Evelyn, his wife, for less than five. But it's as if I have known both forever. For there is, finally, something archetypal, something incarnate in the order of art, that defines their union, as well as their creation.*

As Michael Eigen suggests, one way to view the field of psychotherapy is to see it as a mother bird at which patients keep pecking, in the hope of inciting the development of the broadest possible range of maternal responses and feeding urges. Over the past fifteen years, Samuel Laeuchli, a Swiss theologian with scholarly interests in religion, art and comparative mythology, and Evelyn Rothchild-Laeuchli, an American clinical psychologist, have generated just such a response: highly idiosyncratic, but remarkably attuned

[Haworth co-indexing entry note]: "Samuel and Evelyn Laeuchli." Co-published simultaneously in *The Psychotherapy Patient* (The Haworth Press, Inc.) Vol. 10, No. 1/2, 1997, pp. 143-187; and: *Elaborate Selves: Reflections and Reveries of Christopher Bollas, Michael Eigen, Polly Young-Eisendrath, Samuel and Evelyn Lauechli and Marie Coleman Nelson* (ed: Anthony Molino) The Haworth Press, Inc., 1997, pp. 143-187. Single or multiple copies of this article are available from The Haworth Document Delivery Service [1-800-342-9678, 9:00 a.m. - 5:00 p.m. (EST). E-mail address: getinfo@haworth.com].

*to the relentless pleas of so much pecking. Together, they have combined energies in creating **Mimesis**, an institute for mythic play with centers in Europe and the United States. A group process, "mimesis" uses stories from the great body of mythological literature to confront personal and social issues, and thereby increase understanding, tolerance, and shared community. By exploring the often harsh realities offered by these stories, insight, growth and healing become possible.*

As Sam and Evelyn explain: "Playing a story draws us into its spell. Universal themes–birth, coming of age, initiation, love and intimacy, loss and separation, vulnerability and death–are all manifested in mythic play. We put ourselves into a role, we enter the role, face the other players, and become the role. The role takes over. But by using the story line of the myth, group leaders can ensure a safe and supportive play space for the participants. We then discover that the story has its own inner order, and we are drawn into it. This incarnation, then, is a potential step towards healing and catharsis. The moment of spontaneous play allows for recognition of our own complexity, our unacknowledged selves, our deep humanity."

Participants are invited to "play," spontaneously, within the structure of the mythic tale. This frees the players to create scenes which connect them directly to the basic experiences present in the story, and thereby to their own struggles. There is a chance, then, for both the players and the group as a whole, to be "held" and accepted in the circle of participants, and to express a full range of emotions. Sometimes the play can be outrageously funny, as well as touching or painful. Ample time is given to discuss the scenes generated, and to analyze from a distance when necessary. In this way, players are allowed whatever level of defense is necessary. This ensures a range of expressive possibilities: from the person who will dismiss any personal relevance ("I was just taking on a role . . . "), to the person who will be moved to share deeply personal issues which the stories and process have elicited. Finally, participants will often begin to acknowledge and assimilate what Jung termed "the shadow." In so doing, self-acceptance leads to tolerance and, ultimately, to community.

This interview is derived from two visits with the Laeuchlis. The first took place in October 1994, during the couple's first return visit to Philadelphia, after moving to Switzerland earlier that year. I later visited them in July 1995, in Basel, where they are busy broadening the geographic and therapeutic reaches of ***Mimesis***.

AM: For starters, what are some basic assumptions on which *mimesis* rests?

EL: One principle we accept is that world mythology, including the Bible, Greek, Sumerian and Egyptian myths, fairy tales, Native American and African oral traditions, all provide us with a vast literature which reveals, sometimes boldly, sometimes cryptically, basic truths about the human condition. Myths are universal. They embrace and portray personal, family, and cultural dynamics, and show us the issues of lifetime development. The mythic imagination also expresses parallels to modern psychological notions: for example, the concept of the intergenerational transmission of dysfunction appears in the Orestes cycle, as well as in the biblical concept of the sins of the father being visited on the third generation. The stories both connect us to antiquity and are alive in us right now. What family therapist has not seen some version of Abraham's sacrifice of Isaac? What couples therapists have not seen Adam and Eve after the fall, or, for that matter, experienced the fall in their own relationships?

SL: It is our belief that the stories can be healing partly because they acknowledge these realities. There is no attempt to cover up or sugarcoat the psychological experience. Often coded in symbols, or layered like dreams, the stories speak to us at a depth level. Like great art, this is why they transcend time and context, and can make the experience of playing them out in a group aesthetically satisfying.

AM: Before asking you to illustrate the *mimesis* process in more detail, how did a psychologist and a theologian come together to develop what you call an "institute for mythic play"?

SL: Strangely enough, we first developed this work responding to a theoretical task that had been under discussion for a long time, the so-called hermeneutic problem. For 200 years, an extremely difficult issue has been debated by philosophers, historians, theologians, finally by anthropologists and literary critics: what chance do we really have to ever enter a datum, a text, idea or event of the past?

EL: How could we ever understand and comprehend a culture, a subgroup, for that matter an individual whose frame of reference is different from ours? Is this a process of the mind, of intuition, of critical thinking, of science or even of belief? Does it suffice to "think" about problems, to evaluate text, and consider options and solutions?

SL: We had read Heidegger, Ornstein, Eliade and Kafka; we had been considering Zen, Cabbalah, the questions raised by Yoga and by Sufi cosmology. A huge span of alternative models had begun to emerge. I had started teaching religion and art; the role of ritual in the experience of religion; myth and history; the conflict of cognitive models on ritual and drama from Nietzsche to Bert Brecht and Peter Brook.

It became clear that discourse could not lead us further because we were not able to break out of our own intellectual frame, even one that included alternative approaches to understanding. We were caught in a circle. So I had students who urged me to teach alternative hermeneutics, not as New Age craze, not really as heritage of 1968–which it might or might not turn out to be–but as serious investigation into the data of religion. For nine months, we met every Wednesday night for three hours.

AM: What happened during those sessions? Is it possible to recall some of those "alternatives," as you call them?

SL: We proceeded with three steps. The first was an experiment with the element of silence, of meditation. A well-known anthropologist had written a book on the language of silence: now we not only dealt with such language, we entered it. We wanted to use it for the process of research itself. We examined if and what the element of meditative silence could contribute to the hermeneutic path. So instead of asking historical, philosophical, theological, ethical questions, our question became: how about entering the tale through silence?

EL: Along these lines, we then staged a scene that can be repeated at liberty, if someone has an open enough team to work with. It was a group of about 12 participants, theologians, artists, psychologists, most but not all of them students. We chose a religious text, the famous mythic tale of Abraham sacrificing his son Isaac, with God asking Abraham to kill his son for him. At the end the God prevented the deed.

SL: The research group sat in a seminar arrangement, with the "professor" at the head table, and for 45 minutes, we staged a serious discussion. What is this tale about, what criteria do we use to think about it, how do we come to evaluate it? Since the group came from a mixture of fields, with different interests and access to information and communication, the ideas were extremely varied. And then a major process was added: a one-hour walking meditation. It was practiced as presented by some Sufi groups at the university not long before. The same result can be achieved by many other meditative processes; in fact, we later on did use various forms of meditation.

EL: After the meditation, we returned to the seminar and talked once again about the sacrifice of Isaac. And we made an astonishing discovery, which became a first and crucial entry into an entire process. The discussion differed highly from the one before. The access was much more lucid, the myth seemed different, its terror was much more pronounced. It almost was another tale. The group was not necessarily more unified in its opinions, but the individuals tolerated the differences much more. They shared. They exchanged experiences. They considered. They talked to each other.

The process of silence had changed the process of inquiry. There is an astonishing result in such an experiment. People who meditate have been accused of drawing back into a narcissistic bubble; practicing this kind of mythic approach through silence produced the opposite result: people quite often begin to listen to each other.

AM: But what could you add, if anything, to this opening, which seems to hold such an exclusive, all-encompassing power? There is not much you can do, after all, beyond silence except to be silent. Or *is* there anything more to say?

EL: On first sight, you seem right. All the Quakers can do, so it seems, is to be silent. But as so many Quakers have found out, this step is so often not a dead end, but the beginning of an entire new social experience.

SL: Exactly. A second step consisted in considering the myth in its archetypal force. The term "archetype" has been a difficult one, as there is so much confusion and antagonism surrounding it in academia. But whatever the term, the depth quality of myth, of antique tradition is at stake. What happens when we take myth as actual archetypal experience, when we begin to explore the possibility that the mythic models, in often unexpected ways, speak to issues in our life, as well as to issues not only of research but of the research community?

EL: Let me say something about the background of this second step. Ever since the falling out between Freud and Jung, psychoanalytic writers have generally taken either a Freudian or Jungian position about the meaning and value of religious symbols and experience. The myth is no exception. The Freudian view is quite clear: myth is a concentrate of protohuman horrors. It reveals the pathological archeology of personality and society. Jung was more teleological. He wanted to see in myth a chance to heal, not merely a reflection of illness. The shadow exists to lure us into taking it seriously, no matter the many invalid and futile attempts to change our lives. We try and try the same pathological pattern, because we somehow hope to change it; myth embodies a kind of cultural repetition compulsion.

Through *mimesis*, we found a way to generate a form of experience that could integrate the two viewpoints, while serving the cause of both myth research and depth psychology. We were caught by, but we also accepted as a highly creative sense of process, the see-saw between the pessimism of Freud and the cautious, tentative, at times unreal optimism of Jung.

SL: The third step led us to our work, to the play of myth and hence the process of *mimesis*. It was an extremely arduous path. We really had to do our homework on play. One evening, I remember, we played Adam and Eve with two students whom I was quite fond of. He was a jazz musician and doctoral student; she was an undergraduate, an attractive Italian woman. Playing the scene in front of the tree of life, they began to flirt with each other. It's in the story: the scene of eating the fruit is the step into the loss of childhood, the beginning of sexuality, adolescence, freedom and choice. Now these two began to flirt in a way which was quite uncomfortable. The group was taken aback. Emotionally, she took her clothes off. Here she was, a married woman, and she was having an affair in front of our eyes.

I remember driving home, concerned that these two people had played out, in front of the others, such an extremely uncomfortable sexual scene. It was only when Evelyn entered the work, with months and years of supervision, of practice and inner strength, that I found a way to make the play safe. With Evelyn's therapeutic insights, we were able to create safety. We had to learn to protect the players from their own demons.

AM: Evelyn, it sounds like this is where your psychology background proved crucial.

EL: Yes. I did my studies in clinical psychology. I had also studied anthropology and philosophy. But the paradigms and theories I was presented with in psychology, though part of a good traditional training, lacked breadth and depth. I envied the scope of religious inquiry. I found the more genuine, religiously inspired thinkers to be envied because of their freedom. A freedom I found more in Jung than in others.

Working with Sam gave me a chance to integrate a lot of my training and analytic understanding with other dimensions of group process. Methodology became important, as we tried to find a way *into* the experience, in order to understand our understanding of experience. It was a very satisfying way, not merely an intellectual way, but an experiential way towards a new form of knowledge.

In one of the earliest groups, for instance, where we'd played Moses and Pharaoh, two participants suddenly confronted each other viciously. It was fascinating for me to watch Sam realize what every therapist knows all along: that when you begin to play, the archetypal unconscious rises menacingly. The demons come up. There is no way to stop that. Sam had to start, there and then, to learn about intervention and safety.

SL: I realized I had a tiger by the tail. And what I needed to learn, and what I did learn over the course of the next years from Evelyn, was why and how this emergence from the unconscious invariably takes place at the moment of play. For the next several years, we entered a process of incessant and ongoing evaluation, of reflective work. After each workshop we spent hours examining what had happened, what dynamic we had watched, what kind of interventions worked or might have worked.

EL: We needed structures to make the process safe. We now have hundreds and hundreds of these plays every year, in the U.S. and Europe. Everywhere, every time, when you play myth, within ten minutes people play out and recreate their childhood, their parents, their past, along with the cultural realities that transcend individual history. And they do so in a way which is extraordinarily powerful. Because myth, you see, is very primal; myth is about our human development and experience expressed in a poetic, symbolic and emotionally powerful language. Myth embodies—and play helps to incarnate again and again—these archetypal forces. There is no way to stop this from happening; we can only work to make our contact with these forces constructive and healing. Our work centers on that task.

Sam mentioned Abraham and Isaac, one of our major models of play. Now you can *defend* against what that myth evokes. Such defending has been, throughout history, the function of so much theological, academic and scientific theorizing, an intellectual defense. When you *play* myth, that defense goes; and when it does, what happens can become very healing. But at first it's extremely threatening. We developed many processes to make this lowering of the defenses safe.

SL: Ultimately, that safety is provided by the very *structure* of the myth. It's the myth's very story line that functions hermeneutically as the kind of defense the process warrants. The difference lies in the way we elaborate and talk about the myth. We don't intellectualize it, but we apply and respect its parameters. The play brings up the demons, which reside, so to speak, below the surface of things. The archetypal myth evokes, addresses and at the same time contains ominous issues that get raised.

AM: So you've worked to pinpoint and facilitate a move from *acting* out to *playing* out.

EL: Exactly. I had been trained in play therapy, and really felt that in order to heal, children need to have a safe space, through play, in which to symbolize their experience and conflicts, and in which to work towards resolution. I trusted the children's intuitive sense of what they needed to express and how, within the framework of their own metaphors, they could develop a process of healing. They needed little input from me in terms of directing this process or of interpreting its content. I provided a *being with*, a witnessing and containing of their experience. This presence of a "conscious" other creates safety and limits acting-out. Early in our work together, Sam and I had come to realize that when people would express themselves through intense emotion, it was a short leap into acting out, as a way of not being in the emotion. It is the presence of the therapist, then, aware, present and respectful of unconscious dynamics and defenses, that allows for the predicament of the person to be held, or contained.

It was these elements that we worked to integrate in our groups, so that issues could surface and be addressed gently, and not confrontatively. Ultimately, this led to our own resolution of the problem of acting-out, which no longer takes place, and which necessitates very little if any external control on the part of the group leaders. Again, we accomplished this through very basic interventions, like helping people verbalize their feelings and joining with them emotionally. We try very hard to stay connected with the individuals in this process. Not being alone with what the myth evokes allows it to be experienced without its becoming overwhelming.

SL: The one thing we should point out is that, through *mimesis*, we help teach people to live fully, as human beings. And this means coming to grips with one's suffering. The myths help us come to grips with enormous suffering and pain, even physical pain; people become aware of and share horrendous parts of their experience and they weep, and cry, because we really enter the depths with them. And as a group leader you hold that suffering, you hold it, no matter how painful. It's an incredible responsibility, but it's that part of the process which helps people be less afraid.

EL: A lot of what happens in our groups is the result of countertransference work. The leader constantly monitors his or her own inner process, so that they themselves can stay present and not act out. It's so easy to want to shut down or control the process, out of one's own need to distance emotionally. And though this inner process is a non-verbal one, its effects on the group are clear, especially when it's mismanaged.

SL: Also, as the play elicits all sorts of transferences, it's not uncommon for group members to get angry at us. Everything one says will always and absolutely rub someone the wrong way. The group leader needs to allow for the expression of such aggression without counter-aggression.

For example, we once had a workshop on the struggle of Jacob with the Angel. The powerful scene at the river Jabboc. And here was a European student in Philadelphia. Extremely hurt not only by a sick family, but by the sadism of his culture. At first he was not able even to attend classes, let alone to read a chapter of a book; he admitted to me later on that he would sit in his room with a book open in front of him until 2 in the morning, unable to read even one page.

He entered the play, a tough and merciless Jacob fighting with his Angel. The scene is one of the primal mythic models of confronting our past, the limits of despair, of facing the divine powers with the ominous gestalt of ambivalence. He was enraged beyond sense, our Jacob, having carried for so long so much hurt, guilt and shame, and the dark emotions of generations.

EL: The angel in that scene was played by a therapist who must have known what was about to happen. The troubled Jacob began to attack him viciously. The student-Jacob wanted to act out his usual role, fight his usual fight, repeat the desperate family battle which prevented him year after year from experiencing his helplessness and despair. The angel would not budge. He did not fight back. He did not become sentimental. He simply held his own. He was the mirror of the man fighting the mirror. Our Jacob got nastier and nastier, more and more desperate. The angel held his own. He did not attack, he did not become sadistic; he did not act out, as he easily could have, the very despair of his own past. He was just there, strong, present, compassionate.

SL: At the end the Jacob became quiet. He had finished the fight and he carried the wounds of all the battles he had done with the angels of his life. He was able for the first time to be small and weak, not in defeat but in order to be known and loved. If later on he was able to have a relationship, to complete his education, to do creative work and finally, to marry, it is not in the least the result of these scenes he had played, over and over, with his own angels and demons. Such is the alternative to "acting out," as you called it.

AM: I think most readers will find the richness of the process–the interweaving of myth, ritual, depth psychology, group process, and theater–simply astonishing. Can you say more about the influences behind your work?

SL: Most insights came to us by sheer intuition. Initially, I didn't know Winnicott's work; when I came upon *Playing and Reality*, long after we'd started *mimesis*, it read like a stunning validation and support of our process. Nor did I know Jacob Levy Moreno, the founder of psychodrama, when we started out. In retrospect, I realize how strange this must sound. We basically developed *mimesis* without the ideas of the man who had written "The Theater of Spontaneity." But when I finally did read Moreno, I recognized the great value of his process. That we developed our work before we'd ever read him, however, was important for us. It allowed us to go in our own direction.

AM: What are the fundamental differences between *mimesis* and psychodrama?

EL: We are sometimes challenged because we do not "de-role." Psychodrama de-roles; that means it actively helps the players free themselves from their roles. We believe roles do not need to be shed if there is enough safety in the group. We *are* the roles, whether we like it or not. We are Medea, Cain, Orpheus, Persephone. In mimesis you do not "de-role" because myth contains you. The safety of the group, and the cosmos of myth, allow you to carry your role, which you play one way or another, in your daily life. We work toward integrating parts of self and tolerating moments of dissonance.

SL: Psychodrama is a great movement. But it's also like every other movement: it's like academia, it's like the church. You have great leaders and you have lots of mediocre people, propounding the faith. Moreno himself must have been a genius. Perhaps one of the differences with psychodrama is that, in *mimesis*, we trust the participants more; we control less, intervene less, because we trust the myth.

EL: The use of myth is a major difference. Moreno was also involved a bit with sociodrama, and that involves more than a personal element in the story. We don't necessarily play the personal dynamics of a family or a participant. We use myth, and the myth adds both depth and protection, at the same time. From my own experience with psychodrama, I find that we're less involved with specific techniques; we allow more silence, more ambivalence. We have less of a psychological agenda and, in my experience, we are more concerned with aesthetics and spirituality.

AM: Have you had any "official" or direct contacts with the psychodrama movement?

EL: We once gave a workshop in Washington, at the Academy of Psychodrama, where we were well received. Only one person chided us for not de-roling. But another participant said to us: "You have a trust in the group, and in the tale, which we don't have." That's the real difference. We absolutely trust the group. It's an integral part of what makes the mimetic process. Myth, or what Jung would call the archetypal expression, does the rest.

SL: If Abraham and Isaac were played according to the psychodrama model, father and son might beat each other up. Our friend at the Academy suggested as much. By contrast, what *mimesis* does is to provide a structure. Ritual, and myth, give you a very strong structure. Together, they can help make sense of the 16-year-old kid who comes home drunk, and is met by an angry father. Father and son, they've done that since time immemorial. It's life, with all its drama and tragedy. What *mimesis* does is to give that drama a mythic, or imagistic, structure, from which a resolution can emerge.

AM: Along these lines, Evelyn, how do the principles and foundations of *mimesis* connect with your everyday practice as a therapist?

EL: In my experience, children in spontaneous play are myth-makers and symbol makers; they have an intuitive, integral sense of what needs to be created to transform inner experience, to make life. For adults, stories, or metaphors, can have that function: in a good drama, or in a myth, we reach to a deep level of *primal* experience. This isn't easy for adults, whose struggles are sometimes so painful that they need to be denied. Yet despite their veneer of rationalism, despite a pseudo-scientific aversion to traditional myth and religion that adults often display, we've seen *mimesis* touch such people, and help them move beyond denial.

AM: Similarly, Sam, I know that en route to developing *mimesis* you had already undertaken comparative work in Myth and History, which you first presented in your religion courses at Temple University. This study, if I'm correct, also encompassed a radical critique of academia.

SL: When I first came upon Feyerabend's *Against Method*, it was like a revelation. I found there echoes of what Goethe had said centuries before, and so brilliantly, in his opening of *Faust*. Goethe laughed at the academy; which is to say, at me too! And Paul Feyerabend called science, in his shocking chapter 17, a "myth," in the negative sense of the word. Some of today's academics cannot stand Feyerabend. One of my colleagues practically had a tantrum during a faculty retreat when I quoted the rebellious German philosopher of science. The academic, like the bishop, minister or revival preacher, can be blind to his own mythology.

I recall a panel discussion at Temple, years ago, which I had to chair. A professor of anthropology had stated–it was an old item by that time, of course–that history is just one more ideology, and not even the most useful one. Some of the scholars present were insulted that I had dared even to invite such academic nonsense into the forum. One year later, a Japanese Buddhist proposed the same idea; but perhaps because it was phrased within a different language, it did not receive the same kind of angry response. Still, I am grateful for my academic career. It gave me life.

AM: Returning for a moment to Jung, where do you see the affinities, and the distinctions, between his patterns and yours?

SL: You and I have often talked about Jung, who struggled with myth, shadow, archetype and healing all his life. Our work does have connections with Jung, but it also has a Freudian touch. The hell of life, the *inferno*, is Freud; the archetypal hope is Jung. Our work, every step of our work, is a conflict between Freud and Jung.

In every workshop we do we go back and forth, back and forth. It is, to use mythic language, one ongoing battle between the two tales of creation in Genesis. In the first, the world comes out "good"; in the second, the God throws man and woman out of the paradise.

EL: To give you one example, our first public workshop was fourteen years ago, at a church in Philadelphia. It was a seven hour process–a real ritual, in which we even used masks. After a four-hour play on Orpheus and Eurydice, on that great myth of love and loss, we first had a meditation, and then discussed the experience. During the discussion, there was a young businessman who was very unpleasant: very vocal, very outspoken, he tried to dominate the group.

I had tried very hard to set limits, but to no avail. Suddenly he began to talk very clearly and directly. "My God," he said, "I finally realize what's going on. I don't know anything of what you do, I don't like the church, I don't know what myth is, I didn't even know of Orpheus and Eurydice before today . . . But I want to tell you that four years ago my partner was murdered, and it took eight months to find her body. I had to come to this play to reconnect with the woman they murdered."

SL: Her body had been found just a few blocks from the church where we played. And he had come to our group without any awareness of either the myth or of the fact that our location was near the place where the woman had been found. He had played out the loss of his partner in the morning, defending against it the whole time. And by the end of the day he said: "This is unbelievable. I had to come here, to get in touch with what I'd lost." The myth of Orpheus had become his own. In fact, it already had been his own.

EL: One thing Sam and I do is to listen in ourselves for resonances to the metaphors and stories, and then do transformations. We look for ways to bring the myths to bear on contemporary realities, on lived experience. The way Orpheus, for this man, brought his own loss into consciousness. And just as a person is led unconsciously to identify with and select a mythic figure or character to play out, there's also a lot of spontaneity in the unfolding of his or her personal story. When the myth hits home like that, the variations on its theme are infinite!

I'm thinking now about what you asked before, about how *mimesis* connects with my private practice. I'd read Jung for fifteen years, Freud my whole life . . . but they seem very distant now . . . such models have become less real for me. On another level, having read Winnicott or Jung or whomever, I realize there's an immense amount of insight, immense amounts of knowledge to be gained . . . But these theoretical frames, I believe, are helpful to bring a moment into focus, and then ought to be thrown away. Truly defining an archetype is undoubtedly helpful, but it often can limit you immensely. So I try to bring those elements into my work as needed, and try to let them go right away.

In my training as a psychologist, for example, the concept of self was something fascinating and also very hard to grasp. Every personality theorist had a different definition; every frame looks at the concept differently. But the basic questions persist: "What gets transformed? Who, or what, is interacting in the therapeutic situation?" Now the concept is coming into focus again, as a result of the debates on dissociative experience, split self, and multiplicity.

But again, in doing both group and individual work, I find such concepts not sufficient, though very helpful in understanding my experience with patients, as well as with players in our *mimesis* groups. Here, however, I'm always amazed by the ability of people to take on a role. There's plenty of sociological documentation on role and self, but to see how a role takes over a person is an amazing phenomenon. It's almost like possession. Literally. Time and again people will say: "What came through me? what happened? what did I access in myself? was it something archetypal? or a part of me I'm out of touch with, so that in a way it's not a part of 'me,' of what I know of myself?" You see, then, how this work really brings these questions into focus, and leaves them open.

AM: You both have spoken, time and again, of this element akin to "possession" that unfolds in your work. I get the sense that, in your view, we are somehow inhabited by myths, that there are, *literally*, archetypal forces at work in us.

SL: We experience the archetypal forces in many ways. Perhaps we have the most difficulty dealing with "unacceptable" or unacknowledged inner dynamics. Myth is often cruel. Very brutal, mean, dark. The playing of the dark side is deeply related to getting in touch with the self. One does become possessed, shall we say, but one also comes to repossess what's been split off in life. When people play those mythic tales, they embody a part of self, of consciousness, which is almost always, if it's authentic, dark. People are stunned, when suddenly the myth gets to them, when Oedipus or Cain or Osiris gets to them. They experience dark, sometimes ominous aspects of themselves. They touch what Jung called their *shadow.* And through that shadow, the dark archetypes, or whatever you want to call them, emerge. We see it all the time.

EL: It's what a man who ran a large clinic in Philadelphia once told us. "All therapy is in Dante," he said; because to enter great literature, like therapy, is to enter darkness. And in a strange way, then, myth gives you permission to play your shadow.

SL: And it does so spontaneously, of its own accord. As long as a group is safe, people will suddenly and spontaneously become very dark, and they will play the myth. And the group leader has to be part of that; if I cannot experience the darkness in me, I cannot lead that play. Because the leader functions as the tie-in between myth, self and spontaneity; between the individuals, and the group body. As Evelyn suggested before, it is through the group leader's presence, and his or her own ability to access the mythic depths of experience, that the members of the group can somehow manage to do the same.

EL: I used to do *mimesis* with groups in a hospital, where a patient once said to me: "I finally know what makes this work for me. It is both 'me' and 'not-me.' I can see as much of myself in a role as I can tolerate seeing, and when I become uncomfortable, I can clearly see it's not me, that it is Ophelia, or the character I'm playing." It's that old paradox of subject-and-object: seeing the self as self, and at the same time seeing it as something foreign, against which we need, occasionally, to defend. . . .

AM: Before we go any further, perhaps you can clarify the central term in your discourse. What do the Laeuchlis mean by *myth*?

SL: It is difficult to say. What do you mean by "art"? You get twenty conflicting definitions, by the best scholars. Myth is a cosmos, as Eliade called it, it contains a world of its own. Ancient traditions developed a highly poetic, imagistic form of communication, of imaginative insight. The metaphors were often gods and men, man and woman, society, creation, tragedy, birth and death. And though fairy tales seem different, we are dealing there with a similar code.

Myth is oral, it's not written. Even the Biblical text as we know it is only the last form in which it comes to us. For centuries, even the Bible stories were transmitted orally. And the genesis of such stories is always the Self. So for six thousand years (the Sumerian myth of *Inanna*, for example, dates back that far), something in us developed an imagistic, very enigmatic, very powerful form of communication which may be called myth. In this sense, I am less concerned with theories about man the myth-maker than with the eternal reaches of mythic story and imagery. I share with Evelyn the sense that, if you have to define what Beethoven is, forget it. I only know that if I play the myths out, I can enter something extremely powerful. Evelyn and I both believe that the heyday of theory is long past us.

EL: Theory doesn't work anymore, including Jungian theory, which can present a real roadblock on the way to experience. From our angle, myths are tales, from an antique tradition, which we begin to participate in through play. Like the young businessman in the Orpheus play, I too have experienced miraculous moments of consciousness, of clarity and insight. I've also experienced incredible poetry . . . It's amazing, but when people play out myth they talk poetry! It may be that myth and fairy tales free something in us. It happens with educated professionals as well as with the street kids in the ghettos of South Philadelphia . . . These kids are so dysfunctional, they often can't go to school, but when they play these stories, they also talk with amazing clarity about their experiences and at times show more insight than psychologists and theologians.

AM: Many times, Sam, in private communications, you've put an immense emphasis on *consciousness*.

SL: Here too you have to steer clear of intellectual defense and dogmatism. Of course, I cannot define "consciousness," the way I cannot define art or myth. But listen: you have a group playing the lost paradise. Here is a man or woman playing God. Someone is playing Adam, a woman is playing Eve. The play can go a hundred different ways, you cannot predict how they will play nor what they are about to experience. God commands the man and the woman: "Do not eat from that tree!" But they do. They eat anyhow, and they experience their sexuality. They choose to know; they choose to lose the paradise, to live and to die.

Now a lot of this *play* can be naive, blind, unconscious. God is angry but thinks he is kind, in giving the children freedom. The man is frightened and attacks Eve without being aware of his fear. Eve does not feel happy about having brought about their expulsion, and is more terrified than Adam. But there can be a moment in the play when God, perhaps with fear, or with unbelief, or with a stunned silence, realizes: "I have brought this about! This is my deed, my responsibility! Why have I done so?"

Or it happens, perhaps, that Adam at the end looks at Eve, and says, perhaps with fear, perhaps with pride, perhaps with uncertainty and ambivalence: "I attacked you because you helped me toward a choice! I could not tolerate that you were stronger than me in front of that tree!" Or it may happen that Eve looks back. At the god who never talked to her until he chided her at the end. At Adam who attacked her for giving him a life. And she says to both of them: "Is that what I get for choosing?"

There is consciousness in such play. It is in that instance of insight, that second of clarity. It can be a physical change; an awareness of what is going on in me, in us! Consciousness is a protean force, a movement of my body, my tears about the evil of creation; the song and praise about a creation that has been made possible, the awe about a moment of freedom that has come about. You cannot define, phrase, explain consciousness, but there are scenes when it surfaces.

EL: Consciousness and transformation, both at the same time . . .

AM: . . . two words which are intrinsic to our therapeutic and highly "therapized" cultures. Do you both see *mimesis* as a form of therapy?

EL: Our culture is pretty narrow in its definitions of "therapy." Many experiences are therapeutic. Certainly religious ritual can be very therapeutic, if not actually transformative . . . To the extent that myth encodes depth experience, that it uses metaphor and symbol, it triggers a lot in us that can move us to get in touch with those depths. It frees up, or facilitates contact with, parts of self that aren't normally accessible. It allows for growth, transformation, a sense of aliveness. Now whether that's "therapy" depends, I guess, on how you define therapy.

I've worked in hospitals and clinics with this process, and I've seen patients "choose" stories and myths that would evoke certain specific kinds of consciousness. A given tale, for instance, might help patients prepare for family therapy, or get in touch with crippling core issues, like the connection between eating disorders and early loss. The simple choice, therefore, of a particular fairy tale or myth, could help tap those deeper levels.

AM: Such as. . . .

EL: Cinderella. In the original story there is no fairy godmother. It's a very different story than the one Walt Disney promotes. A child loses her mother at a young age, is neglected by her father, and abused by her step-family. How does such a child grow up, become capable of "meeting a prince," having a relationship? This was the favorite story of women with eating disorders because it so reflected their experience. And the story provides a path of healing.

SL: We struggle a lot with the issue of whether *mimesis* is therapy or not. One thing which helped me was to see in the therapeutic literature considerations of activities not usually regarded as therapy; the therapeutic value of friendship or of having a healthy relationship, for example, or from walking for two hours a day. It's no different from medicine, and the debate there over what really heals people: we have very dogmatic psychotherapies much as we have very dogmatic medical approaches. Like dogmatic, fundamentalist religion.

EL: There are traditional Freudians, Kernbergians, etc., who claim that only what they do is right, and declare everybody else, especially "eclectics," as theoretically "impure." This happens a lot in analytic institutes. Again, religious dogma is everywhere. But getting back to *mimesis*. . . .

SL: It is amazing, Tony, that for fifteen years we have used this process without the participants becoming overwhelmed by the experiences that are evoked in the playing of myth. Nobody has ever broken down. The story and the group provide a framework that allows these experiences to be carried, integrated.

EL: By "broken down" Sam means flooded, overwhelmed. No one's ever had to leave or distance themselves from a group. We really work to create a sense of support, and to make sure that participants don't feel alone in the group. Other therapists who have taken part in *mimesis* have remarked on the immense sense of acceptance and safety they found. People don't feel isolated with their experience, which makes it much more tolerable.

AM: Sam, how do you explain the threat *mimesis* posed to your own community of academic theologians? Though you and Evelyn repeatedly use words like *safety, acceptance*, and *healing*, your experience in the Department of Religion at Temple was not always the friendliest. . . .

SL: Religious traditions are powerful vehicles for myth, and powerful expressions for what goes on inside each and every one of us. Jung knew that, as has every student of myth. Abraham wants to destroy his child; Adam and Eve lose the paradise; life is what we're left with after the Fall. This is very threatening, and many people enter academia because they are terrified of life, and cannot connect with their own issues. I attended C. G. Jung's lectures at the University of Basel, decades ago, and he abruptly stopped teaching because he could not tolerate the academic atmosphere.

Now the scholar may enter the academic enterprise in order to escape precisely this, his own predicament of darkness. You can't blame him, life simply terrifies him. After all, that is exactly how and why I entered the academic career. It would be absurd to deny that path. I give you an example, regarding Abraham and Isaac. One of my colleagues once launched into a sermon over the story, insisting it had only to do with the "historical" fact of being written at a time when sacrifices of children were commonplace. So the story, he says, is about a specific community trying to stop the practice of sacrificing its children! "A wonderful story," he said, over and over!

EL: What this man doesn't realize is that the myth addresses issues inside himself, issues that confront every man and father: the homicidal urges of the father, the eternal issues of power and authority, of faith and submission to the *diktat* of the divine.

SL: Another scholar, the son of a famous New York psychoanalyst, was a good friend of mine. He'd tell me of the fratricidal disputes between his father and analysts of other schools. "It's like three denominations at war with each other," he'd say. "You would not believe the wars I've experienced in my home. It's like murder between religious denominations!" It's the same in academia. There's always a "church," or a school, whose theory or dogma has to be upheld.

AM: What was your actual experience of Temple? How did you manage to bring this work into the classroom?

SL: It was a miracle, for which I thank my department. There were three or four colleagues who thought I had lost it; but there were three or four others who supported me very much. What really helped launch the work, Tony, was the Temple University Center City campus, the downtown "satellite" known as TUCC. With its evening classes and marginal academic audience, TUCC drew people who were not afraid to enter this hermeneutic.

These people, in general, were much more mature than full-time college students in their twenties. We had psychiatrists, secretaries, a black sheriff, Jewish dancers, a Muslim playwright, ministers, professors from New York and rural and suburban Philadelphia and New Jersey, all coming to Philadelphia to take these courses. We were blessed with great participants. These students were people who led a full life, and were genuinely interested in what we did.

And they were not afraid to take chances, to use the mythic path for their own. Once I had two bright and creative people in class, a psychiatrist whose marriage was breaking up, and a woman who was just divorced from a very troubled husband. I could hardly believe my eyes when I saw that they were choosing to play *Orpheus and Eurydice*: I knew of their tragic predicament. They played a stunning scene of loss and wept openly. Years later students would mention to me the impact of that evening. And time and again I've been told how the TUCC experience was the most important academic stage in the lives of many students.

On the whole, I think my department was ultimately extremely helpful. They not only tolerated my work, they also gave me a beautiful and genuinely loving retirement party. So on one level, they did appreciate me. But of course you cannot help, in this work, to threaten the hell out of some academics, the way you threaten the hell out of some churches. It did become difficult for me to attend academic meetings, especially national conventions, where the intellectual defenses were intolerable for me. Where people tried to stab each other to death with quotes. Exactly like Abraham did.

EL: It is excruciating to be in a public situation that so resembles a dysfunctional family, where the unwritten rules say that reality is not to be acknowledged. In such a setting people always act out unconsciously the histories and conflicts of their own personal families, and that's what makes the experience so painful. In such a meeting, everyone is terrified of their own demons.

AM: Evelyn, was there anything similar among your professional affiliations?

EL: Actually, I was fortunate. I worked in an agency in New York, where I used the mimetic process as a part of training in family therapy, and in supervision. I used it with sexually and physically abused young children. Unlike Sam I had a lot of support from my colleagues, who were often risk-takers. I also worked in a private hospital, where the staff asked me to do the process with them, and even the medical director played with us. I've presented *mimesis* at national conferences, to fairly large audiences, and have enjoyed wonderful responses from psychiatrists and psychologists who connect with the process in a personal way, and are fascinated by the power, safety and depth of it. So I've been very fortunate to have my professional colleagues be so supportive.

AM: How did your own personal histories come to bear on the creation of *mimesis*?

SL: I could talk for two hours, Tony, because there is no doubt that my own family history played an immense role. I come out of "clean Switzerland," i.e., World War II, a family that had its Abraham and Isaac, its Cain and Abel, its Adam and Eve–*after* the Fall, that is! The Swiss instituted the stamp for the Jews, the J, in their passports, so that Jews could be easily recognized and turned back at the border. What a heritage I carry on my shoulders. I can still get irrationally enraged about it. I disassociate when I think about Nazism. And the Swiss have acted as if their hands were clean. That lie makes it harder.

I went to the university, where I had brilliant teachers like Jung, Jaspers, and Baumgartner. But I also was imprisoned there by a painful theological unreality. For years and years and years I was interested in theory, in drama, in theater. I was a pianist, a poet and an academic, and did not know what to do with all of this. I had great difficulty with relationships. I had a marriage break up. I went into therapy. There were two sides to my life, the private and the public. I had been caught between the academy and art, between theology and play. I've had a rich academic career, but I also had to break with it, to let it go. And I had psychic experiences that did not fit into the academic models. All this had been hammering at me for decades.

So *mimesis*, for me, is a way to integrate numerous aspects of my own life, and to allow them to coexist. I'm sure it's a way to integrate, on one level, art and the academy. And it finally allowed me to get in touch with my darkness. Previously I had tried various therapeutic interventions. Some of them were quite helpful, some were not. But my first encounter with this field came when I heard C. G. Jung in Basel. I was a 22-year-old student, and I still see him right in front of me.

AM: Paul Tillich was also an influence, if I remember correctly.

SL: Tillich was a great influence in my life. I really appreciated him. I still own an academic cap-and-hood of Tillich's! A kind of transitional gift!

AM: Still I get the sense that even you, Sam, were closeted in the ivory tower, an d in the traditions of the academy, for a long time.

SL: Absolutely.

AM: What made you feel the need to break out?

SL: That's an interesting question. Why did I need to break out? A professor in Basel once put me down in a vicious way, saying, "We in the university think that it's more important for you to play piano, than to read our texts." In a strange way, he was right! He disapproved, but he was on to something.

On one side, I must have had, like every theologian in his career, the illusion that religion is either believing or thinking about Luther, the New Testament, salvation or eternal life. But I also must have known, early on, that the essence of the Reformation, of the Gospels, wasn't in books or in the lectures of professors. And I expressed this by going to museums, by writing poetry. Even early on, when I finished my first academic book, I ended it with a poem. So I must have felt a need to go somewhere else, in a different direction. I finally found a way to break out.

One psychiatrist said to me in a session, "I think you're struggling with your father and your mother, like all of us, but you also take on what your church, culture and history have been battling with for centuries." I inherited this penchant for rationalism; I had contempt for precisely this reason. I struggled with enormous conflicts in my childhood, but what saved me in my teenage years was music. I used to play piano for hours on end. It was the only way to survive my family, the war, the threat of Nazi Germany hanging over my adolescence.

AM: Evelyn?

EL: I grew up in poverty, in a very dysfunctional family. There was a lot of abuse . . . I too remember going into music and art, being absorbed by pictures that were hung on the wall, as a way of handling the pain I felt. I found that I understood metaphor even as a very young child, and learned early on that when people were speaking, often they meant something other than what they were saying. I also found an immense nourishment and comfort, even in pain, when I was in touch with what was real. I loved anthropology and philosophy, but when I decided to do clinical psychology, I found that I was gifted in working with many patients because of my sensitivity to metaphor, to nuance and language.

And that was something that came out of my own pain and struggle, something that had been healing. Literature and art kept me alive as a child, and later as a teenager. I learned to play with language, to hear that what we're doing right now is not what we're doing right now. And I learned to distinguish between when I need to tune into that other level of communication, and when to let it simply happen.

There's a kind of dialectic at play. Theodor Reik puts it wonderfully when he says that we should listen consciously when we hear dissonance in the music; when it's harmony we can simply be in the music. So I developed a respect for this depth of reality, for these often painful depths. Because when you're dealing with what you've always defended against, there's an immense nourishment, and a deep peace. And to share that communally, to share it with others and to grieve with others, gives incredible strength.

AM: "Dialectic" is another key term for both of you: for example, between conscious and unconscious or, as you put it Evelyn, between different levels of reality. Can you elaborate on the concept, and its importance for you?

SL: I give you a crucial scene in my biography. Sometimes these things are best told through stories and images. It was about 1943 or '44 in Basel, the Americans were flying over the city to bomb Germany. It was terrifying. There were 500 bombers at 8 o'clock, night after night, and they came back at 3 o'clock in the morning. Nuremberg gone, München gone, Ulm gone. City after city, gone, just like that. That was my teenage experience.

And so I went to a concert one night, and the planes came back. All the streetcars used blue lights, very dim blue lights; we even had to ride our bicycles with blue lights. The whole city had to be dark. I was waiting that night to take a streetcar home, it was ten o'clock, and for some reason the streetcar didn't come. People imagined there'd been an accident, as the station on Aeschenplatz got more and more jammed with the crowd waiting. There was a frightening tension in the air, although the bombers had moved on. Although we knew they wouldn't bomb Basel, they did occasionally drop a bomb by mistake. Things were tense, waiting in that square for a streetcar for an hour.

Now there was a man in the crowd, a professor of mathematics in Basel, who suddenly yelled at the top of his lungs, in the regional dialect: "The stupid assholes! They don't know that the world is one! It's all mathematical! Everything is clear mathematical unity! The world is one!!"

Can you imagine? In the middle of that tension? That man yelled at us, and amidst the madness of war gave a sermon on the clarity of mathematics. It was a *mimesis*. I had forgotten that story, it only came back to me forty years later, in a meditation of a *mimesis* play. And I again felt his fear permeate his body and mine. That's true *memoria*. "Memoria" of the unconscious. That I would bring up the memory of that story after forty years, shows just how deep the unconscious goes. And that's what takes place in *mimesis*. Something in us is containing dark memory, and the mimetic play is a way of seeking an access to that memory, to not-quite erased levels of experience. The professor communicated terror, and I conjured up that terror decades later.

EL: I think that experientially we have a sense of continuity, a sense of "self," but I think the majority of our experience and knowing is unconscious. We don't understand how to access it, how it's triggered, or resonates with things. I think also that Jung's sense of a universal or transpersonal unconscious is something that my personal experience would support. I've had patients dream details of my life to which they have no access. I do believe, then, that there is another level of connectedness between human beings: a level that's unconscious, and that breaks through to consciousness sometimes spontaneously, but mostly in dreams or in creative moments. I think that most of who and what we are unfolds on another level. You can call it the unconscious, if you like, whose deeper workings are dialectical, weaving in-and-out between at least two levels.

SL: Eight years ago, I began to keep a detailed record of the paranormal manifestations in our work, because some day we'd like to write a book on the subject. So far, we've already collected over one hundred pages of stunning documentation. Along these lines, we just recently gave a lecture in Stuttgart on synchronicity and healing. Americans call these phenomena "psychic"; the Indians, "esoteric" . . . In either case, what we're dealing with is a level of communication, of continuity, which is neither spatial nor temporal.

AM: Somehow *mimesis* seems always to tap into these realities. . . .

EL: My experience has been that when you're in touch with this depth, there are spontaneous synchronicities, psychic connections, "knowings" that come from nowhere. There are many people, both in and outside of academia, who write about these phenomena, and this depth. Mircea Eliade is one. Personally, I don't know what it is; I just know that I experience it. I'll give you an example.

I was finishing my clinical training. I was an extern, and I had as a patient a mildly retarded woman who had been sexually abused. Her language was very limited and the content repetitious. In the course of a session my mind drifted, and I wondered to myself: "Have I paid my car insurance?" She became quiet, looked at me and asked: "Have you paid your car insurance?" I just about fell off my seat! I've had many experiences with patients like that.

I was at Haverford State Hospital in Pennsylvania, working with a man who didn't speak, who had been hospitalized for fifteen years and who, after a long period of time was barely able to make eye contact with me. I had been ill and away for two weeks when, upon returning, he ran up to me and took my hand and said: "I thought the underground was wiped out." And I spontaneously said my first association: "Except for Albert Camus." He smiled and said: "You've read *The Rebel*? That's my favorite book!" And I felt like I had flipped into another dimension. Here's a man, in rags, chronic schizophrenic, hospitalized fifteen years, discussing Camus and Plato with me. He was a graduate student in philosophy when he had his breakdown. And, where did Camus come from in me? I mean, I said to him, "except for Albert Camus," and he replies, "yes, that's my favorite philosopher!" So, yes, I've had many of these experiences; and I think it's that freedom to go back and forth into the unconscious, and to be able to re-emerge from it, that was very healing for that man. Thanks to that breakthrough, to that connection, he began to speak and make contact again.

AM: How does *mimesis* facilitate this? You've both told me of similar stories growing out of your groups.

SL: When you really enter the darkness, when you really know these hidden elements of your life, of your personality and your being, something opens up. Isaac Bentov suggested that there is, in moments of meditation, an entry into a realm of reality that arrests time and space. We participate in different experiences.

It's a constant theme in Rilke's poetry, which is why we so often quote him. There is a different level of reality which goes against surface perceptions, against what we call "everyday reality." When you open up that level, you free yourself. So often people come to a workshop and say they felt compelled to play a role; they knew that an insight, or transformation, was beckoning to them. In *mimesis* something opens up, the way it does in poetry, in therapy, in cabalistic play.

EL: One of the classic stories, from the documentation Sam mentioned, happened in Germany. We were there in a monastery, which the monks had let us use, playing Abraham and Isaac in a closed room. Just as a Swiss psychiatrist picked up his Swiss pocket knife, as Abraham, to symbolically sacrifice his son, at that very moment an old monk walked in and said: "Does someone in this room need my help?"

He had no way of knowing what we were playing. He simply felt, in his meditation, that someone, like Isaac, needed to be rescued; and he came like the angel, offering his assistance just at the moment when the psychiatrist had picked up the knife! We have many such experiences, where events take place that we can't explain. And on this one occasion, it was immensely powerful for the group, of course, that the intervention came from outside.

AM: As a clinician, I've often wondered what happens to these people after a group or workshop of yours? What with the limited time frame of the *mimesis* experience (three to six hours, sometimes condensed into a single session, other times in the context of groups lasting from three to fifteen weeks) what happens to participants who have these fierce insights? After the group dissolves, especially after the intensive, single evening sessions, how do people work with and "through" the insights achieved?

EL: The feedback I've gotten suggests that our use of role play, of dramatic structure, helps. People will come a year later and say, "I've been working with the Isaac in me all year." It's a person's ability to separate out that single element of his or her personality, the ability to look at "the Isaac in me," that allows the rest of the personality to go about its daily functioning. I have not heard from any participant disintegrating or feeling dysfunctional. To the contrary, reports have always been of the type: "It was so fascinating to learn about myself, and to be able to go back and access those newly uncovered parts of self."

SL: Some people, I'm sure, leave our workshops and don't get a lot out of them. But that's life. The greater danger would be if we thought *mimesis* could save the world. It can't. But people do come back, and often.

We had a woman once in a workshop in Germany, who had been sexually abused. She was able through the play to integrate feelings, thoughts, body memories. She was so helped by the experience that she comes back to workshop after workshop. And now we do supervision with her. She teaches at a university in Germany, and she now leads *mimesis* groups.

This weekend we have a group, and some of the people will have been working with us for ten years. There are even four or five medical doctors in that group! So you see, Tony, some people back off, some remain defended, but many others do come back.

AM: Have you, however, either individually or together, envisioned a "working-through" process that can grow out from *mimesis*?

EL: We've developed that over time. We now do what we call "training groups," which are not workshops but ongoing groups. These reflect a group therapy format, where people can really have consistent contact not only with us but with the group. There is enough time to work through issues. So it's not a single experience. We do cycles of six weeks, but then the cycles repeat.

And of course we've also directed many people to individual therapy. A memory of sexual abuse will surface, or an issue will come into focus, and we send people to a good therapist. That usually works well, because the *mimesis* experience, or insight, is generally a signal that the person is ready, and now has the motivation for treatment.

AM: You've frequently mentioned ritual and its mimetic functions. How does ritual help structure experience and meaning in your work?

SL: *Mimesis* itself is a ritual. It's a ritual because it has a beginning, a middle and an end. It has form. At times we use music, we use gesture . . . and it always takes place in a circle . . . We use spatial structures. The ritual is repetition. Even children create rituals. I noticed, when Evelyn described her work with children, that a child has a very innate way to create ritual.

EL: Ritual is the symbolic expression of a very profound inner experience. Play that repeats scenes and themes becomes ritualistic. A child repeats its repetition, and in so doing creates a process that often leads to transformation of the original conflicts. Ritual binds the anxiety while opening up the conflicts.When ritual loses its spontaneous element, it becomes dead. Church rituals can be one of the most exciting and, at the same time, one of the most deadly things imaginable. It's amazing. So we try to create new rituals . . . spontaneously. And to do so we always go back to the story. The playing of myth always involves ritual.

SL: The great rituals in the history of religion always go back to the myth: to the seasons, to the great circle, the cycles of great tales. And ritual always involves the body. In *mimesis*, we don't do a lot of body work, but it's amazing to witness the ways in which people talk, the way they bend, the way they gesture and use their hands. In the university I had to be careful, because in that setting I was already as far out as I could be. So there I did not develop the ritualistic aspect, as we do in our workshops and training groups. At moments what we do is very much group therapy, when we simply sit and talk. At other times we work with the expressions of the body, with what people do with their hands, or their energy. I realize that this talk of energy may seem strange, but one of Jung's former students, Esther Harding, wrote a book on energy, on psychic energy. There is a psychic energy, and it is integrally related to the body. And specific myths evoke specific energies.

AM: Do you sense that ritual is what's been lost in much of contemporary life?

EL: For me ritual is a big part of creating safety. Therapy, even traditional psychotherapy, is a ritual: how we greet patients, how we interact with them, how we sit, how we part at the end of a session, all make for a predictable reality. Ritual gives comfort and creates a sense of trust. Where we have anxiety about loss, or about new contact, we use ritual to bind that anxiety.

We're not aware that most of the rituals we perform are so much a part of our routine. But to create ritual, to take myth and allow yourself to spontaneously create ritual to embody that myth, and then to learn how to use ritual to transform energy, that's what religion is in part . . . It's hard to think or talk in these terms, but I think a lot of religious practice, particularly in the East, has to do with using ritual as a means of transforming energy, and of using that energy for healing.

AM: I usually think of ritual as an integral part of a liturgy, and as a means of fostering community. Does it have similar functions in your work?

SL: As an answer to your question, I'll give an example. We celebrated a wedding recently as a mimetic play. The wedding is a ritual, and it deals with fear, and the hope of co-relationship, and with all the stuff two people bring to it. Every wedding does. Well, one of the stories we play is the wedding at Cana, from the Gospel of John. It's a tremendously profound story. It's a story about a wedding feast, to which Jesus brings his mother–quite a strange thing in itself. And the wine runs out, and the mother says to the servant in charge of the wine: "Look at him, and listen to what he tells you to do." And Jesus gets very angry, and basically says "shut up!" to his mother. . . .

EL: "Who are you to me?" he says.

SL: Exactly! "Who are you? What's going on between you and me?" And out of that comes a transformation, and the water turns into wine. Now, that's a marvelous story! It's one of our major myths of wedding, because you only have intimacy in a relationship if you really break with the parents. And that's what Jesus is doing in the story when he gets angry: he breaks with his mother, he begins to separate from her.

In *mimesis* we take the story line and we recreate the setting, we recreate the ritual. We might actually have a feast, and the wine does run out . . . But you always have this tension played out between mother and son, and the son separates. Psychologically, it is out of this separation that the new wine comes, the wine of relationship and marriage.

There's also a very real, social dimension to all this. For what is marriage about, what is human relationship about? The ritual isn't only in the ceremony: you develop it step by step, over time. *Mimesis* can provide an inkling, a glimpse into all this. Out of our tale we create a ritual which reflects a dynamic of human society; and which in this case points to the crucial moment, to the inner reality, of separation from one's parents. When and if this separation comes, it is a miracle, and truly makes possible the creation of a new family.

EL: You asked about the relationship between liturgy, ritual and community. Theodor Reik said a wonderful thing about unconscious speaking to unconscious through art. When we speak poetry, or myth, the communication goes from unconscious to unconscious; we don't have to understand it. I think the ritual in group process creates safety, and allows people to really enter this "unconscious" community.

Winnicott talks about how, in the process of the therapist just being with a child and observing it play, the child internalizes this "Other." Along these lines, a lot of healing, I believe, happens without verbal interaction. The presence of others *being with* and containing experience is internalized as a community; and without that community, without the sharing it involves, I think healing is impossible. Whether it's the community of a one-to-one therapeutic relationship, or the larger community of family and society that we find symbolized in groups: without that experience, there is no healing. Simply sharing fear and pain and insight and joy is transformative, and without the Other it's not possible.

SL: Rituals, like the Sufi walkaround for instance, really hold the "working-through" process. When you have a safe ritual, you can allow yourself to see things differently, and work them through.

AM: Several times, you've used the term "structure." What do you mean by "creating a structure"?

EL: When people are asked to enter their own underworld, the realm of Persephone, the midnight kingdom of the dark and of naked Ereshkigal, Inanna's sister, they need to feel absolutely safe.

They cannot be left alone with their fear, their uncertainty and the dim, unexpressed knowledge of their own pain. So you have to create a ritual that can hold their experience.

SL: For instance, the Eucharist of the Christian church is a ritual that deals with a grave task, the death of the somatized God. This is my body. This is my blood. The traditional worshiper going to church thinks it is normal liturgical language. It is not. It is language about death, about giving up one's life, about the proximity of death and life.

EL: So the ritual makes it acceptable. You can deal with death if it's contained in symbolic language and acted out in ritualistic form. You are not left alone, you are carried by your community. Our ritual is not the church's ritual, of course, it is not the words of the prayer book; but with many religions of the world, with drama and secular parallels, it attempts to create order. You can proceed with it on your journey. It is all right this way.

AM: What do you need to do for such safety?

EL: To begin with, one person, two persons who are absolutely there for you. Who will not leave you in your pain. That is why group leadership is so basic to our process. At the moment of chaos and loss you stay with each participant and facilitate their being there for one another. It takes training, it takes experience to be able to do so. There is always the temptation to become too active in moments of pain. To give answers, be directive, to tell people what to do. In the worst scenario, to say: "It's not as bad as you think! There is hope!" Such responses destroy safety, they are the denial of hope.

SL: When Virgil was with Dante in the Inferno, he never said: "Don't worry! It's not that bad!"

EL: He stayed with him, he strengthened him, he did not leave him. But it's trickier than it sounds. Emotional abandonment can be quite subtle.

SL: I tell you a story. An extreme story, to be sure, it does not need to be played out on this level of intensity all the time–though it does frequently happen this way.

There was this woman, originally from Eastern Europe, who participated in our work for the first time and decided to play Cassandra. What does it take, for a person, to become Cassandra? The psychic woman who foresees her own tragedy, who ends her life as the lover of the victor of Troy, murdered by his enraged wife, Queen Clytemnestra . . . We had three people playing the scene. Three adults playing four-year old children on a playground. How does the sensitive, troubled one become Cassandra? The woman replayed her childhood; her two playmates were quite nasty to her. They laughed at that intractable girl. They began to tease her.

So one of the "nasty" children, a Basel psychiatrist, teased Cassandra. "You're no good! Your dad is no good! My dad is better than yours!" Cassandra began to cry. She cried and cried and cried. She was in my arms for perhaps half an hour crying.

We discussed the play afterwards, and the woman Cassandra, a talented artist, shared her memories and emotional reactions. Her father, a railroad engineer, had driven trains to Auschwitz. Her mother had worn the fur coat of a Belgian woman gassed in the ovens. The scene had brought back her childhood pain. These experiences were part of her becoming Cassandra. She had indeed been Cassandra in her life.

EL: What makes that scene safe? *That she was not left alone.* That in the midst of recalling the terror of her childhood with a destroyed, alcoholic father, she had people who would go the way with her, as she went it a second time. She felt safe recalling that story because she was held, literally and figuratively, and not abandoned.

SL: Afterwards a professional who had participated in the play asked me, almost in fear: "How did you dare play this? Were you not afraid?" I was not. It felt absolutely safe. I trusted her intuitive sense that this was her moment to remember and share.

EL: We work hard to see that the individual's defenses are not overwhelmed, but that the participants themselves can decide when it's right to open up to new awareness. Sometimes as a group leader you sit on the edge of your seat, deciding when and when not to intervene.

SL: The Cassandra in question returned many times more. We played many more scenes, in the years to come, coming to terms with a tragic childhood.

EL: Another thing that helps is that we play in a circle. The circle has an order. It holds, it creates trust. The circle is the alternative to the lectern, to the "chair" or pulpit. Of course there is authority, responsibility. Sam used his role, his authority, when he held that precious person in his arms. We try very hard not to abuse our position of authority, to use it for purposes of narcissism, of self-gratification. Our authority can be challenged, given up, surrendered.

SL: The person who leads the group is allowed to cry. To be sad. That too is part of the structure: that the pain is acknowledged by the leadership. If we cannot acknowledge the pain in ourselves, the play is not believable.

EL: Of course some cannot tolerate the pain, but they too are supported. Their defenses are shored up. They are helped to distance. It's a dance of opening and closing, each group and each person has its own rhythm.

SL: And structure is present already in the order of myth. The structure lies in the language of myth, but not merely in its language; in its imagery, but not merely there. It lies in the quality and specific power of mythic imagination. Medea and Jason is perhaps the worst love story, or not-love story, of antiquity, as told by Euripides. The mythic structure in Medea holds us: this is part of the darkness of our planet, or our history. People do awful things to each other. The loneliness and pain, the rage and fear are beyond comprehension.

EL: When this is expressed in myth, it touches us all, and is part of all of us. Hence it strengthens us. The pain is never merely my own. Death is not merely my own.

SL: And the ritual provides structure. There is an opening to it all. There is a closing. The ritual can be broken. It can be retold, rewritten. Chaos is allowed, change is allowed. Even chaos has an aesthetic power.

AM: One aspect of your work, of which I've only learned today, involves your efforts with underprivileged youth. Can you talk about that?

EL: We've worked with adjudicated youth, and homeless, acting-out, inner-city black teens. I've worked in Coney Island with pre-schoolers who were abused. These are kids who will not talk to a social worker, and for whom the normal therapeutic approaches are bankrupt. They can't sit in a seat. But when you give them the opportunity to play a role, it's so incredibly pleasing to them.

We've played Abraham and Isaac, which is an abuse story, and these kids will sit for two hours afterwards and talk about the abuse in their families. They'll ask questions like, "Why did God let that happen to me? what does it mean? why didn't I get rescued?" From there, then, they can and often do go to the social worker, and really engage in therapy for the first time.

SL: Those kids are tough. And they all want to play God. And God is always played as the white policeman, or the judge. They love to play God; and they'll play the most vicious God you can imagine. It's a tragic reality they know all-too-well.

EL: I've taken certain stories and transformed or adapted them as part of the therapeutic process with groups. If we play the good Samaritan, for instance, it's not the Samaritan's role that we privilege, but the priests and the pharisees who walk by and let the person on the road suffer. And it is so cathartic for these kids. They play the parole officer, they play a teacher at school, they play the social worker, and they laugh and cry . . . Then we all ask together: "What would *really* help this person who's hurt? What does he or she need? How can we be the Samaritan?"

Their insights then go directly to what *they* need: what they need to be safe, what they need to trust, learning all the while that they can trust and be safe with each other; that their suffering and their common experience has given them a bridge to connect with each other, and a sensitivity to what is needed to be emotionally empowered.

With inner-city kids, we've also played stories like Hansel and Gretel. These are safe ways to bring up very, very painful themes that these kids normally are unwilling to touch, like abandonment, or uncaring parents: themes which, dealt with in more traditional ways, usually prompt a lot of aggression as a defense against the real deep pain these children feel. We've seen young people able to cry together, able to share their own stories, of homelessness and abandonment.

A lot of times, with black inner-city kids, we did biblical stories, because some grandmother or aunt or other relative knew the Bible; and it helped these kids feel incredibly validated to see that their story had actually been written. "My story's in the Bible," they'd often say . . . and it was for them an incredible opening . . . To sense, somehow, that "my experience is bigger than my experience . . . " To feel that there was something intrinsically valuable about them . . . "As painful and as hard as this is, I'm important, and it has a reason. . . . "

SL: I learned a great deal from that, Tony, because some Old Testament scholars will tell you that playing Abraham and Isaac has nothing to do with us today. But these black kids know differently. Abraham and Isaac is their story; they've all been Isaac . . . all of them, and they know it. So, in a sense, they know more than we did when we thought we did "research."

EL: We played Abraham and Isaac once, and I'll never forget the words of one boy: "But, God can't do that, that's blood . . . that's a father and a son. Blood don't kill blood." And then he said: "This God needs a social worker; is he on drugs?" And it was so powerful, and so true. These kids took risks no theologian would take.

SL: We learned a lot. We only wish we could have done more.

EL: I remember playing with 4-year-old children, and asking them to make up their stories. One was that the baby food has glass in it, and that we have to get the glass out of our food because it's killing the children. The stories that these poor, hungry, abused kids made up and played were so often filled with anguish, and yet so caring. We had one little boy who was unable to speak, and could only sing. The rest of the children said that singing was important, and their group needed a singer; so they gave him the role as the group's singer. I mean, the kids were so immensely loving with one another. Kids who were very aggressive, very violent were immensely therapeutic with each other when given a frame within which to express their predicament and work towards resolution.

AM: There's another question I have about the process, in light of the postmodern idea of "multiple selves," or the less controversial concept of internalized objects and object relations. How does a participant come to identify with only one mythic character? Isn't it likely, given the range and force of myth, that more than one character in a story might resonate within a person?

EL: We often do role-reversals, so that a person who has played the rebel child then gets to play the good child. Or, if someone's played Abraham, taking his son to be sacrificed, we flip the roles so that the same person plays Isaac. So we do give the opportunity for people to play multiple roles, to see how the different roles interact, and to find and identify other parts of themselves. The very notion, and persistence, of introjects points to the fact that we all have all the roles in us: so that we don't define ourselves only as "the victim," but allow ourselves to know and own the sadist within as well. And when this is done in play, and often with humor, it is a safe kind of recognition that takes place.

SL: That gets to heart of any good therapy. Cain on one level is also Abel, and Abel is Cain. The roles get switched, they get reversed within oneself. In this regard, I want to tell a story, one that you yourself were part of, Tony. There was an evening when we played the myth of Inanna. You played Inanna's father, the father who could not bless his daughter. The process was a painful one for you, and must have summoned so many of your own demons. Well, like I said, sometimes we reverse the story, and play its opposite. It's another way of getting to the core of the myth and its meaning.

There was another time, in my TUCC course, when I'd decided to risk an intervention, and play the "dark mirror"–the inverse of a myth. So I recounted a story of Evelyn's.

EL: There was a patient of mine, from New York, who was a delightful but quite troubled woman. She had never separated from her family of origin, or perhaps one could say they never allowed her to separate. Each time she tried to establish herself in her own life, often through a relationship, her father would threaten to "have a heart attack" if she left. Only this wasn't the usual cliché. He really did end up in intensive care each time she tried to leave. And each time she fell into a depression and attempted suicide. With therapy the woman's life began to improve. Things were saner. In the beginning it was rough, especially since her parents had opposed and muddied every step towards change. But step by step the woman grew stronger. She found a job, and also met a man, a good man who loved her a great deal. After months of discussion and much growth, the woman decided to marry. I warned her, meanwhile, that her family might not tolerate this latest development. That in all likelihood, they'd oppose and fight it! Which is exactly what happened. . . .

SL: One night Evelyn and I were home having dinner, when the phone rang in our kitchen. I immediately recognized the woman's voice, and passed the phone to Evelyn. What I overheard was fascinating: "That's incredible! But of course I'll support you! You're absolutely right! Go for the wedding! You do have the right to your own life! I'll see you tomorrow."

EL: That afternoon, the woman's father had gone to her house and announced he'd been diagnosed with cancer. He was saying in a way: "If my daughter leaves, I'll punish her still. Even at the cost of my own life!" Perhaps he really couldn't tolerate losing her. I supported the woman in her intention to marry. And the father did not prevail, he did not succeed in destroying the daughter. Two months later, she was married. Three months later, the father died.

SL: I'm sure you see the connections with Inanna, whose father sends demons to drag her back when she tries to leave him. The night after, in another class, we changed the story line a bit, to fit the real-life story of Evelyn's patient. And as often happens the drama was intense, at times even violent. The people in the class were intensely divided; some were utterly shocked: "We will never allow a wedding feast!" For these students, it seemed, the father was more important than the daughter. But a greater number supported the idea: "The wedding will take place! We have a right to live our lives!"

At the end of classes, I'd ask my students to turn in a journal where they've recorded their impressions and reactions to the *Mimesis* semester. One student, a dancer, wrote something very important about the class on Inanna. She began with the premise that her parents weren't dead, and that there was no cancer in her family. But in every other respect, the brutal atmosphere of oppression, manipulation and emotional control was the same in her family as it was in that of Evelyn's patient.

The student had no independence, no life of her own; she was always being controlled, every day, via countless phone calls, endless tears, and the weight of pain and suffering. The student wrote that our class on Inanna had uplifted and excited her: "I couldn't fall asleep until five the next morning!" Your own drama, Tony, and of the Inanna from New York, whose father would not bless her, allowed the student to come to grips with the entanglements of her own family. The inverse of the myth, derived from the account of an actual and contemporary psychotherapy, was gut-wrenching but healing nevertheless. The student ended by thanking me for providing her with a new and important "vista" onto her life. She had begun to explore the self.

EL: I had many patients play an abusive father: women, for example, who were abused. It wasn't rare that one would say: "Oh my God, I never understood what was going on inside him; I never before understood his predicament. Now I do." Or, "I never knew why my mother was so passive. But playing the role, I understand her now." Because those introjected parts of self are activated, the process allows the person to embody them, and to know the introjects experientially, within themselves.

AM: And yet, from my own limited experience with *mimesis*, I'm always amazed by how a person feels called by, or ticketed for a specific role.

SL: People are often "called." They get drawn to the darkest, the most hidden side of their own personality, and that's what they play out.

EL: The word "dark," here, is not meant in a judgmental sense. It doesn't refer to evil, or to what's bad . . . but has more to do with a sense of hiddenness . . .

SL: . . . of pain . . .

EL: . . . and what's unknown.

SL: The unknown, when it opens up, is truly beautiful. When you watch people begin to struggle with different parts of the self, it can be inspiring. There is so much courage. And you see Abel come to grips with Cain, and you see Cain realize that to kill Abel is also to kill a part of oneself. These struggles are in me, and in all of us. What we do is to help them develop, in safety . . .

EL: . . . so that these roles become markers for moments of our own experience, as well as recognized parts of self. The myths really become ways through which we organize our own knowing of ourselves. Eliade talks about a mythic shock, about a quality of transformative experience generated outside of normal time-space contexts. You know when you're in it, and so does the group. A group will shift into that moment together, and somehow be transformed. In *mimesis* it happens all the time. It's a kind of moment that energizes, that gives meaning and, at a very deep level, organizes experience.

AM: Amidst all the shocks, what happens to you two as group leaders?

EL: I'm a human being too. Sometimes a part of me says: "Oh, I'm tired, why did I have to come here tonight? . . . " On another level, it's an immense grace to be able to receive and share with other people the depths of which we've spoken. To be able to be that honest and open, there's an aesthetic to it. I believe that reality is basically an aesthetic, and that it's healing and nourishing to be able to experience it fully, even when it is deeply painful. There's an immense beauty to such moments of honesty.

SL: Time and time again, Tony, despite our own ambivalence about doing another evening of workshops or training sessions, we come out of it, and are refreshed, alive . . . You are filled with life through contacting life.

AM: And yet, in your positions as group leaders, isn't there the inherent risk that you yourselves might be defended against what the other participants evoke and distill?

EL: I don't think the group can reach the depths unless we can go there. I really do believe that. Take the emotions, for instance: if a therapist can access a level or a depth of emotion within themselves, it's like lighting a fire in the patient. Through his own ability to access an emotion, an empathic therapist can hand back to a patient the patient's own experience. And it works that way in a group as well. If we were somehow blocked, I think the group would also be blocked.

SL: We have first to be conscious of our own stuff. That has to be worked and played through first. It's our responsibility, something very basic. Otherwise, how could we be strong enough to embody and carry the group's toxicity? How could we otherwise hold it? But let me conclude with one more story. It's as good a way as any to give a true sense of what we do, of what *mimesis* is all about. And it's as much Evelyn's tale as mine, for we were both in it.

A friend of ours, a therapist from the East Coast, works in a clinic for abused women. One Christmas, when together with her husband and two children she visited us in Yardley, she told us a story from her practice. There were two women whom she'd been seeing weekly. One was German, a woman who'd been mutilated in body and soul by two horrific, racist, sadistic parents. Her mother was a very angry woman; her father, an alcoholic, had been dead for a year. The other woman was Jewish, the daughter of a concentration camp survivor. Her father was a depressed man, a man crushed by life, out of work and joyless. Both women were twenty-eight years old, very ill, with no friends, and no partner. Our therapist friend would see them both on Tuesday evenings, back-to-back. The two women didn't know each other, and had never exchanged a word; they'd only brush each other's life in silence, every week, in the waiting room, as one exited the consulting room and the other prepared to enter.

The following semester, I invited our friend to my course at TUCC on "Religion, Myth and Healing," where she retold the story of her two patients. The model we were playing was a combination of two famous mythic traditions, "the Stations of the Cross," the Catholic ritual of going through stations on your way to death, and the legend of Jesus meeting the eternal Jew on his way to Golgotha. The meeting between the person in despair and the savior. Who is the savior, and who is the victim? I told the modern tale. Then two women in the class recreated the roles of our friend's patients. One woman was German, and chose to play the Jewish patient. The other was Jewish, and played the German patient. The evening was moving, as the two women met, but didn't speak. Still, they'd felt each other's presence, and became aware of each other. The scenes were real, a ritual, a truly profound pantomime.

Suddenly, the women began to speak. The drama intensified. Taking turns they presented each other with the story of their past, their families, their ancestors. Each told the story of her tragedy. The power of their encounter was immense. After the class the two students whose lives had been touched stayed around for an hour, and continued to talk. The German and the Jew.

Christmas, two years later. Our therapist friend was again our guest, and told us the next "station" in the story. After three years of therapy, the women began to change, and develop. One evening, the wounded German woman–who would occasionally have trouble breathing–had a crisis. Though her life had improved, on this one evening she couldn't breathe, and was rushed to the emergency room of the local hospital. And do you know who received her there? It was the Jewish woman, who regularly preceded her every Tuesday night! The Jewish woman, a nurse, welcomed and treated her German counterpart–her German "enemy." And the two women recognized each other, and gave birth to a miracle.

After the meeting in the hospital, the two women never again crossed paths without talking to one another. It is our therapist friend who waits for both in silence. The recognition that the drama prefigured in our class had become a reality in the lives of the two women. But the story isn't over. I was telling this story in another class, as an example of the impetus, the task of change. I was only telling the story, we weren't playing it out. Except that on this occasion, again years later, the German student who'd played the Jewish patient had just returned from Germany to complete her master's degree. After class one evening she told me of her life, of her mad, dishonest parents, corrupted by the false piety of so much German Protestantism. With no life of their own, the parents had abused their sons and daughters in the name of "parental" power and authority. Not only did the couple have no life–they had no "self." For their daughter, my student, playing, *being* the Jewish woman had helped her experience the tragedy of her own family.

EL: But there's still one "station" along this Via Crucis of which to tell. Last spring, Sam and I were teaching in Hamburg, when this same student visited us unexpectedly from Philadelphia. Her cousin, with whom she grew up very closely, like a precious sister, was dying. And even as she was dying, her own family, parents, aunts and uncles were forcing upon her their denial and emotional dishonesty, abusing her as they'd always done. With only a week left to live, the student told us, the young woman had mustered the strength to break with her sick family. I got to speak frequently with the woman, who in the months of agony surrounding her cousin's death furthered her own healing process, and became more and more conscious of her past. She'd speak of the two women from Brooklyn, of how privileged she felt to have participated in their healing encounter. In three months' time, she not only touched, but revived, the "self" her family had wounded. And you know, Tony, I don't think we exaggerate to call this a "miracle."

WORKS CITED

Camus, A. (1956). *The Rebel: An Essay on Man in Revolt* (tr. by A. Bower). New York, Knopf.

Feyerabend, P. (1975). *Against Method: Outline of an Anarchistic Theory of Knowledge*. Atlantic Highlands, NJ, Humanities Press.

Moreno, J. L. (1987). "The Theater of Spontaneity," in *The Essential Moreno* (ed. J. Fox). NY, Springer.

Goethe, J. W. von (1992). *Faust, a tragedy. Part 1* (tr. by M. Greenberg). New Haven, Yale University Press.

Winnicott, Donald W. (1971). *Playing and Reality*. London, Tavistock Publications.

Wolstein, D. and S. N. Kramer (1983). *Inanna, Queen of Heaven and Earth: Her Stories and Hymns from Sumer*. New York, Harper and Row.

SAMUEL AND EVELYN ROTHCHILD-LAEUCHLI: SELECTED BIBLIOGRAPHY

Books by Samuel Laeuchli

Jesus und der Teufel: Begegnung in der Wüste (Mit klinischen Beiträgen von Dr. Evelyn Rothchild-Laeuchli). (1992). Neukirchen, Neukirchener Verlag.

Die Bühne des Unheils. (1988). Stuttgart, Kreuz.

Das Spiel vor dem Dunklen Gott. (1987). Neukirchen, Neukirchener Verlag.

Religion and Art in Conflict. (1980). Philadelphia, Fortress Press.

Articles on *Mimesis*

Evelyn Laeuchli and Samuel Laeuchli. "Mimesis: Healing through Mythic Play," *Second Opinion*, 1994, 19:4.

Evelyn Laeuchli. "Lot's wife looks back: biblical stories as therapy and play," in Bjoern Krondorfer: *The Bible and the Body*. Philadelphia, Trinity Press, 1992.

Samuel Laeuchli. "The expulsion from the Garden and the hermeneutic of play," in Bjoern Krondorfer: *The Bible and the Body*. Philadelphia, Trinity Press, 1992.

Evelyn Laeuchli and Samuel Laeuchli. "Mimesis, the Healing Play of Myth," *Quadrant: The New York Journal of Analytical Psychology*, 1989, 22:2.

Samuel Laeuchli. "Orpheus and Eurydice: The Healing Dimension of Myth," *Listening*, 1987, 22:2.

Polly Young-Eisendrath

> You yourself are a conflict that rages in itself and against itself, in order to melt its incompatible substances . . . in the fire of suffering, and thus create the fixed and unalterable form which is the goal of life.
>
> –C. G. Jung

Polly Young-Eisendrath is an internationally recognized Jungian analyst and author. Formerly of Bryn Mawr College, she is a Research Psychologist and member of the Medical Staff at the Institute of Pennsylvania Hospital in Philadelphia, as well as in private practice in Vermont. As one might expect, a long list of publications and credits highlights her professional career. An incredibly prolific and tireless writer, Polly is also a sparkling theorist and a speaker of brilliant clarity. In fact, it was at a talk she gave years ago, at The C. G. Jung Society of Philadelphia, that I first heard her. Rarely had I been in the presence of anyone who combined such intellectual acuity with the eloquent courage of their ideas.

"Courage" is a word that our times may find outdated. Some may think it is relegated to an earlier period of this century's intellectual history, a term most readily associated with the likes and works of Paul Tillich, Rollo May, perhaps Albert Camus. And yet, in the few hours spent talking with Polly, it's a word that pushed itself into consciousness, and stuck. A self-professed Jungian, feminist, postmodernist, contructivist and student of Zen Buddhism, not only

[Haworth co-indexing entry note]: "Polly Young-Eisendrath." Co-published simultaneously in *The Psychotherapy Patient* (The Haworth Press, Inc.) Vol. 10, No. 1/2, 1997, pp. 189-225; and: *Elaborate Selves: Reflections and Reveries of Christopher Bollas, Michael Eigen, Polly Young-Eisendrath, Samuel and Evelyn Laeuchli and Marie Coleman Nelson* (ed: Anthony Molino) The Haworth Press, Inc., 1997, pp. 189-225. Single or multiple copies of this article are available from The Haworth Document Delivery Service [1-800-342-9678, 9:00 a.m. - 5:00 p.m. (EST). E-mail address: getinfo@haworth.com].

has Polly juggled all these hats in the face of more than one uncompromising orthodoxy; she's often done so while walking a tightrope, without ever compromising her personal, professional, and intellectual integrity. As she explained during our meetings, not without a touch of sadness: "It has been really uncomfortable to be a Jungian feminist, partly because I'm not well-received by either group. The Jungians are suspicious of my feminism, and the feminists are suspicious of my Jungianism. . . . " The tensions inherent in this kind of predicament are clear. In claiming adherents, ideologies can often take prisoners. And yet, with courage and the strength of her ideas, Polly remains freely loyal to both camps, ever-intent on the construction of bridges and syntheses that can help make sense of the postmodern complexities in which we live.

The following interview, which focuses primarily on themes developed in Polly's 1991 ***Jung's Self Psychology: A Constructivist Perspective****, took place over the course of two days, September 13 and October 11, 1994, at Philadelphia's Institute of Pennsylvania Hospital.*

AM: As a starting point I'd like to cite the title of a lecture of yours, which seems to encompass your clinical and research interests at this time: "Myth and Body: Pandora's Legacy in a Postmodern World."[1] What is your understanding of post-modernism as both a historical moment and cultural sensibility, and if there is such a thing as a "postmodern world," what distinguishes or characterizes a postmodern patient?

PYE: My understanding of post-modernism is that it's a critique of enlightenment philosophy. Whereas people had in earlier periods assumed enlightenment premises or taken them as reality or fact, post-modernism questions idealism, the idea that there are categories of the mind, or a kind of transcendent good, that are somehow given to us as scientific facts through the physical world. It's a critique of enlightenment ideas from the perspectives of both rationalism and of science. I also see it, in some ways, as a linguistic philosophy, a way of looking at language. I know that postmodernism extends to art and to many other fields but, in my view, the

1. Lecture first delivered October 1993 at Colorado College, Colorado Springs, CO.

questions and the concerns arise out of ideas and language. What post-modernism represents for me is a philosophy that's congruent with so many of my beliefs.

I think these beliefs were incipient in me before I could have really talked about them. They certainly led me to feminism, to a questioning of the sort of cultural truths I had inherited . . . Is there a postmodern patient? I think there is, though it's a very complicated issue. I would say the postmodern patient presents a kind of depression or despair that involves a questioning of the values and truths that have evolved into the central culture, the male culture, that has dominated our society. What I'm describing as a postmodern patient is the person who basically says: "I don't have a religious faith, I don't have any sense of spirituality, I can't really believe in rationality, and I don't believe in the received knowledge of my culture. So I have nothing to believe in; I'm really lost." I've seen that kind of patient among younger people, particularly college students. I've seen it among people who have actually studied post-modernism, who have been affected by multiculturalism, or even by popular culture. I'm thinking particularly of people who come to this point of despair through listening to a lot of contemporary music. The postmodern patient, then, is the sort of patient who despairs of ever having any kind of meaning system that allows for a base to one's existence.

AM: From a brief description of your lecture, being a Jungian analyst at this time in history is not particularly comfortable in most intellectual or psychological circles. Can you elaborate on this sense of discomfort? There seems to be an implicit tension between a Jungian *weltanschauung* and the kind of postmodern turn you've described. . . .

PYE: Most people who read and are interested in Jung, I believe, read him either as an idealist or as a realist. They believe that archetypes either refer to categories of the mind that are Kantian-like, eternal and extended over time, and through which we move as human beings; or, that archetypes have something to do with genetics and genetic patterns that shape human beings. Very few Jungians really understand that terms like *archetype, genetics, idealism* and so on are all human ideas. They are all aspects, expressions of the human community. They aren't real things. They aren't pointing us in some way to a transcendent truth in themselves. Most people who come to and use Jung's ideas believe that they're dealing with something that's eternal, than's transcendent, whose movements are like those of morphogenetic structures.

So, the Jungian position as it's received is essentially a kind of realism. It may be an idealist realism, but it's a realism. It's the idea that the "really real" lies outside of human interpretation. But as a post-modern constructivist, I cannot understand Jung's ideas that way, or I would simply not be a Jungian. What I've done is to take his ideas further, in the direction I think Jung was moving; but certainly when the world looks at me as a Jungian psychoanalyst, whether it's my Freudian colleagues or my colleagues in psychology, they assume that I believe in these kinds of universal categories that transcend human culture. Now those very categories also have been connected with a certain kind of racism and anti-semitism in Jung . . . So it's often uncomfortable for me to be a Jungian because I have to explain that I don't take this idea–of *archetype*, of the *collective unconscious* or whatever–to mean that we're talking about the "really real" that's transcended. Rather, I take the idea as a product of its time, but as an idea that's fertile, that moves forward, I think, with constructivism and postmodernism to something that's more interesting to me than the Kantian category is at this point in history.

AM: What would you say, then, distinguishes you as Jungian, given this radical interpretative break of yours?

PYE: What distinguishes me as a Jungian is that I believe that it's useful to theorize universals. In other words, I think that once you realize that this is all human interpretation, that we're not talking about *the* truth, then you have the question: "Is it possible to say anything about all human beings, or are human beings so thoroughly shaped by their local culture that you simply cannot?" Can I say anything about another person without making a really big mistake from the point of view of my own ethnocentrism? What I would say as a Jungian is that, yes, you can. . . .

My idea of an archetype refers to the human predisposition to form an image, a coherent image, in a highly charged emotional state, and it is these emotional states that all human beings experience that make up what's universal. And there's quite a lot of empirical work to support this view. Human emotions are universal, and they do predispose us to organize a particular kind of image; moreover, there are configurations of human relationship, using Bowlby's terms like attachment, loss and separation, that are also universal and predispose human beings towards certain archetypal images: images like "good mother/bad mother," "good father/bad father," "divine child/terrible child" and so on. I believe it's very useful to talk about universal images that transcend culture. I don't think I would be thinking that way were I not Jungian . . . I might, if I were a Freudian, say that the Oedipus complex is universal, but I happen to think it's dependent on a particular family configuration. In general, Freudians don't worry a lot about universals, though they often take them for granted . . . So what I think is particularly Jungian about me and my work is my concern for universals in the application of a developmental model. While Jung didn't have a very advanced developmental model, he certainly believed there were stages of life that were important, and that predisposed people, again, towards certain kinds of experience the world over.

AM: In your book *Jung's Self Psychology* you write that Jung believed that the subjective organization of self was motivated by an archetype. You then go on: "We simply mention here that *self* is a coherent expression of certain universal features of individuality that are connected with self-conscious emotions, i.e., pride, shame, guilt and envy." In light of what you just said, is there a reason why the universal features you cite as examples are limited primarily to emotions that are widely regarded as negative?

PYE: Let me back up and say a few things about the self first, and then go on to the issue about the emotions connected to the self. In his book *The Origins and History of Consciousness*, Erich Neumann talks about centroversion and the predisposition in the human personality to come up with a central organizing image. Because of the complexity of the human nervous system, and because we are such complex beings, it seems that we could not manage our experience without a central organizing image. This idea fits very well with a lot of research that's been done on the brain, and presented in works like Daniel Dennett's *Consciousness Explained.* Any number of theorists who are looking at consciousness would say that the sense of unity in the human being masks a fundamental diversity; that we have a way of presenting and explaining ourselves as though we were unities, although that's not what's going on from the point of view of the brain. There's just so much more diversity than we experience when we talk about "I," or of a unified sense of self. So, my sense is that the whole issue of the universality of self, of individual subjectivity, arises out of the complexity of our being, and is not contingent on self-conscious emotions. I would say self-conscious emotions are probably the first emergence of this property of being human, of having a self. What I consider to be the universal properties of self are what I call the "invariant principles" of agency, coherence, continuity and emotional arousal. What I mean is that in any individual subjectivity, in any culture, you'll find these features. The way language relates to those features is another issue. There are cultures, for example, where there are no personal pronouns; in which, if you weren't thinking about the idea that self is universal, you might say: "In this culture, people don't really have an individual sense because they don't have any words for 'I' or 'me.' " But what they do have are verb forms that refer to locations, to the origin or source of actions . . . So their particular sense of agency involves an image of themselves as specific beings capable of causing something to happen.

Now this apparent need of human beings, to have a central image, is a very important and major part of human life. It is the first big sign of the emergence of these self-conscious emotions. In other words, infants are not born with a sense of "I"; in all likelihood, they're not even born with an experience of being located in a particular body; they're probably too divergent in their responses. They haven't yet cohered and differentiated into self and other. But somewhere around the middle of the second year of life, infants in all cultures begin to locate themselves in the body. We know this from experiments that have been done on self-recognition. Michael Lewis, for instance, has done experiments where rouge is put on the nose of the infant, and the infant is then put before a mirror. Prior to the age of eighteen months, infants don't seem to recognize the mark, but seem to view themselves and the image in the mirror as the same thing. But around eighteen months or so, they start to discover the mark on the nose. When they see it in the mirror, they know it's also on the nose, and it's very exciting for them to discover that they are located in the image they see in the mirror . . . that that image also reflects the body, and so on. . . .

AM: That hints of Lacan's mirror stage. . . .

PYE: Yes it does, though it's much later than Lacan says, and I think for good reason. I don't think the infant is as well organized early on as Lacan does, or as Melanie Klein does. While infants have a lot of capacities, and while we continue to discover how responsive they actually are, I just don't think that the nervous system is sufficiently well-organized to be able to locate a mirror image at six months. In all fairness to Lacan, however, he does allow for a range of time for the event to unfold, as he situates it somewhere between the ages of six and eighteen months. And it certainly does happen at around eighteen months for most infants, unless there's a real developmental disability: but even in such cases, the beginnings of these self-conscious emotions are evidenced. They're not all negative, actually, because pride is not a negative emotion; but pride, shame, envy, guilt, embarrassment are the emotions that are associated with this emergence of the sense of self as separate from other people.

You ask about the way universal human emotions are categorized, how there seem to be more negative ones than positive ones . . . What does this say about human beings? It's only recently that some theorists are trying to look at this picture. Mihaly Csikszentmihalyi, in *The Evolving Self*, says that human consciousness tends towards negativity under all conditions. He believes that if a human being is left alone unstructured, the person will become depressed. All of us have a tendency towards negative feelings, much more than towards positive ones, and he believes that's because there is a kind of instinctual tendency towards competence in human beings, so that we're never satisfied, we never feel fully competent . . . We're always trying to make things better essentially, so that it's part of our genetic package to see things negatively more than positively. This keeps us trying to improve everything, whereas other animals don't try to keep improving their situation.

AM: That sounds like a contemporary take on the insatiability of desire.

PYE: Yes, the insatiability of competence. In the lack is the drive to make something better. So, if you want to refer that back to self-conscious emotions, not only are there more negative self-conscious emotions but there are more negative primary emotions as well. And so, it could be that the human being's sense of self is more negative than positive, and is infused with more negative feelings.

AM: I was wondering, after reading a number of your books and articles, if there were a more basic element of discomfort throughout your own professional journey. More specifically, I was wondering about your parallel commitments to both feminism and the Jungian approach to depth psychology.

PYE: It has been really uncomfortable to be a Jungian feminist, partly because I'm not well-received by either group. The Jungians are suspicious of my feminism, and the feminists are suspicious of my Jungianism. The influence of feminism on my thinking has a clear date. It was when Shirley Chisholm ran for President of the United States, and I believe that was 1974. At that point, I was working at a black university in North Carolina, where I was involved in the Civil Rights Movement and the Black Power Movement. I was interested in black liberation, in how oppression translates into liberation; but until then I didn't think that women were oppressed. I hadn't really awakened to what was going on with gender. I thought the Women's Movement was mostly about middle-class women complaining and burning their bras, which all seemed silly to me. But Shirley Chisholm brought race and gender together, in terms of oppression, and a light went on inside of me. I thought, "Of course, it's the same thing." Around that same time, I had my first child, and read *Of Woman Born* by Adrienne Rich. Reading *Of Woman Born* crystallized for the first time in my thinking a whole critique of culture, because what Rich says in the book is that the institution of motherhood is different from the experience of motherhood. Women have no voice in really speaking about their experiences of motherhood; we're visited upon by the institution, and at that point we're forced to comply with a whole set of institutional values about what it means to be a mother, without any reliable sense of our own experience of being a mother. When I read the book, I was in a terrible dilemma about my own feelings. I loved my baby, but was often irritated by her, and afraid of some of the feelings she aroused in me: some very destructive feelings, especially when she was crying, or would wake me up at night. I couldn't find these feelings referenced anywhere in any of the child development books, and I thought maybe I was crazy. But when I read Adrienne Rich, and found my experience expressed in her book, my mind opened up enormously. She gave voice to the fact that not only aren't these experiences written, but that women had not even begun to express their own experiences as mothers. As women, all we had was a patriarchal institution of motherhood. I suddenly saw that a lot of my experiences weren't unique or weird or crazy; they just hadn't been entered into the cultural record. That was for me the beginning, when I began to read everything feminist that I could get my hands on.

By that time I had already been reading Jung, and hadn't even thought about the sexism in his work. In fact, I thought it was great that there was a depth psychology where women were even mentioned in a positive way. It was in 1974, then, that I gave a talk on "Jungian Psychology and Women Today," which was really about feminism and my beginning understandings of it. From that time on I began thinking of both of these influences in a dialectical relationship, particularly in regard to *anima* and *animus* and similar concepts, in terms of what they meant from the point of view of patriarchal culture, and what they could mean from a feminist perspective. And as I developed that perspective, I stayed in the closet in a weird way. When I was with my feminist friends, I never spoke about my interest in Jung; and when I was with the Jungians, I never spoke about my interest in feminism. I did that probably until about 1982 or so. I kept these things apart, hidden one from the other.

Then, in 1982, I became very uncomfortable that there were no black Jungian analysts. I had started my own psychoanalytic training in 1979, and I'd been at enough meetings and conferences to have seen that this was a very racist group, as there were no people of color. I assumed we had to be racist, because there would be some people of color if we weren't. So I wrote an article for *Quadrant* called "The Absence of Black Americans as Jungian Analysts." After I wrote that piece I promised myself I would never be silent about my beliefs. I would be straightforward and bring all these discontinuities together in actually speaking to people about them. Since then I've had a very hard time, particularly as a Jungian. There have been many occasions when I've been personally attacked for being an animus-dominated woman because of my ideas. So it's been very uncomfortable, but very fertile. Sometimes I feel very sad when I think my work's not read because I'm in this funny predicament of being feminist and Jungian, and that because of this I fall through the cracks. A lot of the Freudians and feminists don't read me because I'm Jungian, while the Jungians don't read me because I'm feminist . . . That's been the sadness of it. I feel that my work is only narrowly responded to because my group identity or affiliation is in conflict . . . I do wish I had more colleagues who were both Jungian and feminist. Overall, I would say that feminism has been the bigger influence in the long run, due in part to the fact that there's been too little development of Jungian thought. I do make use of Jung's ideas, as I make use of Andrew Samuels' and a few others—but there is a whole body of Jungian work out there that I don't make use of, because it's too realist.

AM: How then did your Jungian background, your feminism, and your postmodern sensibility all come together to influence your theory and practice of therapy?

PYE: In a single word, constructivism. From a formal perspective, constructivism is the big circle in which these other things take place. On another level, I could say also Buddhism, but that's more of a personal issue. By constructivism I mean the position that human interpretation is primary in all that we experience, that we simply don't have access to another world, other than the human world. Into that I can fit my understanding of Jung, my understanding of feminism, my understanding of developmental psychology, and still feel like I have a coherent world view that is deeply meaningful to me. This is a very, very optimistic slant, different from the "deconstruction" which I think is very pessimistic. Constructivism, as a system of thought, probably didn't come into my universe until the mid-1980s. Although my interests and influences might have come together in me experientially, I couldn't say there was coherence in my thinking until then. In fact, I lacked coherence, since the different approaches and systems of thought I was interested in didn't really combine easily with each other, except through the aesthetic appeal they had for me.

AM: A central part of your theory is the notion of what you call a "dissociative tendency" of the human personality. In *Jung's Self Psychology,* while you avoid any direct references to post-modernism, you still talk about personality being characterized by "multiple organizations" or "multiple voices." You also talk about diverse enactments of one's being. Is this, in essence, an aspect of your theory that is most consonant with post-modern thought? Is constructivism the way you deal with this dissociative tendency?

PYE: Yes. I consider constructivism to be an aspect of post-modernism. I think of post-modernism as the critique and constructivism as one of the outgrowths of that critique. Deconstruction is another outgrowth. I tried to differentiate myself from deconstructionist efforts because, while I think they involve an interesting and skeptical approach, I think they're also part of the pathology of post-modernism.

AM: Which is?

PYE: Despair. I find that my post-modernism is of the affirmative type. To me the idea that there is the possibility of coherence, of continuity, in our experience as human beings . . . that we are not only discontinuous, or dissociated . . . that idea makes more sense. If you are truly a dyed-in-the-wool deconstructionist, or a certain kind of dyed-in-the-wool post-modernist, you really don't believe in coherence. I certainly believe that the human personality is best theorized as dissociative, that subjectivities are multiple and that, again, because coherence is so much of an aspect of the self, we have a tendency to speak about ourselves singularly. There are a number of different hypnotic experiments that are very interesting in this regard. In one a large number of people were hypnotized and given the post-hypnotic suggestion that after they came out of trance, they would crawl around on the floor. When the investigators then went up to the individuals to ask them the reasons for their crawling around, every person had an explanation like "I think I dropped my watch," or "I'm looking for my pen," or "I thought I saw a speck of dust on the carpet." People came up with a coherent, singular explanation for something they were doing that was completely irrational. But nobody said: "I don't know why I'm crawling on the floor!" Isn't that interesting? That's the way we are as people. We are driven towards this singular, coherent sense of self, and come up with the most preposterous reasons for what we're doing, that may have nothing at all to do with what's actually going on. For me, that's a very good illustration of how we can seem rational when in fact we're very irrational.

AM: When I first approached you about this interview, not only were you receptive to the idea of discussing the nature and theory of self experience, but you also hinted that some contemporary theorists writing about the idea of multiple selves do so "as if they'd invented the wheel." You went on to suggest that Jung had postulated a "decentered self" long ago, before there was anything fashionable about the concept.

PYE: Absolutely! That's a wonderful piece of Jung's discovery. Not only did he talk about almost this inner theater of the *shadow*, the *persona*, the *anima* and *animus*, of all these characters going on within the person; he insisted on talking about them as personalities, and not merely as concepts. He wanted to give them images of subjectivity, rather than call them something abstract, like "superego" or "id." I think through his early work with schizophrenics, when he was at the Burgholzli, he saw clinically that people actually are profoundly dissociated. He also studied with Janet, from whom the idea of a psychological complex originally comes, and who had a very well organized personality theory of dissociation. Janet probably is the original theorist of dissociation. Then Jung studied with him, and further developed the idea of psychological complex. Jung always talks about the autonomous nature of the complexes, which means that each complex has a separate, core expression. As I suggested earlier, a person may be enacting a subpersonality that is really related, for example, to early relationship with mother, or early relationship with sister. So while the subpersonality is being enacted in the present as though it's taking place right here, the person is going to have a rational explanation for its enactment, and not understand that what is really occurring is the emergence of a subpersonality, emotionally cued by something in the environment. So, when I think of people like Stephen Mitchell, who in his book *Hope and Dread in Psychoanalysis* puts forth a theory of the discontinuity of the self, I don't see any awareness of Jungian personality theory and how it already encompasses that idea of discontinuity. And Jung develops the idea in a way that's far more useful clinically. A lot of the contemporary psychoanalytic theorists, who are either drawing on Lacan or on object relations theory for a model of dissociation, might benefit from looking at Jung. I think too many people ignore him . . . But that comes back to the whole issue of how Jung is seen, and to the political issue of Jung's alleged anti-semitism.

AM: If I read you correctly, you see the self as the nucleus around which the ego complex of an individual forms. The ego complex is then further constellated, much like a molecule by electrons, by the highly individualized expressions of what Jungians call the *persona*, the *shadow*, and the contrasexual archetypes. Are these the subpersonalities from which you derive your notion of a decentered self? Or is the idea more complex?

PYE: It's a little more complex than that. I imagine that there exists a central tendency for coherence that is the self: the tendency to organize a sense of individual subjectivity that underlies a big part of the way human beings operate with each other, and in regard to themselves and the world. So we have a tendency towards unity. My sense is that the organization and development of psychological complexes, or subpersonalities, has to do with relationships to other people and the ways in which those relationships are cast through the emotions. Emotions are predispositions to have a particular image, or to relate in a particular way. (A hyper-aroused infant, for example, will have a tendency towards negative emotional states, a tendency to form negative psychological complexes with mother, father, brother and so on. Overall, this kind of infant will in all likelihood develop along a certain trajectory, perhaps towards depression or certain kinds of anxiety.) The ego complex, then, in the way that I imagine it, doesn't really start developing until about eighteen months, when the self-conscious emotions emerge together with the organization of a separate individuality: of an "I" as separate from "you," or of an "in-here" as separate from "out-there." I don't think that organization is primary; I don't think people are born with it. I think it's secondary, and comes into being around eighteen months. And then it's elaborated. In our culture, the ego complex is assumed to be the genuine sense, or core, of the personality. We assume that the sense of individuality, of separateness, is really the most authentic sense of personality, rather than other psychological complexes which may have more to do with relationship.

Yesterday, for instance, I was in a couples session, where the husband, a painter and very intelligent man, made the statement that what bothers him so much is that marriage is like a prison camp, and that so much has to be sacrificed to stay in the marriage. He said that the issue of freedom, and how one deals with that issue, is constantly a problem. I found the whole metaphor so interesting, because I had just been reading an article in *Trycycle*, a Buddhist magazine, about the differences between Asians and Westerners who go into *sesshin*, or intensive meditation retreats. The article explained how Westerners tend to describe their experience, after a week in intensive meditation, as self-realization; whereas Asians tend to describe it as repentance. Asians will talk about the week's experience in terms of their relationships with other people, how they want to become more compassionate, or want to be forgiven . . . Westerners will say: "I have no feelings of repentance . . . It's been wonderful simply to be with myself and have this authentic experience of my self." We cast things so much in terms of our sense of a separate self, of being an individual; and so we value the ego complex in the personality, and often take that complex to be what the personality is. And, like the case of my patient in his relationship with his wife, if the ego complex doesn't feel too good, it can mean something is off-center. For my patient, it meant something about the relationship was deadening and imprisoning him.

AM: For people not familiar with Jungian terminology, I'm wondering if you can explain the meanings of terms like "ego complex," "shadow," "animus" and "anima". . . .

PYE: The term, ego, in Jung's work is very similar to the term ego in Freud's work. Jung thought of the ego as the center of consciousness; he doesn't worry, however, as Freud does, about the ego's relation to language, whether language is essential to consciousness. He says basically that there has to be a seat of consciousness in the personality, which is the ego: so anytime that you are conscious, you are somehow relating through the ego. After 1944, Jung revises his theory of psychological complexes which, contrary to many Jungians, I see as a momentous event in the history of his work. Initially, his idea of a psychological complex was that of an associated field of emotionally charged material around some kind of core issue. The core issue was something emotionally charged, around which associated experiences would cluster. Jung investigated these processes through the association experiments he performed after he came back from studying with Janet. In his early theory, Jung believes that the collective unconscious, envisioned as the substrate of the human psyche that is common to all people, is organized by archetypes which, at this point in his work, are similar to Kantian categories. They are eternal forms that organize the collective aspect of the psyche, whereas the personal unconscious is organized by psychological complexes, derived from actual, lived experiences that have become emotionally charged. So from 1916 to about 1944, Jung is almost talking about two different phenomenologies: that of the collective unconscious, operating somewhat apart from human experience, and that of the personal unconscious, seen as the repository of all of our personal experiences.

It's then after 1944 that Jung changes his theory, partly because he's interested in innate releasing mechanisms, in ethology and evolutionary biology. He begins to see, in fact, that what he'd called "archetype" resembles an innate releasing mechanism. It's an emotional situation in which we're predisposed to act and see things in a certain way; in which there's a predisposition to form an image in an emotionally charged state. He then looks at his theory of complexes, and suggests that the nucleus of a complex probably involves an archetype. The complex, then, is seen not simply as an emotionally charged experience or cluster of experiences: in fact, the reason why the complex is so long-lasting, why it's not dissolved by analysis, is because it has at its core an archetype, which is connected to this predisposition to form a coherent image. So Jung begins to see how an individual's mother complex has at its core the mother archetype, meaning that a negative mother complex will share in some ways with somebody else's negative mother complex. The themes will be the same and the images will be similar. As he begins to think about this he realizes that even the ego complex has an archetypal core, the self, which is the central, organizing archetype. So he starts to unite the collective and the personal unconscious, putting them in a framework that is very digestible to a constructivist, because at the core of the personal complex is this universal tendency to form an image in an emotionally aroused state. That tendency then, is repeated throughout the life-span. Jung therefore moves away from the idea of the archetype as a mental category, and towards the idea of the archetype as being connected with universal human emotions.

What I call "ego complexes," as a result, are in line with Jung's later idea of the ego being a complex as well. He even says the ego is only one complex among many, and is itself an unconscious complex: that is, it's unconsciously defended, even though a part of its function is to mediate consciousness, or is basically experienced as consciousness. Now, clinically, how do all these complexes relate? Jung had an early theory about these interrelationships, which to some extent I question. His view was that the persona complex rests primarily on the surface of the personality, and is compensated by the shadow and then by the ego complex. The ego complex, in turn, is more central than the persona, and is itself compensated by the anima or the animus, the contrasexual complex. The way I tend to see this picture is that in different individuals there will be different kinds of charges of emotional meaning, different interconnected complexes. For some individuals, the ego complex is very emotionally charged, and the self-conscious emotions are extremely powerful. Or, at different times throughout the life-cycle, other complexes may become dominant. But in different individuals, different unconscious complexes will be very important because of their experiences: because of trauma, or living with a depressed parent, or having a particularly rivalrous relationship with a brother or sister. As a result, there will be a kind of dialectic in the personality between the very strongly charged unconscious complexes and the ego complex. Clinically, then, the personality may be dominated by the unconscious complex, contrary to the ego's own view of itself. What you see is something like an alter-personality that comes onto the scene and takes over: as happens, for example, in a depressive state, where an identification with a negative unconscious complex, often an earlier parental complex, occurs.

The shadow is otherness, however otherness is conceived. It is the projection of the alienated aspects of the personality, the aspects of oneself and one's experience that one does not want to look at, entertain or identify with. It's the projection of those aspects into other people, or into the world, or onto animals, or whatever. And, contrary to what Jung thought, I find that the shadow often emerges towards the very end of an analysis. Whereas Jung believed that the persona and the shadow were among the earlier emergences, in my opinion it's the parental complexes that are the first to surface in treatment. I believe that the persona is really just one of the defenses of the ego complex: by "persona" I mean the ways we want to appear, the particular roles we unconsciously adopt, through which we present ourselves socially. So I tend to think of persona as a defense of the ego complex, rather than having a particular relationship to the shadow.

AM: In context with the elimination of Jung's original demarcation between a collective and personal unconscious, you've pointed to affinities with object relations theory. . . .

PYE: I actually think of the way I use analytic psychology as an object relations theory. I do think that Jung's theory is similar to that of Melanie Klein, whom I've always considered to be the founder of object relations. I consider Jung to be similar to both Melanie Klein and Harry Stack Sullivan, because of the way in which the psychological complexes are the mix of one's subjective experience and what objectively happened. It's a mix that's impossible to tease out, since a psychological complex is a subjective, very subjective image of an experience with another person. To me, that's very much like an internalized object. Differently from Klein, however, who puts an emphasis on phantasy, on infantile configurations of negative and positive (while suggesting that it really doesn't matter what the parents or environment were actually doing), for Jung the actual experience does matter, since a psychological complex is made up not only of the archetypal core but of its associations with actual experience. But similarly to Klein, he also acknowledges those early configurations to be universal: there's always going to be the great and the terrible; there will always be dichotomies in human experience and in the ways we experience ourselves emotionally. So, from a Jungian point of view, a psychological complex is the product of personal life, with a universal at its core.

AM: In the course of a Jungian analysis, how do you understand what is termed a "rearrangement of psychological complexes"? Can you explain how the rearrangement unfolds, and how tools like myth or transference are brought to bear by a Jungian on the therapeutic outcome?

PYE: Things vary from case to case. In particular I think there's a difference between those people who have been traumatized in childhood and people who have had a neurotic childhood. With trauma, you're dealing with a lot more dissociation. A corrective emotional relationship is a big part of the treatment when there's been trauma. In a neurotic situation it's a little different. Take a situation where the depressive mother complex is dominant in a personality, and basically colors a great deal of the patient's emotional experience. Through an analysis, the ego complex and the positive side of the mother complex would come into greater dominance. What that means is that the person's experience is reorganized along different coordinates, so that at the end of the analysis, the person has the possibility of being freer in the moment, without replaying most interactions as a repetition of a depressive relationship with the mother.

A case I'm working on right now involves a woman who had a narcissistic mother who was not abusive but somewhat neglectful. The mother was a heavy drinker, and probably depressed too. (I think narcissism also goes with depression. . . .) The daughter was sexually abused by an older childhood friend, and then enacted the sexual abuse with her own brother. She was never able to talk about any of those experiences with mother, whom she constantly felt she was disappointing. This makes me think she was never an idealized, self-object for the mother. I think the mother perceived the daughter as not being feminine enough, and basically distanced herself from the daughter early on because the daughter did not satisfy her own narcissistic needs. So, this woman grew up with a very dominant, negative mother complex that colored most of her experience: this meant that no matter how successful she was at what she did, she derived almost no feeling of satisfaction from any of her successes. Nor was she able to feel emotionally close to other people, with the exception of her children. Over time this woman came to feel that her life was deadened. She increasingly became depressed until, by the time she came into treatment in her 50s, she was living her mother's life. She was so driven by this complex that, even though she had done all sorts of things differently from her mother, she felt depressed, empty, unable to find joy in her daily experiences, unable to be in touch with her husband, or to feel in contact with him. Her personality was unconsciously dominated by this complex. Her ego was weak in response to it. She wasn't able really to analyze any of this. She wasn't able to reflect on it.

This is where transference comes in for me. Transference, countertransference and my experience and interpretation of both, are the primary ways I work in therapy. I see dreams and any kind of mythic interpretation as adjuncts to the use of the transference. In a sense, I take dreams to be messages about the transference; I look at them from the point of view of what they say about the treatment. I do believe very strongly that therapy, as a contained experience which we hope is mostly benign, is a corrective emotional relationship. In this woman's case especially, I felt that it was over time, in her relying on my ability to see her, to mirror her in a positive way, to contain what she brought, that she gradually developed a different kind of mother complex: I became like a positive mother, providing the experience of a positive mother which she could internalize. She feels me as a loving figure who knows her and reflects her, and this gives her hope and confidence. She's come to understand and analyze really what has happened to her, so that she can step back from this tendency towards emptying her experience of meaning, towards a depressive re-enactment of her mother complex. She's not through with the analysis yet, because she hasn't quite integrated all of this so that it goes smoothly. She will notice that she's identified with her complex, and then be able to get out of it.

But rather than being able to notice it when it kicks in, it will usually take her a day or two. What I work with in the sessions, very often, is her way of feeling with me, what she basically places into me and what she takes out of me. In the beginning and over time these dynamics had to do with the negativity of the mother and the mother complex; now, they have to do with other things, like competition and rivalry. So there's a move in the analysis to a more distinctly Oedipal stage, where I continue to work, in any case, at that intersubjective level. I may interpret in terms of the mother complex, or occasionally use myth. And though I don't use myth very often, with her I sometimes think about the emotional drama of Demeter, of Persephone. Recently, she herself brought up the myth of Sisyphus, because there is an element of that myth that's very strong in her personality.

Near the end of treatment I might be more disposed to talk in terms of mythic themes, as I then tend to be freer in what I say about my own imagistic responses. At the beginning of treatment I talk less, and I'm less likely to say something that's just going through my mind. I may be drawing on mythic themes in my own thinking about cases, but I rarely speak about them in the treatment.

AM: I'm interested in exploring the complementary dynamics or dimensions of the therapeutic process in which the patient's, as well as the therapist's, self or selves are dialectically elaborated. My emphasis, here, is on the word *labor*, on the conscious and unconscious work that therapy involves. In simpler terms, then: how do patient and therapist "elaborate" each other? And how does this rearrangement of selves, through the labor of therapy, make it possible for the patient to deal differently with the world?

PYE: If there's an overriding theme here for me it's the dialectic. Jung says that if the opposites are in the right kind of dialectic relationship, there's a transcendent function. That transcendent function is the ability to move back and forth between these two sides of the dialectic. If the two sides are not in the right kind of relationship, however, there is no transcendent function, and what you have is a kind of "stuckness": on one side, consciously or in an enactment, on the other side in how the unconscious responds. Some very similar concepts to the Jungian's transcendent function are Winnicott's notion of potential space and play space, and concepts in Buddhism that deal with freedom from obsessions. In Buddhist terms, when you're free from obsessions you aren't captured by a particular point of view, but are able to move between points of view, to be free on many levels. The way the dialectic unfolds in treatment, however, is so complex, because there are so many different dialectics going on. There's subject-object: the sense, the experience, of an Other standing before or against the self. Here, now, I experience you as object, I experience myself as subject. If I experience that in a very stultified or rigid way, then I'm separated from you. I don't experience the potential for flexibility in who's subject and who's object, the possibility that you and I are somehow fluid. So that if the Other is rigidly objectified, there tends to be a strong separation in one's experience, and the entire dialectic tends to be handled through projection and projective identification, trying to get other people to behave as you want them to.

Another kind of dialectic is between conscious and unconscious. This involves the way we experience something as an aspect of our own doing, our own agency, and the way we experience it as "doing" us, as acting upon us. That too is always going on in treatment. It's what Roy Schafer and Don Spence talk about, the difference between a "happening" and an "action," and the way we experience the two in our lives. Is one the victim of circumstances? Or do we actually help bring about events? At any particular moment, it becomes a matter of responsibility: did you enact this, did you bring this out of your own action? Or did this just "happen," out of nowhere? That kind of dialectic is going on all the time in treatment, and often centers around the issue of blame . . . blaming the self or blaming others . . . blaming the therapist and blaming oneself.

Another dialectic is the dialectic of gender, which can also play out as a dialectic of sexual orientation. If there are two people of different genders, then that fuses with the subject-object dialectic: it complicates further the issue of whether you can understand me, whether you can see me in my gender because of our gender difference, how much are you captured by that difference, how much therapist and patient handle and relate to each other, back and forth, through projection. Then, from a Jungian point of view, there's also the gender-based dialectic going on within each individual: if I'm consciously female, but unconsciously male, when the self is of a particular gender but there's a subpersonality of another self of the opposite sex. So things get very complicated around issues of gender and the way we attribute meaning in regard to gender.

For example, many women I've seen over the years tend to project their authority into men. Even with the women's movement, we're so socialized to believe that men are authorities, that women still tend to be uncomfortable with a female doctor or a female boss. How we imagine the opposite sex, and what qualities we attribute to or are carried by the gendered Other, is a very important part of the dialectic of therapy. I think that dialectic often doesn't come up with certain Freudian psychoanalysts because they assume those qualities are universal. They assume, because of the reproductive system, that women are women and men are men, and that there's a certain boundary in that. I agree that we are constrained by our embodiment, but the forms of meaning that embodiment assumes change throughout the life cycle. And if you don't pay attention to the fluidity of it, I think you again get stuck in projection. You get stuck with the sense of these big differences between the sexes that can't be bridged, which then invariably get handled through projection. So you have all these dialectics going on in treatment, as well as the dialectics of transference and countertransference.

One other dialectic I'll mention is between projective identification and the transcendent function, or play. The dynamic of projective identification is a deadly serious one, and carries with it a feeling of danger. It usually develops when the patient perceives the therapist in a fixed and inflexible way, denying the therapist a fuller reality. There's a feeling of danger about this dynamic which isn't at all playful. But if you can move out of the feeling and into the space of play, you can then enter into and experience the transcendent function. It's difficult to describe, but this is where the cutting edge of my thinking is. I believe a lot of psychopathology is connected to projective identification, to ways in which people enact their psychological complexes so as to engage other people in the evocation or reenactment of trauma. This is a very difficult thing to see in one's own experience, because we project constantly, in order to grow and develop. We project aspects of ourselves and regularly meet up with resistances to our projections, and it is from this dynamic that we learn to distinguish self from not-self. But since we can't stop projecting, and because we do it so much, it just feels like reality. It's hard to glean at a particular moment: Am I projecting something into my partner, my child, my boss? Am I evoking this enactment? Or is the other person just doing something that I find deeply offensive or really troubling?

The earmark of projective identification as a problem is what Eigen, I think, calls "kidnapping." You get the feeling of being carried away into a space where there is no freedom, only a seriousness that's distinctly different from play. Conversely, when you're in the play space, you can move back and forth between different meanings, and none of those meanings seems to be heavy or confining. Instead, when you're in a projective identification, people sometimes have the sense that they will die if they can't convince you of being right. That treatment dynamic, or that dialectic, between projective identification and the play space or transcendent function is, I think, the very basis of what makes dynamic psychotherapy really helpful. Of course, there have to be all the rituals of therapy. You need to have the containment, and so on. But once everything else is in place, you need to have this dialectic. You need to go crazy with the patient, go into the projective identification, but then you need to be able to come out into the play space. Ideally, you need to be able to do both in a treatment hour, because it's only when the patient is actually able to go crazy with you, and when you feel crazy too, that stepping out of the madness is meaningful.

AM: You refer in *Jung's Self Psychology* to how contemporary depictions of knowledge, in ecology and biology, for example, are circular or cyclical, and thus reflect Jung's idea of the mandala as the archetypal image for the self. In the day-to-day elaborations of clinical work, how do therapist and patient work, on the one hand, with the experience of the self's timeless circularity; and, on the other hand, with the linear directionality of the Western ego, and the very linear constraints of the fifty-minute hour?

PYE: From everything we know about being human, we are absolutely constrained by time's arrow. There's a beginning and an end to our lives, at least from the point of view of the ego complex. The force of linear time is strongly present in all human interactions, and is a very big component in a psychoanalytic treatment: what with the beginning and the end of the session, the idea that treatment begins and ends, and that we will know each other for only a part of life. The therapy relationship itself requires enormous sacrifice, the sacrifice of any kind of fluid relationship. Whereas in other relationships people can nourish the fantasy of forever, in therapy, ultimately, you can't. So there is a strong imposition of linear time on the therapeutic dynamic. How does circularity enter into it? We can think of psychological complexes as being the first enactments of a kind of internal theater, of a performance that is going to be played out again and again, in different places, in a person's life. This involves a circular repetition, what Freud called a repetition compulsion. What a good treatment should do is churn the repetition compulsion into a spiral, transform the circle into a spiral. Whereas the person, coming into treatment, may have constantly been repeating the same dynamic in every new relationship or situation, in leaving treatment that person will sometimes repeat the dynamic but be able to see it, entertain it in the play space, and be free of it, so as to move on to another level in which those same themes will be repeated again. In other words, in everybody's life and throughout the lifespan, the themes of attachment, loss and separation, of the primary emotions of fear, aggression, joy, and curiosity, are being continually repeated through new experiences; but optimally, each time that a loss is experienced, it is a somewhat different experience of loss, although articulated within the same general theme.

In treatment, therefore, it's through the psychological complexes that you get into the circularity of repetition. Then, hopefully, through the transcendent function, the movement into a spiral occurs. The way I see the ideal development of a human life is that it starts with the circularity of the repetition, of carrying out unconsciously a dynamic that was set up before a person could have any knowledge about it; then, gradually, through self-reflection, through consciousness, you become somewhat free of the dynamic, and move on. Then you repeat the dynamic again, but see it from a different perspective. It's similar to a passage in Eliot's *Four Quartets*, in "Little Gidding," where the poet says:

We shall not cease from exploration
And the end of all our exploring
Will be to arrive where we started
And know the place for the first time.

In a successful treatment and a successful life, again and again, you return to that place–but it's not the same place. It's a place you recognize, that's not foreign, from which you can reorganize and go on.

Finally, even though the focus is on the subjectivity of the patient and the patient's suffering, the therapist too must be changed in the treatment. Because if that isn't happening, then the therapist is not in any way entering into the craziness of the patient, and is not in any way really engaged in the transcendent function. The therapist must make new discoveries in the treatment, and be subjectively changed for the treatment to be effective. I don't mean that therapists should talk about themselves and their own pain in the treatment, but that through this whole aspect of working with the patient and the patient's experience, one's own subjectivity is engaged. All of us have these common emotions and these common experiences of attachment, separation and loss. As a result, there's no way a patient of any sort cannot have a lot in common with me–because we're both human beings. This idea is also very Jungian: because there are universals, I know I'll have a lot in common with the patient, and so I too must change in the treatment.

AM: Throughout your writings, you've paid close attention to Jung's relationship with Eastern philosophies and to Buddhism in particular, citing letters where he says things like: "The whole course of individuation is dialectical, and the so-called 'end' is the confrontation of the ego with the 'emptiness' of the centre." What was the influence of Zen on Jung's thought, and what role, if any, has Eastern thought had on your work?

PYE: Nobody knows for sure what the total influence of Zen Buddhism was on Jung's ideas. He did meet with Hisamatsu, and that meeting now has been documented in an excellent book called *Self in Liberation: The Jung-Buddhism Dialogue*. He'd read a number of translated Chan and Zen texts, and apparently was reading a book on Chan, by Helen Lukes' husband, when he was on his deathbed. So Jung was strongly influenced by Buddhism, and turned increasingly towards Eastern thought after his heart attack and his recovery in 1944–when he had the out-of-body experience he describes in *Memories, Dreams and Reflections*. This, even though in his early work he stood firmly on the idea–one that he never totally rescinded–that Westerners should pursue their development through Western forms and, somehow, Easterners should pursue their development through Eastern forms.

Essentially, Jung was very influenced by Zen Buddhism as it began to surface in the West. He realized–though he doesn't say this–that Buddhism adapts itself to the culture that it enters. Buddhism does not represent a specific Eastern tradition: it was able to move, for example, and change, from India to China to Japan to Southeast Asia, by adapting itself to the culture at-large. Thus Jung began to sense that Buddhism could become a part of depth psychology, and began to use the idea of the empty center in talking about his concept of the self: a concept which earlier had seemed very much like a Hindu concept of the self, like Atman, or the eternal soul. In his letters particularly, he now talks about the self as the empty center, and not the self of the imago, not the eternal self. Influences aside, however, he never did integrate his ideas into a theoretical position. Still, my sense is that too many Jungians ignore the later development of Jung's concept of the self. They take the concept of the self from the middle part of his work, and relate it to the Christian idea of the soul, suggesting all the while that Jung was talking about an individual soul. My sense is that, by the time Jung entered the 1950s, he was rethinking his notion of the self; there is a real distinction, you realize, between the idea of the self as individual soul and the self as empty center. In his later ideas he says that self is also an attitude towards relationship, that it necessarily orients one towards relationships with others. This is not in his earlier work. At the time of his introductions to the Tibetan texts, *The Great Liberation* and *The Tibetan Book of the Dead*, Jung was moved by these texts but as yet not distinctly influenced by them. It was only later, when he began to read Zen Buddhism, that the influence was integrated into his thinking.

As for me, I think that a certain aspect of spirituality is very personal, and since I don't like the confessional approach to things, I won't go into all the details of my personal experience. I became a student of Phillip Kapleau's when I was 23 years old. I belonged at the time to the Rochester Zen Center, an affiliation which marked a very big shift for me, as I'd grown up a very devout Catholic. I came to the Center in a very serious way, differently, perhaps, than the way some people came to Zen around the same time in the '70s. Later, after about 2 1/2 years, I left, because I felt the practice was too severe, and was actually repeating for me a lot of the fear that I'd felt in the Catholic church. At the same time I felt very devoted or, let's say, transformed by Buddhism and by its religious beliefs. Buddhism doesn't have a dogma, you see, but a practice, and a set of beliefs; so when I left the Rochester Zen Center, after having taken my vows, I told Kapleau–with whom I did not have a very close relationship–that I was leaving, because somehow the place just didn't seem suited to me at the time. I told him I had other things I wanted to pursue, but still wanted to consider myself a Buddhist. I remember him saying that some people need to pursue an individual path, and that he didn't seem particularly obstructive or concerned.

So I left, and over the twenty years that followed, I hung around with the Quakers and was very influenced by Quaker communities. I've written my books at Pendle Hill, and have always felt a carry-over, or link, between Quakerism as a mystical form of Christianity and Buddhism. For one, both of them have great respect for revelatory experiences, something you don't find in too many forms of Christianity. Still, I felt, throughout all those years, that I had remained a Buddhist. I never was attracted to Tibetan Buddhism, which was the prominent form here in Philadelphia. I couldn't find a teacher that I liked. I would go to different teachers' talks but was never particularly impressed. Then, quite by accident, two years ago when I was in Burlington, I ran into Phillip Kapleau. It was so remarkable to meet him again, on so many different levels, but it also became totally clear to me that he is my teacher, that he's always been my teacher, and that I've never been satisfied with anyone else. Now, I've become very close to him. I write to him, and go to visit and sit with him in Florida, where he's now partially retired at 82. I have a personal relationship with him now that I would never have been able to imagine with a teacher. So between Vermont and Florida, and with the other geographically scattered centers of Kapleau's lineage, I now feel I have a community. I can call myself a Buddhist, and I do have a teacher.

But that's just the formal side of my affiliation. I have now read a considerable amount of Buddhist philosophy and I've been most impressed with the philosophy of the middle way, as expressed primarily in the work of Nagarjuna, a second-century Indian philosopher who was a follower of Buddhism but returned a lot of the concepts to their original meanings. What I've found in reading Nagarjuna is that his philosophy of the middle way is a form of contemporary constructivism. He focuses especially on language, and on what it is that language represents. Does it represent reality, or is it a construction based on people's experiences? And he answers, really, that language is a construction, and that as a result our concepts will always change. We will not have, as a result, permanent concepts of the truth, or of the divine. Because of that, he suggests, we should regard our language and concepts lightly. . . .

Nagarjuna talks about the conventional use of language and the formal use of language; how we should be aware that, while we speak conventionally as though we know the truth of things, in a formal way we actually don't. As a Buddhist, then, this guards against the position of claiming to know the essence of transcendence. Such a position can only thrust a person into an opposition with someone who takes a different position. According to Nagarjuna, then, the way to walk the middle path is to acknowledge the way one sees things for now, but without any claims to absolute knowledge. It's sort of what Richard Rorty says about claims to truth: constrained as we are by embodiment and cultural perspective, we cannot claim the gods' view from on-high. Nagarjuna, like the Buddha, says even wars are fought over this very issue, over competing truths about the divine. This, then, is one area in which Nagarjuna's philosophy is very similar to constructivism, but there are many others as well.

Where psychotherapy is concerned, another thing I like very much about Nagarjuna is the way he talks about the "Noble Truths" of Buddhism. The first Noble Truth is translated usually as "all life is suffering"; but it can also be translated "life is dissatisfaction," or somehow "unsatisfying." Seen in this light, the focus shifts, to the issue that human beings are often dissatisfied with their experiences, and to the apparent primacy of negative primary emotions. *Dukkha*, then, is suffering; or, as I tend to think of it, all development involves suffering in human life. When we develop, from the time we learn to walk or speak, we suffer in that development. That suffering, though, is caused in great part by a kind of grasping. Thus, when the second Noble Truth raises the issue of desire, and the idea that suffering is caused by desire, it can be very misleading for Westerners. Many people seem to have the impression that Buddhism is preaching against desire, against involvement in the world. I think nothing could be further from the truth. The Buddha's followers were known in his lifetime as the most joyous of spiritual groups. That to me is what Buddhism is in essence: a joyous, alert, engaged form of practice. Our grasping, however, has more to do with trying to hold on to the idea of permanence in the midst of impermanence, wanting things to be as one wants them to be, and not as they are. Nagarjuna says it is more difficult for us to let go of our obsessions than to let go of, say, various aspects of greed: like our love for sensual experience or food or whatever. It's easier for people to give up things they enjoy sensually, or to go without physical comforts, than to give up their obsessions. Because those obsessions–what I would call psychological complexes–are undergirding the way we all create reality. So it is through these obsessions that suffering is caused.

What Buddhism offers is a method for breaking these obsessions, or for alleviating the suffering that goes with letting go of the obsession. In that way it is similar to psychotherapy. In Jung's words, a great deal of our suffering is neurotic, or unnecessary, suffering. Both Buddhism and depth psychology recognize that to let go of one's obsessions, and to break through them, so that they no longer constitute the world, is a way to suffer less and be freer. Personally, I have a very strong sense that contemporary constructivism, and perhaps some other branches of postmodernism, are in some ways the upwelling of a Buddhist orientation within Western culture.

AM: Earlier, we talked about the atom or molecule as your metaphor for the self-ego axis. In *Jung's Self Psychology*, you write: "The ego complex rotates around the self in a unique energy field." Speaking of postmodernism, now, I was wondering how the metaphor might apply in a world where coherence of the personality, and thus of the very ego complex, seems to be increasingly at risk. In Jungian terms, if our masks keep multiplying to such an extent that we can't hold onto them all, is the *persona* destined for psychosis?

PYE: I want to emphasize that what you've cited is a metaphor. I even have some reluctance to use spatial metaphors for the person or the mind. I prefer relational metaphors to spatial ones; but in Jung's concept of a psychological complex, he uses that metaphor of the atom. But I do want to say one thing about that metaphor. When you observe the atom subatomically, it looks like it's mostly space; it's not matter as we recognize it. There are such huge spaces between the subatomic particles that it's hard for physicists even to tell how the particles interrelate with each other and hold the atom together. Isn't that interesting? This adds even more relevance to the metaphor. But your question, if I'm not mistaken, is about the coherence of the personality. . . .

AM: On the one hand, my question addresses the sense of coherence, as this applies to the idea of a permanent self. On the other, however, if we entertain the Buddhist or postmodern idea that the self is impermanent, it seems to have a Jungian correlate in the concept of *personae*, of the socially acceptable masks we all wear. In this light, within an exceedingly demanding and increasingly complex postmodern world, is there a risk that our masks might multiply beyond our control? On a general level, how real is the risk of serious psychic fragmentation?

PYE: I don't know. There is a traditional way of looking at the self or the structure of personality, the idea that it changes and stays the same, or that there are certain character formations that are very difficult to change over time and thus stay the same. The old Jungian point of view, from the middle period of Jung's work, saw the self as the coherent center which somehow pulls together the whole personality, as the nucleus of the atom would. If we look at the atom with what we know about it now, we see that the nucleus does not effect a very strong pull on any of the atom's other parts. Physicists really cannot figure how the atom keeps its structure together. Now, the way I see things, I don't think the persona is a big issue in all this; I really don't. I think that people increasingly live with multiple personae without really much distress about it. There's a certain amount of distress because, if you think of the culture as the larger container in which people exist, it's now permissible to have six different communities in your life that don't interact at all: one at work, one at the club or gym, one at church, another perhaps in the family. So you have different identities and different personae in a lot of different places in your life, but I don't think this is a source of much anxiety among people.

A hundred years ago, everything would take place in one's neighborhood or little town, and everybody knew each other in all one's roles all the time. Nowadays that's not the case, and the roles don't overlap very much. But what I feel holds this scenario together is the fact that this is the contemporary *weltanschauung*: it's what people today take to be normal; it's not something crazy or weird. Embodiment, on the other hand, being in this bodily form, requires a coherent image. It just does. We cannot have very multiple images of ourselves. We cannot be really dissociated and function very well; and I think it's because our nervous system is so complex, always functioning behind the scenes, on so many different levels and in very contradictory ways. Erich Neumann thought that the self, this unitary self, arises out of a process of centroversion, which is the pulling together of the disparate aspects of the personality into one such unitary image. It just goes with having this particular form of embodiment . . . I'm not sure what a good metaphor is, but there's got to be somebody "at home," let's say, there's just got to be somebody that we can call into: a person who tries, in various ways, to say, "I am the same person that I was when I was fifteen, that I was when I was three," and so on. I don't think we can operate without that function right now.

AM: My question is: Is that function increasingly at risk?

PYE: I don't think so. What I hope is increasingly at risk is believing in the reality of that function. See? To me there's a difference between the function, let's say, of coherence and continuity, between the experience of being a continuous being, and the sense that somehow that experience is the reality of one's existence: that one *is* this continuous being. This relates to something I learned the other day. The pancreas, apparently, replaces all of its cells in a 24-hour period, so that we have a new pancreas every day. And yet, we all have a pancreas that continues over the course of our lifetimes. Now, it's relatively easy for us to say: "OK, I get it, I don't really have exactly the same pancreas but the functional properties continue." Now, if we could only feel the same way about the self! I think, then, that this is the kind of movement presently underway. This in itself is a sort of postmodern critique: that the self as a function is constantly being replaced, while its structure remains continuous. In other words, we're never without a self under reasonably good circumstances. Even when we sleep, there is a dreaming "I" or self that's separate from the other characters in the dream. Sometimes that self may be an animal or, under rare conditions, even an object; and it can certainly take on a different gender. The point is, however, that there is a perspective within the dream that is of the "I" or the self. That function, therefore, seems to be very important and very central to our being human.

AM: I'd like to address the connection between this function and the human capacity for symbolization. You write in *Jung's Self Psychology*: "Only new symbolic meaning that is assigned to experiences can constitute true 'development' or a change in adaptive attitude." Later in the same book, you recognize that "modern and postmodern cultures offer little in the way of initiation into symbolic life . . . Without the means of translating mythological images into personal meaning, many people lack the ability to sustain a symbolic life." I was wondering if you could expound on this. Yours seems to be a pessimism, or a kind of realism, that at least acknowledges our culture's lack of a capacity to promote a symbolic life; at the same time, however, you argue that the capacity is essential for any kind of transformation to take place.

PYE: When I did *Jung's Self Psychology*, I was trying to stay close to Jung. I was in a dialogue with Jung. In *You're Not What I Expected*, there's actually a passage on the mythopoetic consciousness and self awareness in which I develop the idea more from my own perspective. What I think is going on is the breakdown of the mythopoetic framework. Now, when Jung says that meaning is based on a symbolic connection, I agree; but I also agree with Robert J. Lifton about the symbolic connection to immortality. I think that the big symbolic issue for us is death, and the recognition of our own death. It is this issue that brings into question all of our activities and all of our relationships, and calls into question their meaning. Lifton talks about the symbolic connection to immortality as a connection to a sense of something bigger than oneself: it can be a connection through history and tradition, through one's children, through nature, or through various kinds of religious activities.

When I talk about symbolic connection, then, I am primarily talking about the symbolic connection to something bigger than us. But, you ask, can there be any kind of universal symbolic development without mythopoetic culture, and can you expect it in psychotherapy? I would say yes. I think it's more difficult now to feel the consensual validation of other people with regards to the forms of symbolic development one takes. I was working recently with a woman who, in her early 40s, is going to graduate school after departing from a very unique, highly dogmatic Christian tradition. All of her old structures for symbolic connection are breaking down. She's coming into new meanings which won't be reflected when she goes back to her home. Meanwhile her graduate-student peers, while they reflect the new meanings, don't know her old symbolic connections. And so this woman has no place where she can be consensually validated within the total framework of all that's developing for her symbolically. Except for therapy. This is the one place where someone knows what happened before, what's happening now, and what she's moving towards; this also makes her very afraid that she's so dependent on me for this reflection.

So, we have this emerging problem with shared meaning. Our society right now is very chaotic. One sees a lot of violence, a breakdown in family structure, to a large extent because there's not a lot of shared meaning. We don't have the traditions to carry us through. But I also believe that we're in a chaotic period of transformation, and that there is movement towards something new. It would be such a huge, huge step for human beings to achieve the deep recognition that what they take to be self is truly impermanent. Yet this is so beyond our mythopoetic traditions, because these have functioned primarily from the vantage point that there is a kind of lifelong connection between permanent individuals, as well as with a permanent divinity on whom we relied, in turn, for our very permanence and transcendence. Within that kind of framework, you can go about all of your activities knowing that you're going to exist forever someplace else, if you get it right here on earth. So that whole structure would have to break down. Anyway, I believe that the universality of human development rests on the constraints of embodiment. When I get angry at certain deconstructionists, or some of the pragmatists and other postmodernists, it's because I believe they've forgotten about human embodiment. They're talking as though we are a species of infinitely variable organizations, that we're these little heaps of person that can be organized in thousands of different ways, representing endless different kinds of meaning, so that you could bring together a person from an Eskimo culture and a person from New York City who wouldn't even be able to recognize each other as human. To me this scenario is simply crazy, because both will be hard-wired for the same emotions. They can hug, they can smile, they can raise their fists, and all of that's understandable between them without any kind of issue about culture.

We lose sight of the universal sometimes right now, because we think so much in terms of local meanings and the breakdown of the large cultural meanings. Moreover, this particular form of embodiment that we're in is so demanding of a being: it requires so many things to be complex, to know about one's own death, to have these emotional dependencies. We are so affected by grief at the loss of loved ones, for example, so much more than other species. These are the kinds of things that are universal and keep us connected to each other as a species.

AM: At the very end of your book, you talk about the self as "the knowledge that comes from suffering." That's a marvelous, stunning equation. In a world as complex as ours, can psychotherapy generate for a patient the kind of compassion that Buddhists would say leads to "right action?" Is there an ethical dimension that naturally emerges or, like the self, that spirals out of the work of psychotherapy?

PYE: I really think there is. For the ritual of psychotherapy to be effective, it has got to have a strong ethical base. It is that ethical base, the containment of all of the particularly negative emotions, without retaliation to the patient, together with the ongoing regard and respect for the patient's developments, symbolic meanings, and so on, that results in the patient's ability to see herself and others in a more compassionate light. Then the patient starts to go "Aha! The reason why people abuse me, or the reason why father did this, is because father was abused. Now I can see father more compassionately, I can even see Ronald Reagan more compassionately, because I see what goes into the making of a personality. At the same time, I can also see that people are personally responsible for what they do, that there's a line between things that just happen to you and the things that you do intentionally. So, I can see where Ronald Reagan may be personally responsible, and thus hold him responsible at the same time I exercise my compassion." I think people come out of psychotherapy, when it's done well, with a much stronger sense of compassion. They can see what's common in human life, how we all get into bungles, because they've seen it and experienced it all for themselves: in the company, one hopes, of a compassionate witness. Of a person who's been able to regard all this without retaliating.

In closing, I want to say a few things about Lacan and his writings–from what I know of them. I always find his gender theory interesting but too patriarchal, ultimately. I think he regards the whole issue of the father as so significant–what with "the Name of the Father," and the father as the source of language–that I think he sometimes loses track of this sense of the universal human emotions that transcend language. Where I do find him extremely useful, however, is in the ways I think he's similar to Jung. I think his model of the Real, the Imaginary and the Symbolic fits very well with Jung's ideas. There are parallels, for example, between the archetype and the Real; between the psychological complexes and the Imaginary; between the world of culture and symbol and the Symbolic. I also think that Jung and Lacan–and this doesn't very often get spoken to–are both right on when it comes to the Other:

regarding the importance of understanding the way the Other is constructed, and the way Otherness influences and dialogues with self. For Jung it's the anima/animus dynamic, contrasexuality, the projection of the Other into the opposite sex. For Lacan that's there too, but he adds the idea of the mirror image, where what is translated into the representation of the self as it gets projected is the imaginary object of desire. I think that Lacan actually is most useful in regard to the whole issue of desire, of the object of desire, and the importance of Otherness. I don't always agree with him, but he does get me to think about the subject-object dimension of human meaning: how I experience myself as subject of desire, or as object of desire; and how one can lose the sense of subjectivity by locating oneself more as the object of desire, rather than the subject of one's own desire.

AM: But there is also a major difference, arguably, in your respective ideas of decentering. In Jung, and in your thinking, the course of the ego complex seems to differ markedly from Lacan's. Perhaps we can close with this. Lacan seems to suggest, in a fierce critique of ego psychology, that a decentered self is possible only via a dissolution of the ego. You seem to point to an active process of decentering, something that apparently involves a decision which is both age-specific and part of a developmental program. Is this so?

PYE: I don't think of the process exactly as a decision, nor do I think it's really age-specific. I'd say it's more event-specific. What seems to me to take place is a recognition of helplessness, and by helplessness I mean the experience of being unable to organize one's ordinary defenses. That seems to me to be the first step towards dissolution of the ego, rather than the multiple-self scenario. When you experience that kind of helplessness, you recognize the limitations of your own construction of yourself. From there, finally, you take steps towards a sense of the personality having a center other than the ego.

WORKS CITED

Csikszentmihalyi, M. (1993). *The Evolving Self.* New York, Harper Collins.
Dennett, D. C. (1991). *Consciousness Explained.* Boston, Little Brown and Co.

Eisendrath, P. Young (1987). "The Absence of Black Americans as Jungian Analysts," in *Quadrant: The New York Journal of Analytical Psychology,* 20:2.

Eliot, T. S. (1943). *Four Quartets*. New York, Harcourt, Brace and Co.

Evans-Wentz, W. Y., ed. (1954). *The Tibetan Book of the Great Liberation*, London and New York.

______ (1957). *The Tibetan Book of the Dead*. London and New York.

Jung, C. G. (1973). *Memories, Dreams and Reflections* (Recorded and edited by A. Jaffe. Tr. by R. and C. Winston). New York, Pantheon Books, 1973.

Meckel, R. and Moore, R., eds. (1992). *Self in Liberation: The Jung-Buddhism Dialogue*. New York, Paulist Press.

Mitchell, S. (1993). *Hope and Dread in Psychoanalysis*. New York, Basic Books.

Neumann, E. (1964). *The Origins and History of Consciousness* (tr. by R. F. C. Hull). New York, Pantheon.

Rich, A. (1976). *Of Woman Born*. New York, Norton.

POLLY YOUNG-EISENDRATH: SELECTED BIBLIOGRAPHY

The Gifts of Suffering: Development through Difficulty (1996), New York, Bantam.

A Cambridge Companion to Jung (ed., with T. Dawson, 1996), Cambridge, Cambridge University Press.

You're Not What I Expected: Learning to Love the Opposite Sex (1993), New York, William Morrow.

Jung's Self Psychology: A Constructivist Perspective (with J. Hall, 1991), New York, Guilford.

Female Authority: Empowering Women through Psychotherapy (with F. Wiedemann, 1987), New York, Guilford.

The Book of the Self: Person, Pretext, Process (ed., with J. Hall, 1987), New York, NYU Press.

Hags and Heroes: A Feminist Approach to Jungian Psychotherapy with Couples (1984), Toronto, Inner City Publications.

For Product Safety Concerns and Information please contact our EU representative GPSR@taylorandfrancis.com Taylor & Francis Verlag GmbH, Kaufingerstraße 24, 80331 München, Germany